EXTERNAL FACTORS
FOR ASIAN DEVELOPMENT

The **Japan Institute of International Affairs (JIIA)** is a private, non-profit, and independent research organization founded in 1959 through the initiative of former Prime Minister Shigeru Yoshida, the first president of the JIIA.

The JIIA's mission is to contribute to the formulation of Japan's foreign policy through organizing study groups on regional and global issues, international conferences, symposiums and seminars, and joint research projects with other domestic and overseas research organizations and universities. The JIIA also invites foreign researchers to Japan and assists them with their research activities, and it issues a wide range of publications as a result of these activities.

The **ASEAN Foundation** was established by ASEAN leaders in 1997 to boost ASEAN's effort to promote region's co-operation in various fields of social and human development such as science and technology, youth, women, health and nutrition, education, labour affairs, disaster management, HIV/AIDS prevention and control, children, population, and rural development and poverty eradication, culture and information, environment, drug matters, and civil service. The Foundation was established to promote greater awareness of ASEAN, greater interaction among the peoples of ASEAN as well as their wider participation in ASEAN activities.

The ASEAN Foundation deems that the most beneficial and effective means to attain its objectives is focusing on human resources development projects such as education, training, seminars, workshops, exchanges, network-building, fellowships and information dissemination.

The **Institute of Southeast Asian Studies (ISEAS)** was established as an autonomous organization in 1968. It is a regional centre dedicated to the study of socio-political, security and economic trends and developments in Southeast Asia and its wider geostrategic and economic environment.

The Institute's research programmes are the Regional Economic Studies (RES, including ASEAN and APEC), Regional Strategic and Political Studies (RSPS), and Regional Social and Cultural Studies (RSCS).

ISEAS Publications, an established academic press, has issued more than 1,000 books and journals. It is the largest scholarly publisher of research about Southeast Asia from within the region. ISEAS Publications works with many other academic and trade publishers and distributors to disseminate important research and analyses from and about Southeast Asia to the rest of the world.

Asian Development Experience Vol. 1

EXTERNAL FACTORS
FOR ASIAN DEVELOPMENT

Edited by

Hirohisa Kohama

JAPAN INSTITUTE OF INTERNATIONAL AFFAIRS

ASEAN FOUNDATION

INSTITUTE OF SOUTHEAST ASIAN STUDIES, Singapore

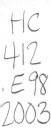
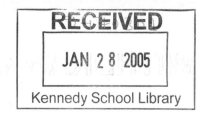
First published in Singapore in 2003 by
Institute of Southeast Asian Studies
30 Heng Mui Keng Terrace
Pasir Panjang
Singapore 119614
http://bookshop.iseas.edu.sg

ISEAS Library Cataloguing-in-Publication Data

Asian development experience. Volume 1, External factors for Asian
    development / edited by Hirohisa Kohama.
    1. Economic assistance, Japanese—Asia, Southeastern.
    2. Economic assistance, Japanese—Asia.
    3. Japan—Foreign economic relations—Asia, Southeastern.
    4. Asia, Southeastern—Foreign economic relations—Japan.
    I. Kohama, Hirohisa.
    II. Title: External factors for Asian development
HC412 A865 v. 1   2003

ISBN 981-230-192-5 (soft cover)
ISBN 981-230-196-8 (hard cover)

Printed in Singapore by Utopia Press Pte Ltd
Typeset by International Typesetters Pte Ltd

Contents

List of Tables

List of Figures

Contributors

Hirohisa KOHAMA is Professor of Economics at the Faculty of International Relations, University of Shizuoka, Japan

Masayoshi HONMA is Professor at the Department of Agricultural and Resource Economics, University of Tokyo, Japan

Kaoru ISHIKAWA is Director-General at the Multilateral Cooperation Department of the Ministry of Foreign Affairs, Japan

Fukunari KIMURA is Professor at the Faculty of Economics, Keio University, Japan

Masahiro OMURA is Minister, Permanent Mission of Japan to the International Organizations in Vienna, Japan

Yasuyuki SAWADA is Associate Professor at the Graduate School of Economics, University of Tokyo, Japan

Shujiro URATA is Professor at the School of Social Sciences, Waseda University, Japan

Matsuo WATANABE is Research Fellow at the Center for Asia-Pacific Studies of the Japan Institute of International Affairs, Japan

Hiroyuki YAMADA is a Ph.D. student at the Graduate School of Economics, University of Chicago, USA

Acknowledgements

The three volumes bring together essays from a two-year research project, "Asian Development Experience" that commenced in November 2001. The principal objective of the project was to investigate the dynamic factors contributing to the remarkable success of ASEAN economies. We particularly focused on the role of external factors, domestic policy reforms and governance as well as regional co-operation, which have received lesser attention in the past literature of the field.

We would like to thank Saori Honma and Katsuya Ohara of the Japan Institute of International Affairs (JIIA) for their dedication to this research project and the contributors to the volumes for making the editors' job so easy. We would also like to acknowledge the tireless support of Triena Ong and Dayaneetha De Silva of the Institute of Southeast Asian Studies (ISEAS) for realizing the publication.

The research project was undertaken with the financial support of the Japan-ASEAN Solidarity Fund, contributed by the Japanese Government and managed by the ASEAN Foundation.

1
Introduction: Aid, Trade, and FDI for Economic Development in East Asia

Hirohisa Kohama

East Asian countries including Japan were poor in the mid-1960s. Table 1.1 shows the country's income level in 1965 and 2000. We can make income comparisons between the years 1965 and 2000 for 92 countries in the World Bank database. Japan's income was $910 in 1965, which was about a quarter of the US' income. Japan's income was lower than some Latin American countries such as Argentina, Puerto Rico, and Venezuela in 1965.

Other East Asian countries were also poor in 1965. For example, the per capita income of Korea and Thailand were $130 and $140 respectively. Income levels of Korea and Thailand were lower than some Sub-Saharan African countries such as Congo, Gabon, Ghana, Mauritania, Niger, Zambia, and Zimbabwe in 1965.

Generally speaking, East Asian countries performed rapid growth, but Sub-Saharan African countries were stagnant as shown in Table 1.1. External factors such as foreign trade and investment and good policy environments explain the good development performance in East Asia. Good policy environments are crucially important for development. Figure 1.1 is the simulation result of the income level of Zambia by Bill Easterly (Easterly 1999, Easterly 2001, p. 43). Zambia's income would have been very much higher if aid had gone into investment which would have gone to growth.

Burnside and Dollar (2000) found that aid has a positive impact on growth in developing countries with good policies but little effect in countries with poor policies.[1] Although Easterly, Levine and Roodman (2003) admitted that the Burnside and Dollar (2000) finding that aid raises growth in a good policy environment has had an important influence on policy and academic debates, it is not as robust when they used the extended database.

Foreign aid played a catalytic role for development. We made an analysis not only of the role of aid for development but the role of trade and FDI (Foreign Direct Investment) from the standpoint of policy coherence.

The Foreign Ministry of the Netherlands argues the "Policy Coherence for Development" as follows:

> Policy coherence for development means taking explicit account of the potential impact of policy decisions on poverty in developing countries. This implies that governments must always examine how decisions in other areas relate to goals and efforts in development cooperation. The idea is that policy areas should reinforce one another. For example, in addition to assisting farmers in developing countries with production, rich countries can eliminate import barriers to their products as part of their commercial and agricultural policies.
>
> Coherence issues arise at the interface between development cooperation and many other policy areas: trade, agriculture, food safety, fisheries, intellectual property, the environment, international finance, tax policy, migration, peace and security, etc.[2]

In this connection, we discussed agricultural exports of Indonesia, the Philippines, and Thailand in Chapter 7, and FDI in Chapter 8.

Major analyses of this volume are the following. In Chapter 2, Hirohisa Kohama presents the brief history of economic development in post-war Japan and a historical overview of the expansion of Japan's official development assistance (ODA). He argues the structure of Japan's aid, determinants of Japan's aid allocation and the role of aid for economic development in East Asia.

Chapter 3, by Yasuyuki Sawada and Hiroyuki Yamada, looks at Japan's ODA and poverty reduction by a cross-donor comparison and comprises a case study of Malaysia. Sawada and Yamada investigate the effectiveness of Japan's ODA in reducing recipients' poverty. They compare the effectiveness of eleven donor countries, i.e., France, Germany, Japan, Netherlands, U.K., U.S.A., Canada, Italy, Finland, Norway, and Sweden. Then they investigated the effectiveness of Japan's ODA in Malaysia over thirty years. They find that in the late 1990s, grant allocations of Japan, the Netherlands, U.K., Canada, Norway, Sweden were consistent with the poverty targeting. They also find that while Japan's bilateral ODA allocation to Malaysia have concentrated on economic infrastructure, Japan's aid significantly contributed to poverty reduction in Malaysia.

Shujiro Urata discusses the upgrading technology in ASEAN countries and Japan's ODA in Chapter 4. He argues that technology, not only in the form of engineering technology but also management know-how, plays an important role in achieving economic development, and that domestic technological capability plays a crucial role in the success or failure of absorption of imported technology. He finds that ASEAN countries are lagging behind the developed countries and the NIEs in technological capability. Recognizing the importance of good technological capability in achieving economic development, he argues that ASEAN countries, as well as donors of economic assistance to these countries, have made efforts to upgrade their technological capability. He presents anecdotal evidence showing that economic assistance has had favourable impacts, although it is difficult to quantify the contribution of technical assistance to upgrading technological capability.

Masahiro Omura makes an analysis of the role of Japan's ODA for Indonesia's agricultural development especially in rice production (Chapter 5). He examines experiences in Indonesia's development focusing on the era of the Soeharto Regime, examining in particular the significance of ODA in agricultural development. He focuses on the umbrella method; a system which organizes the various forms of assistance of technical cooperation, grant aid, and loan aid under unit objectives and for specified sub-sectors and specified geographical areas.

Chapter 6, by Matsuo Watanabe, is an analysis of ODA as a catalyst for foreign direct investment and industrial agglomeration. He investigates the contribution of infrastructure development financed by ODA to attracting FDI and to the formation of industrial agglomerations, with reference to the automotive industry in Thailand. He argues that the success of the Thai automotive industry is evidenced by the expansion in the volume of production and exports which has been the largest among ASEAN member countries. This expansion has been facilitated by a concentration of investments in the industry (known as 'agglomeration') from foreign parts suppliers, including those in the Eastern Seaboard (ESB) area. He investigates how the agglomeration of the automotive industry has taken place in Thailand. Special attention is placed on the shift in concentration on new investments over the last two decades in accordance with the development of infrastructure in the ESB and Bangkok Metropolitan area – a large part of which was financed by Japan's ODA in the same period. He finds that the development of the ESB area has substantially contributed to attracting investments in the automotive industry (as well as other industries) which has led to agglomerations.

In Chapter 7, Masayoshi Honma reconsiders the roles of agricultural exports through assessing the performance of three Asian countries, Indonesia, the Philippines and Thailand over four decades. In the 1960s, the agricultural export performance was similar among Indonesia, the Philippines, and Thailand. But afterward, the three countries have shown different performances in agricultural exports. One important factor explaining the differences is the ability of agricultural exports to diversify and adjust when the market conditions changed. He argues that there are a lot of opportunities to gain from agricultural exports.

In Chapter 8, Fukunari Kimura analyzes the role of government and ODA in Southeast Asia (SEA). He understands that the development pattern of the SEA countries is fundamentally different in many aspects from the pattern of preceding economies such as Japan and Korea in which industrialization started from import substitution by local indigenous firms. He understands that the role of FDI is different from that in Latin America and other parts of the world in terms of the number of countries involved in international production/distribution networks. He argues that market forces are important, but the policy framework is not simple laissez-faire. He explains economic logic behind the formation of international production/distribution networks and discusses the importance of government policies.

Kaoru Ishikawa discusses Japan's new approach to nation building based on people-centred human security in Chapter 9. He points out the importance of the role of rule making in light of a newly emerging situation in the world, as well as people-centred approach to build communities and the role of communities in nation building. He argues Japan started to seek a new way of development assistance based on this understanding.

Notes

[1] Main messages of the World Bank (1998) are the same, because David Dollar is one of the main authors of World Bank (1998).

[2] http://www.minbuza.nl/default.asp?CMS_ITEM=552B39A9D9804A508C7.

References

Burnside, Craig and David Dollar. "Aid, Policies, and Growth." *American Economic Review*, Vol. 90 No. 4, September 2000.

Easterly, William. "The Ghost of Financing Gap: Testing the Growth Model of the International Financial Institutions." *Journal of Development Economics*, Vol. 60, No. 2, December 1999.

Easterly, William. *The Elusive Quest for Growth: Economists' Adventures and Misadventures in the Tropics*, Cambridge, Mass.: The MIT Press, 2001.

Easterly, William, Ross Levine, and David Roodman. "New Data, New doubts: A Comment on Burnside and Dollar's 'Aid, Policies, and Growth' (2000)". NBER Working Paper No. 9846, July 2003.

The World Bank, *Assessing Aid – What Works, What Doesn't, and Why*. Washington, DC: World Bank, 1998.

Table 1.1 Per Capita Income in 1965 and 2000

	1965		2000		2000/
Country	US$	US=100	US$	US=100	1965
Algeria	260	7.1	1,580	4.6	6.1
Argentina	1,230	33.5	7,450	21.7	6.1
Australia	2,250	61.3	20,120	58.5	8.9
Austria	1,310	35.7	25,230	73.4	19.3
Bahamas	1,910	52.0	14,860	43.2	7.8
Barbados	530	14.4	9,460	27.5	17.8
Belgium	1,750	47.7	25,070	72.9	14.3
Belize	360	9.8	2,880	8.4	8.0
Benin	120	3.3	390	1.1	3.3
Bolivia	260	7.1	990	2.9	3.8
Botswana	90	2.5	3,070	8.9	34.1
Brazil	270	7.4	3,630	10.6	13.4
Burkina Faso	80	2.2	220	0.6	2.8
Burundi	70	1.9	110	0.3	1.6
Cameroon	140	3.8	580	1.7	4.1
Central African Republic	90	2.5	280	0.8	3.1
Chad	120	3.3	200	0.6	1.7
Chile	660	18.0	4,810	14.0	7.3
China	100	2.7	840	2.4	8.4
Colombia	300	8.2	2,020	5.9	6.7
Congo, Dem. Rep.	330	9.0	90	0.3	0.3
Congo, Rep.	170	4.6	590	1.7	3.5
Costa Rica	410	11.2	3,820	11.1	9.3
Cote d'Ivoire	200	5.4	680	2.0	3.4
Dominican Republic	240	6.5	2,120	6.2	8.8
Ecuador	220	6.0	1,070	3.1	4.9
Egypt	180	4.9	1,490	4.3	8.3
El Salvador	290	7.9	2,000	5.8	6.9
Fiji	290	7.9	2,160	6.3	7.4
Finland	1,790	48.8	25,090	73.0	14.0
France	2,040	55.6	23,990	69.8	11.8
Gabon	390	10.6	3,190	9.3	8.2
Ghana	230	6.3	330	1.0	1.4
Greece	800	21.8	11,730	34.1	14.7
Guatemala	300	8.2	1,690	4.9	5.6
Guyana	320	8.7	860	2.5	2.7
Haiti	80	2.2	500	1.5	6.3
Honduras	220	6.0	860	2.5	3.9
Hong Kong, China	690	18.8	26,410	76.8	38.3
Iceland	2,460	67.0	30,250	88.0	12.3
India	120	3.3	450	1.3	3.8
Ireland	1,040	28.3	22,870	66.5	22.0
Israel	1,440	39.2	16,710	48.6	11.6

Table 1.1   Per Capita Income in 1965 and 2000   *(continued)*

Country	1965 US$	1965 US=100	2000 US$	2000 US=100	2000/ 1965
Italy	1,260	34.3	20,130	58.6	16.0
Jamaica	610	16.6	2,820	8.2	4.6
Japan	910	24.8	35,420	103.1	38.9
Kenya	100	2.7	350	1.0	3.5
Korea, Rep.	130	3.5	9,010	26.2	69.3
Kuwait	3,580	97.5	17,900	52.1	5.0
Luxembourg	2,160	58.9	41,860	121.8	19.4
Madagascar	130	3.5	250	0.7	1.9
Malawi	60	1.6	170	0.5	2.8
Malaysia	330	9.0	3,250	9.5	9.8
Malta	510	13.9	9,130	26.6	17.9
Mauritania	150	4.1	390	1.1	2.6
Mexico	490	13.4	5,100	14.8	10.4
Morocco	220	6.0	1,180	3.4	5.4
Nepal	60	1.6	240	0.7	4.0
Netherlands	1,650	45.0	25,260	73.5	15.3
Niger	180	4.9	180	0.5	1.0
Nigeria	120	3.3	260	0.8	2.2
Norway	2,080	56.7	34,530	100.5	16.6
Oman	100	2.7	6,180	18.0	61.8
Panama	550	15.0	3,250	9.5	5.9
Papua New Guinea	160	4.4	670	1.9	4.2
Paraguay	210	5.7	1,460	4.2	7.0
Peru	390	10.6	2,060	6.0	5.3
Philippines	190	5.2	1,020	3.0	5.4
Portugal	480	13.1	11,190	32.6	23.3
Puerto Rico	1,060	28.9	10,550	30.7	10.0
Rwanda	40	1.1	240	0.7	6.0
Saudi Arabia	480	13.1	8,120	23.6	16.9
Seychelles	320	8.7	6,730	19.6	21.0
Sierra Leone	160	4.4	130	0.4	0.8
Singapore	540	14.7	23,350	67.9	43.2
South Africa	540	14.7	3,060	8.9	5.7
Spain	710	19.3	14,760	42.9	20.8
Sri Lanka	160	4.4	890	2.6	5.6
St. Vincent and the Grenadines	180	4.9	2,750	8.0	15.3
Sudan	120	3.3	310	0.9	2.6
Sweden	2,860	77.9	27,420	79.8	9.6
Switzerland	2,590	70.6	39,650	115.4	15.3
Syrian Arab Republic	280	7.6	950	2.8	3.4
Thailand	140	3.8	2,020	5.9	14.4
Togo	110	3.0	290	0.8	2.6
Trinidad and Tobago	770	21.0	5,250	15.3	6.8

Table 1.1   Per Capita Income in 1965 and 2000   (*continued*)

Country	1965 US$	1965 US=100	2000 US$	2000 US=100	2000/ 1965
Tunisia	230	6.3	2,100	6.1	9.1
United States	3,670	100.0	34,370	100.0	9.4
Uruguay	670	18.3	6,150	17.9	9.2
Venezuela	1,110	30.2	4,310	12.5	3.9
Zambia	260	7.1	310	0.9	1.2
Zimbabwe	290	7.9	440	1.3	1.5

Source: WDI CD-ROM 2003.
Note: Per capita GNI in current US$. Last column is the ratio of income in 2000 to that of 1965.

Figure 1.1   The Gap between the Linear Aid-Investment-Growth Model and the Actual Outcome in Zambia

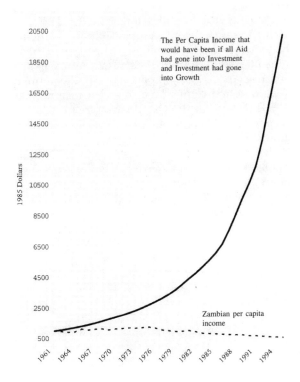

Source: Easterly (1999).

2

Japan's Development Cooperation in East Asia: A Historical Overview of Japan's ODA and Its Impact

Hirohisa Kohama

1. Introduction

Japan's economy was not fully developed in the 1950s. I think that Japan, in the high-growth period, can be described as the forerunner of Asia's newly industrializing economies (NIEs). Japan had balance of payments difficulties until the mid-1960s. The country started its Official Development Assistance (ODA) programme in the form of technical cooperation in 1954 and commenced the ODA loan programme at the end of the 1950s. At first Japan's ODA loans were fully tied aid. The tied aid in those days can be rationalized in the light of the balance of payments difficulties.

In the process of the post-war reconstruction of its economy, Japan utilized World Bank loans. Japan's development experiences had implicit influences on its aid policy. There are some misunderstandings about the economic development of East Asia. In the case of Japan, a common misunderstanding is that the rapid industrialization in post-war Japan was led by the government, especially by the industrial policy of the Ministry of International Trade and Industry (MITI). This is not true.

Take the case of the steel industry, which was one of the leading industries in Japan's high-growth era from 1955 to 1973. Many non-Japanese economists had the misunderstanding that large-scale investment could be made without risk in the steel industry due to the government's heavy protection and promotion. What caused the rapid enhancement of the international competitiveness of the steel industry was not industrial policy but the entrepreneurial decision to import innovative modern technology, such as the Basic Oxygen Furnace (BOF) and continuous casting.[1]

In what economic environment does such innovative entrepreneurship fully function? This is a basic question, not only for economic development in general but also for aid principles. A competitive economic environment and "social capability" are crucial for enhancing the international competitiveness of the industry.[2] It seems to me that competitive economic environments are realized not only in a liberalized economy but also in a protected and oligopolistic economy (Ohkawa and Kohama 1989, Chapter 8).

It is difficult to explain this idea rigorously, but we can derive lessons from historical facts in post-war Japan and other East Asian countries in order to understand the economic development of East Asia (mainly Japan, the NIEs, and the members of the Association of Southeast Asian Nations or ASEAN). When we find a mechanism that promotes the innovative behaviour of private companies in protected and oligopolistic markets, we should modify the policy conditionality of the International Monetary Fund and the World Bank loans to developing countries.[3]

In Section 2, I briefly discuss Japan's post-war economic development in order to understand the background of Japan's aid policy. In Sections 3 and 4, I discuss economic co-operation to East Asia and the expansion of Japan's ODA and its policy. In the last section, I present my view on East Asian dynamism and the role of development cooperation.

2. Japan's Post-War Economic Development and its Policy

2.1 Change in Economic Structure in Post-War Japan

Japan started heavy industrialization in the 1950s. Generally speaking, heavy industry includes the metal, chemical, and machine industries. We understand that heavy industry has two subsectors. The required level of technology for traditional heavy industry, such as the steel and shipbuilding industries, is different from that for the new heavy industry, such as the computer and mechatronics industries. The latter can be called technology-intensive industries. The rapid change in the industrial and trade structure in post-war Japan will be reviewed in order to understand that light industries, such as textiles and food processing, were the leading industries when Japan moved toward rapid economic growth. The rapid shift of key industries will be discussed below: a clear decline of light industry and the rise of traditional heavy industry, followed by technology-intensive industry. Such a shifting pattern has been transferred to the NIEs, with certain time lags, and then to the ASEAN countries, China, and other countries. The smooth diffusion of dynamism from more developed countries to less developed countries is a major reason behind the dynamic economic development in East Asia.

Let us look briefly at the change in the share of shipment value of 21 subsectors in the manufacturing industry. In 1955, the early phase of rapid economic growth, the shares of the textile and the iron and steel industries were 16.2% and 9.6%, respectively. The textile industry share decreased sharply and was as low as 1.0% in 2000. The iron and steel industry share was larger than 9% of the manufacturing total up to 1970 but started to decline later in that decade, dropping to 3.9% in 2000. Instead, machine industries have expanded rapidly.

Table 2.1 shows changes in the export structure of Japan for 1953–2000. Textiles were the largest export items in the early phase of Japan's post-war economic growth. Textile export share was 40.3% in 1954 and 30.1% in 1960, but it declined to 12.5% in 1970, 4.8% in 1980, and 1.8% in 2000. In the latter half of the 1950s, about one-fourth of Japan's export expansion was accounted for by textile export expansion. The contribution ratio of textile exports to total export expansion was 23.1% in 1955–60, but it decreased to about 8% in the 1960s, 2.5% in the 1970s, and less than 1% in 1980–85.

Steel was the leading export industry up to the mid–1970s. The steel export share was less than 10% in 1960, but it increased to more than 15% in 1965 and 18% in 1975. However, it has been on a downward trend since the mid–1970s. The export share of steel decreased to 11.9% in 1980, 4.3% in 1991, and 3.1% in 2000. The machinery industry is the leading export industry in Japan. The machinery export share was 25.5% in 1960 and increased to 46% in 1970, 63% in 1980, 72% in 1985, and 75% in 1990. Since the mid–1960s more than half of Japan's export expansion has been attributed to the expansion of machinery exports. In the latter half of the 1970s about three-fourths of Japan's export expansion was explained by machinery export expansion. For the period of 1980–85, 93% of Japan's export expansion was accounted for by machinery export expansion. Compared with the export contribution ratio of 1965–70 and that of 1980–85, the contribution of machinery total, general machinery, electric machinery, transport equipment, and precision instruments increased by 38.2%, 10.8%, 8.1%, 11.3%, and 8.2% respectively.

The transport equipment, mainly automobiles, export share was the largest subsector in machinery export in 1985. The automobile industry has become one of the leading export industries of Japan. In 1955, Japan exported only two passenger cars, but Japan's car exports increased remarkably over those 30 years. In 1985, Japan

Table 2.1 Export Structure of Japan(1953–2000) (%)

	1953	1954	1955	1960	1965	1970	1975	1980	1985	1990	1995	2000
Total	100.0	100.0	100.0	100.0	100.0	100.0	100.0	100.0	100.0	100.0	100.0	100.0
Foodstuff	9.4	7.6	6.2	6.3	4.1	3.4	1.4	1.2	0.8	0.6	0.5	0.4
Textiles	36.1	40.3	37.3	30.1	18.7	12.5	6.7	4.8	3.6	2.5	2.0	1.8
Textile fibres	n.a.	n.a.	2.9	2.0	1.8	1.0	0.8	0.5	0.4	0.3	0.3	n.a.
Textile yarn	n.a.	n.a.	29.1	22.7	13.5	9.0	5.2	3.9	2.8	2.0	1.6	n.a.
Clothing	2.9	3.4	5.2	5.4	3.4	2.4	0.6	0.4	0.4	0.2	0.1	n.a.
Chemicals	5.7	5.5	5.1	4.5	6.5	6.4	7.0	5.3	4.4	5.5	6.8	7.4
Non-metallic minerals	4.9	4.6	4.7	4.2	3.1	1.9	1.3	1.4	1.2	1.1	1.2	1.2
Metals and metal products	15.1	15.6	19.2	14.0	20.3	19.7	22.4	16.5	10.6	6.8	6.5	5.5
Iron and steel	10.9	10.3	12.8	9.6	15.3	14.7	18.2	11.9	7.8	4.4	4.0	3.1
Non-ferrous metals	n.a.	n.a.	3.3	0.6	1.4	1.3	1.0	1.5	0.8	0.8	1.0	1.1
Metal products	n.a.	n.a.	3.0	3.8	3.6	3.7	3.2	3.0	2.0	1.6	1.6	1.3
Machinery	15.9	13.5	na	25.5	35.2	46.3	53.8	62.7	71.8	74.9	74.7	74.3
General machinery	n.a.	n.a.	na	na	7.4	10.4	12.1	13.9	16.8	22.1	24.1	21.5
Electric machinery	n.a.	n.a.	na	na	9.2	12.3	11.0	14.4	16.9	23.0	25.6	26.5
Transport equipment	n.a.	n.a.	na	na	14.7	17.8	26.1	26.5	28.0	25.0	20.3	21.0
Precision instruments	n.a.	n.a.	na	na	3.9	5.7	4.7	7.9	10.1	4.8	4.7	5.4
Others	12.9	13.0	na	15.3	12.1	9.9	7.4	8.1	7.7	8.5	8.2	9.5

Source: Ministry of Finance.

exported more than four million passenger cars. The recent leading export industries are very export-oriented. The export/production ratio of passenger cars was less than 5% in 1960, but it increased to 22.8% in 1970, 40.0% in 1975, 56.1% in 1980, and 57.9% in 1985.

2.2   Balance of Payments and World Bank Loans to Japan

As mentioned at the beginning, Japan's trade and current account balances were negative until the mid–1960s, as shown in Figure 2.1. Balance-of-payments management was one of the most important economic policy issues of Japan at that time. In addition, Japan borrowed money from the World Bank for infrastructure and basic industry investments, as shown in Table 2.2. Japan was a recipient country of World Bank loans at the beginning of the 1960s. The crucial point of external financing is not the absolute amount of external debt, but how to use the money efficiently based on the long-term perspectives of the economy.

Figure 2.1   Balance of Payments in Post-war Japan: 1946–1970

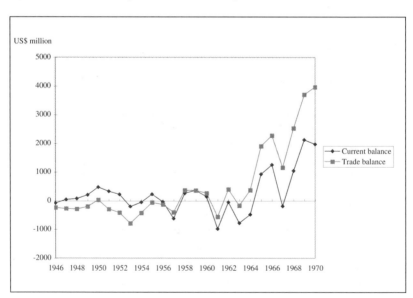

Source: Bank of Japan.

Table 2.2   World Bank Loans to Japan

Year	Project	Loan (US$1,000)
1953	Power plant	21,500
	Power plant	11,200
	Power plant	7,500
1956	Steel plant	5,300
	Steel plant	2,600
	Machine toold for car plant	2,350
1957	Ship engine plant	1,650
	Ship engine plant	1,500
	Steel plant	20,000
	Agricultural land development	1,330
	Agricultural land development	1,133
	Non-project	984
	Non-project	853
	Irrigation	7,000
1958	Steel plant	8,000
	Power plant	37,000
	Power plant	25,000
	Steel plant	33,000
	Steel plant	10,000
	Power plant	29,000
	Steel plant	22,000
1959	Power plant	10,000
1960	Steel plant	24,000
	Steel plant	20,000
	Freeway	40,000
1961	Steel plant	6,000
	Steel plant	7,000
	Power plant	12,000
	Shinkansen (bullet train)	80,000
1962	Freeway	40,000
1963	Freeway	75,000
1964	Freeway	50,000
1965	Freeway	25,000
	Power plant	25,000
	Freeway	75,000
	Freeway	25,000
1966	Freeway	100,000
TOTAL		862,900

Source: World Bank/Tokyo Office(1991), pp.114–117.

2.3 Development Policy in Post-War Japan

Japan's post-war economic development and policy experiences had substantial influence on its aid policy. It is not explicit, but it is important to formulate the basic aid policy of the Japanese government. Many economists, especially non-Japanese economists, misunderstand the role of the government, or Japan's industrial policy, in the process of rapid economic growth in the post-war period. My understanding is that industrial policy is an interaction mechanism between the private sector and the government. In this context, we believe it is useful to study the Japanese experience to understand the characteristics of Japan's aid policy. Relevant anecdotes on Japan's industrial policy are presented in Ohkawa and Kohama (1989, Chapter 8).

Many non-Japanese argue that the Japanese government, in particular MITI, played a crucial role in the rapid industrialization and export expansion of post-war Japan.[4] It is true that the Japanese government, in particular MITI, implemented various industrial and export promotion measures in the post-war period. However, MITI did not always lead the private sector, and private companies did not always respond as expected by MITI.

The most important factor to explain the rapid economic growth was not industrial policy but the dynamism of the private sector. Of course, industrial and export promotion policies played their own role. However, the implementation of industrial policy was in a manner assisting the efficiency-oriented management of the economy based on the dynamism of the private sector, or, in other words, the market mechanism. The Japanese government just provided basic infrastructure and a competitive economic environment. This is the secret of Japan's post-war economic success.

The static and naive view that intervention in the market through industrial policy causes distortions in the market and gives rise to economic inefficiency is not warranted in economic development, which is a dynamic process. Economic development is a long-term process of structural change. Insofar as competitive conditions are ensured even in a protected and oligopolistic market like post-war Japan, entrepreneurs have a strong incentive to improve productivity and international competitiveness. Industrial policy designed to promote the private sector's initiative to improve competitiveness seems to be rational from the standpoint of long-term development policy. Japan's industrial policy basically stressed private-sector vitality and initiative. Based on this view, I have doubts about the stereotypical liberalization conditionality of the IMF and the World Bank.

The private sector sometimes did not follow what MITI said or did not react as expected by MITI. Japanese manufacturers have been very enthusiastic about technology improvements and new technology imports. Before trade liberalization, Japanese manufacturers came under the pressure of competition with foreign companies. This is one of the reasons why they were eager for technology improvements in order to improve their international competitiveness.

Protection policy can be rationalized from an economic standpoint when the protected industry is an infant industry. However, it is very difficult to identify an infant industry *ex ante*. Protection policy in the course of import substitution tends to be prolonged. There exist many examples of the failures of prolonged import substitution in Latin American countries.

In post-war Japan, especially in the early phase of rapid economic growth, domestic industries were heavily protected and promoted. However, all business people, economists, and government officials knew that Japan should open the domestic market in the 1950s. They knew that trade liberalization would be carried out in the 1960s and followed by capital liberalization.

We understand that protection policy in certain development phases can be rationalized from an economic standpoint, as mentioned above. The crucial issue is how to maintain and promote efficiency-oriented economic management in a protected market. For this purpose, the government should announce a schedule for liberalization. Gradual and step-by-step liberalization is desirable, but the liberalization schedule should not be substantially changed by political pressure once it is announced. Private manufacturers should make every effort to improve their competitiveness by the scheduled time of liberalization.

Japan's experiences, namely, efficiency-oriented economic management, severe competition in a protected and oligopolistic market, and the consciousness of international competition, have important implications for contemporary developing countries. In order to realize the above-mentioned private initiatives, political stability, continuity of economic policy, and the supply of basic infrastructure are indispensable.

3. Economic Cooperation to East Asia and Japan's Presence

3.1 Japan's Development Cooperation

Japan started aid-giving in the 1950s, as mentioned at the beginning. The trend of Japan's economic cooperation is shown in Figure 2.2. Japan's ODA was less than US$500 million in the 1960s. It started to increase in the 1980s. It was reported that Japan's ODA increased to more than

Figure 2.2 Selected DAC Members' ODA.

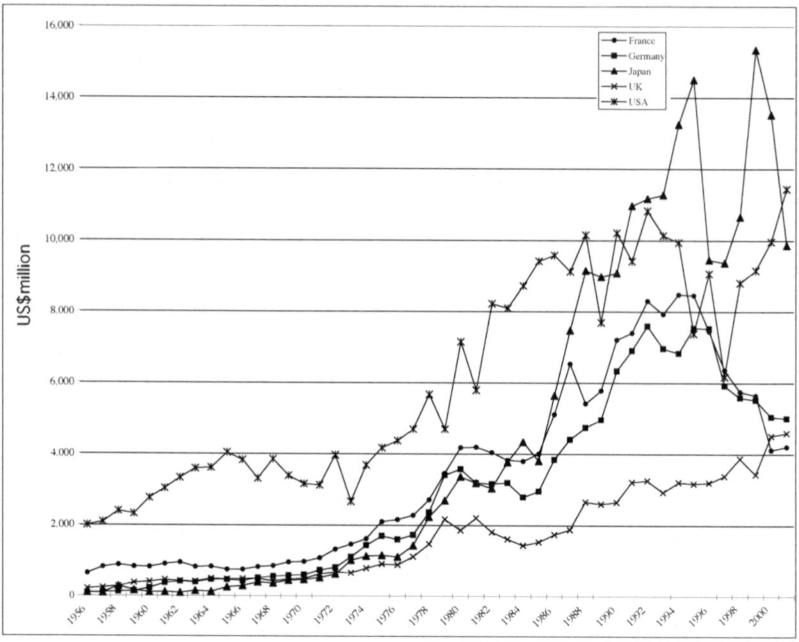

Source: DAC.

$10 billion in 1991. Japan was the world's top donor from 1991 to 2000. Japan disbursed more than $15 billion of ODA in 1999. This was about 27% of the total amount disbursed by members of the Development Assistance Committee (DAC). Japan's per capita ODA was more than $100 in 1999. Although Japan's ODA budget has been declining since 2001 due to the country's huge fiscal deficit, Japan is still the second largest donor after the United States.

Japan's ODA budget has been declining recently, but the Japanese government intended to expand ODA in the 1980s and 1990s. The government announced the first medium-term plan for ODA expansion in 1978. Major targets are shown in Table 2.3. In addition to the ODA value expansion, ODA quality improvement targets are also included in the third, fourth, and fifth plans.

Japan's ODA presence in developing countries is getting stronger and stronger. In 1970, Japan's ODA was the largest bilateral ODA in six recipient countries. This number increased to 28 countries in 1990 (Table

Table 2.3 Japan's Medium Plan of ODA Expansion

1st Plan (3-year doubling plan: 1978–80)

Base year: 1977 (ODA performance=US$1.424billon)
Target year: 1980 (ODA target=US$2.848billon)
Target year (1980) ODA performance: US$3.304billon

2nd Plan (5-year doubling plan: 1981–85)

Base period ODA: US$10.68billon (1976–80 total)
Target period ODA: US$21.36billon (1981—85 total)
Target period ODA performance: US$18.07billon (1981–85 total)

3rd Plan (6-year doubling plan: 1986–92)

Base period ODA: US$18.07billon (1981–85 total)
Target period ODA: More than US$40billon (1986–92 total)
Target period ODA performance: US$62.36billon (1986–92 total)

4th Plan (1988–92)

Base period ODA: US$24.96billon (1983–87 total)
Target period ODA: More than US$50billon (1988–92 total)
Target period ODA performance: US$49.27billon (1988–92 total)

5th Plan (1993–97)

Target period ODA: US$70–75billon (1993–97 total)
Target period ODA performance: US$57.78billon (1993–97 total)

Source: OECF (1998), p. 439; Japan's ODA 2002 CD-ROM.

2.4). In 2000, Japan was the top donor for 54 developing countries. Among these 54 countries, Japan's ODA is larger than the financial flows from international organizations in all except 11 countries.[5] It is often suggested that the quality of Japan's ODA is low. Japan's grant ratio and grant element (GE) are in the lowest group among the DAC member countries. The tied aid ratio is also an indicator of aid quality. When Japan started ODA loans in the late 1950s, the tied aid ratio was almost 100%, which means that all aid money was used to import Japanese goods. However, Japan's tied ratio of ODA loans has declined remarkably and is now one of the lowest among the DAC member countries.

Table 2.4   List of Countries where Japan's ODA is the Largest among Bilateral Donors

1970	1980	1990	1995	2000
Burma	Bangladesh	Bahrain	Argentina	Argentina
Cambodia	Burma	Bangladesh	Bahrain	Azerbaijan
Iran	Indonesia	Bhutan	Bangladesh	Bahrain
Kuwait	Iran	Bolivia	Bolivia	Bangladesh
Philippines	Korea	Brazil	Brazil	Brazil
Qatar	Malaysia	Brunei	Brunei	Cambodia
	Maldives	Burma	Butan	Central Africa
	Nepal	China	Cambodia	China
	Pakistan	Cyprus	Chile	Dominica
	Paraguay	Ghana	China	Dominican Republic
	Philippines	Grenada	Colombia	El SaSalvador
	Saudi Arabia	Indonesia	Dominica	Fiji
	Sierra Leone	Laos	Dominican Republic	Gambia
	Thailand	Malaysia	Equador	Ghana
	UAE	Maldives	Fiji	Grenada
		Nepal	Ghana	Guatemala
		Nigeria	Grenada	India
		Pakistan	Guatemala	Indonesia
		Paraguay	Honduras	Iran
		Philippines	India	Kazakhstan
		Qatar	Indonesia	Kiribati
		Saudi Arabia	Jordan	Kyrgyz
		South Korea	Kenya	Laos
		Sri Lanka	Kiribati	Malaysia
		Thailand	Kyrgyz	Maldives
		Tonga	Laos	Mauritania
		Turkey	Malaysia	Mongolia
		Western Samoa	Maldives	Myanmar
			Mexico	Nauru
			Mongolia	Nepal
			Myanmar	Nicaragua
			Nepal	Oman
			Oman	Pakistan
			Pakistan	Palau
			Panama	Palestine
			Paraguay	Paraguay
			Philippines	Peru
			Saint Vincent	Philippines
			Saudi Arabia	Saint Christofer and Nevis
			Seychelles	Saint Lucia
			Singapore	Saint Vincent
			Solomon Islands	Saudi Arabia
			South Korea	Sri Lanka
			Sri Lanka	Swaziland

Table 2.4 List of Countries where Japan's ODA is the Largest in Bilateral Donors *(continued)*

1970	1980	1990	1995	2000
Burma	Bangladesh	Bahrain	Argentina	Argentina
			Syria	Syria
			Tanzania	Tanzania
			Thailand	Thailand
			Tonga	Tonga
			Trinidad and Tobago	Trinidad and Tobago
			UAE	Turkey
			Vanuatu	Urguay
			Viet Nam	Uzbekistan
			Western Samoa	Viet Nam
			Zambia	Zimbabwe
			Zimbabwe	
(6 countries)	(15 countries)	(28 countries)	(55 countries)	(54 countries)

Source: Ministry of Foreign Affairs, *Japan's ODA*, various yearas.

The geographical distribution of Japan's ODA and its structure are shown in Tables 2.5–2.9. The share of Japan's bilateral ODA to Asian countries was 98% in 1970 and more than 70% in the 1970s, but it decreased to 60% in 1990 and 57% in 2001. This reflects the fact that Japan's aid is extended to countries with which it has close economic relations, such as trade and direct investment.

The major recipient countries of Japan's ODA in 1990 and 2001 are shown in Tables 2.10 and 2.11. Asian countries, such as Indonesia, China, and India, are the major recipients of Japan's ODA. As a rule, poorer countries are the recipients of financial grants. Tanzania was the largest recipient of Japanese grant aid in 2001. The top 20 recipient countries of Japan's ODA loans (cumulative value until FY 2001) and the economic growth rate of these countries are shown in Table 2.12. For reference, the economic growth rate by income group and region is shown in the table. We cannot identify the causality, but the economic growth rates of these 20 countries are relatively high.

The proportion of Japan's ODA loans to total bilateral ODA was more than 60% in 1991, but, as shown in Figure 2.3, this proportion is declining.[6] The sector distribution of the ODA of major DAC member countries in 2000 is shown in Table 2.13. Aid for economic infrastructure is the largest sector of Japan's bilateral ODA. Its share was 32% in 2000, and this share was much higher than the DAC average. The high share of ODA loans is one of the remarkable characteristics of Japanese aid. This is partly due to the high share of Japanese ODA loans in total bilateral ODA.[7]

Table 2.5   Geographical Distribution of Japan's ODA in 1990 and 2001
(Net disbursement)

1990   ($ million)

	Financial grant	Technical assistance	ODA loans	ODA total
Asia	639.16	707.39	2,770.00	4,116.55
East Asia	38.61	275.51	520.59	834.72
Southeast Asia	273.00	351.24	1,755.00	2,379.24
South Asia	327.55	76.30	494.41	898.25
Others	4.34	4.34	0.00	4.34
Middle East	113.24	96.06	495.35	704.65
Africa	423.23	124.89	243.63	791.75
Latin America	117.17	199.10	244.92	561.20
Oceania	61.40	32.00	20.13	113.53
Europe	0.00	11.85	146.11	157.96
Eastern Europe	0.00	5.38	147.73	153.12
Others	19.85	474.06	0.00	493.91
Total	1,374.05	1,645.35	3,920.16	6,939.56

Source: Ministry of Foreign Affairs.

2001   ($ million)

	Financial grant	Technical assistance	ODA loans	ODA total
Asia	727.51	1,088.26	2,404.71	4,220.48
East Asia	67.05	373.28	254.36	694.69
Southeast Asia	316.72	548.76	1,252.04	2,117.52
South Asia	298.98	120.89	736.99	1,156.87
Others	44.75	45.33	161.32	251.40
Middle East	177.86	135.47	-26.14	287.19
Africa	614.42	223.34	13.57	851.33
Latin America	269.62	302.99	165.61	738.21
Oceania	48.41	44.67	8.43	101.50
Europe	41.96	42.52	31.61	116.10
Eastern Europe	2.19	32.75	31.71	66.65
Others	26.88	1,105.48	4.86	1,137.22
Total	1,906.67	2,942.73	2,602.64	7,452.04

Source: Ministry of Foreign Affairs.

Table 2.6 Geographical Distribution Structure of Japan's ODA (1990)
(%, net disbursement)

	Financial grant	Technical assistance	ODA loans	ODA total
Asia	46.5	43.0	70.7	59.3
East Asia	2.8	16.7	13.3	12.0
Southeast Asia	19.9	21.3	44.8	34.3
South Asia	23.8	4.6	12.6	12.9
Others	0.3	0.3	0.0	0.1
Middle East	8.2	5.8	12.6	10.2
Africa	30.8	7.6	6.2	11.4
Latin America	8.5	12.1	6.2	8.1
Oceania	4.5	1.9	0.5	1.6
Europe	0.0	0.7	3.7	2.3
Eastern Europe	0.0	0.3	3.8	2.2
Others	1.4	28.8	0.0	7.1
Total	100.0	100.0	100.0	100.0

Source: Ministry of Foreign Affairs.

Table 2.7 Japan's ODA Structure by Region (1990) (%, net disbursement)

	Financial grant	Technical assistance	ODA loans	ODA total
Asia	15.5	17.2	67.3	100.0
East Asia	4.6	33.0	62.4	100.0
Southeast Asia	11.5	14.8	73.8	100.0
South Asia	36.5	8.5	55.0	100.0
Others	100.0	100.0	0.0	100.0
Middle East	16.1	13.6	70.3	100.0
Africa	53.5	15.8	30.8	100.0
Latin America	20.9	35.5	43.6	100.0
Oceania	54.1	28.2	17.7	100.0
Europe	0.0	7.5	92.5	100.0
Eastern Europe	0.0	3.5	96.5	100.0
Others	4.0	96.0	0.0	100.0
Total	19.8	23.7	56.5	100.0

Source: Ministry of Foreign Affairs.

Table 2.8   Geographical Distribution Structure of Japan's ODA (2001) (%)

	Financial grant	Technical assistance	ODA loans	ODA total
Asia	38.2	37.0	92.4	56.6
East Asia	3.5	12.7	9.8	9.3
Southeast Asia	16.6	18.6	48.1	28.4
South Asia	15.7	4.1	28.3	15.5
Others	2.3	1.5	6.2	3.4
Middle East	9.3	4.6	−1.0	3.9
Africa	32.2	7.6	0.5	11.4
Latin America	14.1	10.3	6.4	9.9
Oceania	2.5	1.5	0.3	1.4
Europe	2.2	1.4	1.2	1.6
Eastern Europe	0.1	1.1	1.2	0.9
Others	1.4	37.6	0.2	15.3
Total	100.0	100.0	100.0	100.0

Source: Ministry of Foreign Affairs.

Table 2.9   Japan's ODA Structure by Region (2001) (%)

	Financial grant	Technical assistance	ODA loans	ODA total
Asia	17.2	25.8	57.0	100.0
East Asia	9.7	53.7	36.6	100.0
Southeast Asia	15.0	25.9	59.1	100.0
South Asia	25.8	10.5	63.7	100.0
Others	17.8	18.0	64.2	100.0
Middle East	61.9	47.2	−9.1	100.0
Africa	72.2	26.2	1.6	100.0
Latin America	36.5	41.0	22.4	100.0
Oceania	47.7	44.0	8.3	100.0
Europe	36.1	36.6	27.2	100.0
Eastern Europe	3.3	49.1	47.6	100.0
Others	2.4	97.2	0.4	100.0
Total	25.6	39.5	34.9	100.0

Source: Ministry of Foreign Affairs.

Figure 2.3 Share of ODA Loans in Japan's Total Bilateral ODA

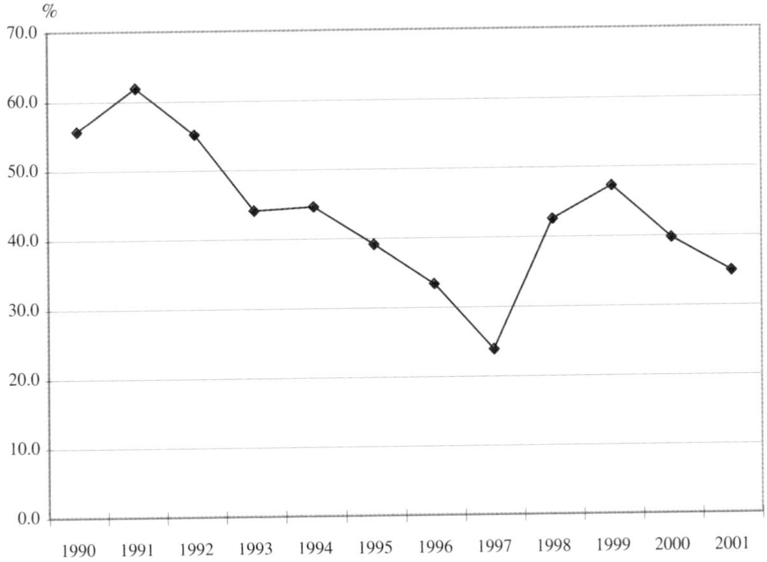

Source: JBIC (2003).

Table 2.10 10 Largest Recipient Countries of Japan's Bilateral ODA (1990) (net disbursement, $ million)

	ODA total	ODA total (% share in bilateral ODA total)	Financial grant	Technical assistance	ODA loans
1 Indonesia	867.78	12.5	53.38	108.68	700.72
2 China	723.02	10.4	37.82	163.49	521.71
3 Philippines	647.45	9.3	91.15	61.98	494.31
4 Thailand	418.57	6.0	76.02	96.34	246.21
5 Bangladesh	373.57	5.4	131.66	19.98	221.94
6 Malaysia	372.62	5.4	1.77	58.54	312.31
7 Turkey	324.21	4.7	0.34	15.25	308.62
8 Pakistan	193.55	2.8	56.06	11.54	125.96
9 Sri Lanka	176.07	2.5	74.39	16.58	85.10
10 Poland	149.85	2.2	0.00	2.12	147.73
Total	4,212.87	60.7	527.59	554.50	3,164.61
Bilateral ODA total	6,939.87	100.0	1,374.05	1,645.35	3,920.16

Source: Ministry of Foreign Affairs.
Note: This table lists top ten recipients of Japan's total bilateral ODA.

Table 2.11 10 Largest Recipient Countries of Japan's Bilateral ODA (2001)

ODA total   (net disbursement; $ million, %)

	ODA total	% share in bilateral ODA total
1 Indonesia	860.07	11.5
2 China	686.13	9.2
3 India	528.87	7.1
4 Vietnam	459.53	6.2
5 Philippines	298.22	4.0
6 Tanzania	260.44	3.5
7 Pakistan	211.41	2.8
8 Thailand	209.59	2.8
9 Sri Lanka	184.72	2.5
10 Peru	156.52	2.1
Total	3,855.50	51.7
Bilateral ODA total	7,452.04	100.0

Grant aid   ($ million, %)

	Grant aid	% share in bilateral grant aid total
1 Tanzania	241.32	12.7
2 Bangladesh	169.22	8.9
3 Cambodia	79.89	4.2
4 Philippines	66.75	3.5
5 Honduras	60.48	3.2
6 Vietnam	51.58	2.7
7 Nicaragua	51.26	2.7
8 Nepal	49.72	2.6
9 Jordan	49.10	2.6
10 Indonesia	45.16	2.4
Total	864.47	45.3
Bilateral grant aid total	1,906.67	100.0

Table 2.11   10 Largest Recipient Countries of Japan's Bilateral ODA (2001)
(continued)

Technical cooperation   ($ million, %)

	Technical cooperation	% share in bilateral technical cooperation total
1 China	276.54	9.4
2 Indonesia	117.27	4.0
3 Thailand	90.12	3.1
4 Vietnam	86.71	2.9
5 Philippines	84.70	2.9
6 Korea	66.07	2.2
7 Malaysia	52.21	1.8
8 Brazil	44.37	1.5
9 Cambodia	40.11	1.4
10 Laos	39.41	1.3
Total	897.52	30.5
Bilateral technical cooperation total	2,942.73	100.0

ODA loans   (net disbursement; $ million, %)

	ODA loans	% share in bilateral ODA loans total
1 Indonesia	697.64	26.8
2 India	505.52	19.4
3 China	386.57	14.9
4 Vietnam	321.25	12.3
5 Pakistan	159.55	6.1
6 Philippines	146.77	5.6
7 Sri Lanka	133.46	5.1
8 Peru	124.01	4.8
9 Thailand	116.97	4.5
10 Azerbaijan	87.69	3.4
Total	2,679.42	103.0
Bilateral ODA loans total	2,602.64	100.0

Source: Japan's ODA 2002 CD-ROM.

Table 2.12   20 Largest Recipient Countries of Japan's Bilateral ODA Loans and Growth Rate

Country	Cumulative value until (million, commitment)	GDP growth rate 1980–90	GDP growth rate (%) 1990–2001
1 Indonesia	3,639,292	6.1	3.8
2 China	2,829,275	10.3	10.0
3 India	2,009,946	5.7	5.9
4 Philippines	2,005,486	1.0	3.3
5 Thailand	1,919,278	7.6	3.8
6 Malaysia	879,657	5.3	6.5
7 Pakistan	826,169	6.3	3.7
8 Vietnam	766,733	4.6	7.7
9 Korea	645,527	4.2	2.0
10 Sri Lanka	588,914	4.0	5.0
11 Bangladesh	552,347	4.3	4.9
12 Egypt	437,819	5.4	4.5
13 Myanmar	426,567	0.6	7.4
14 Turkey	424,556	5.3	3.3
15 Peru	358,345	–0.1	4.3
16 Brazil	304,923	2.7	2.8
17 Mexico	229,568	1.1	3.1
18 Jordan	204,425	2.5	4.8
19 Kenya	172,833	4.2	2.0
20 Tunisia	165,962	3.3	4.7

Source: Japan's ODA 2002 CD-ROM; WDI-2003.

Reference Table   Growth Rate by Income Group and Region (%)

	1980–90	1990–2001
Low income countries	4.5	3.4
Middle income countries	2.9	3.4
Lower middle income	4.0	3.7
Upper middle income	1.7	3.1
Low and middle income countries	3.2	3.4
East Asia and Pacific	7.5	7.5
Europe and Central Asia	2.1	–1.0
Latin America and Caribbean	1.7	3.2
Middle East and North Africa	2.0	3.0
South Asia	5.6	5.5
Sub-Sahara Africa	1.6	2.6

Source: WDI-2003.

Table 2.13 Sector Distribution of ODA (2000) (commitement, %)

	Japan	USA	UK	France	Germany	Italy	Canada	Austraria	Sweden	DAC average
Social infrastructure	23.6	39.1	26.8	39.1	44.5	20.5	31.7	53.5	30.7	31.7
Economic infrastructure	32.0	13.8	6.5	4.5	13.9	2.8	4.5	8.8	8.2	16.5
Agriculture	6.1	4.0	6.3	5.2	4.6	4.3	4.5	6.5	2.0	5.1
Industry*	8.1	—	13.9	12.6	15.3	17.9	12.6	8.5	4.8	10.1
Food aid	0.6	11.0	12.5	4.6	6.0	10.6	14.3	11.1	20.2	7.7
Programme aid**	29.6	—	34.0	34.0	15.7	43.9	32.4	11.6	34.1	28.9
Total	100.0	100.0	100.0	100.0	100.0	100.0	100.0	100.0	100.0	100.0

Source: Japan's ODA 2002 CD-ROM.
* includes multi-sector aid.
** includes debt relief and administration costs.

3.2   Financial Flows to East Asia

As is well known, in its initial phase of industrialization, Korea was heavily dependent on external financing. Figure 2.4 shows Korea's dependency on foreign capital in the initial phase of industrialization. When Korea started the first five-year plan, nearly 80% of gross domestic fixed capital formation (GDFCF) was financed by external sources. Even in the third five-year plan period (1972–76), which is the start of heavy industrialization in Korea, the foreign capital/GDFCF ratio of Korea was still higher than 20%.

Accumulated foreign borrowing in Korea was a big policy issue around 1980. In terms of external debt, Korea was among the worst 10 in 1980. But by 1990 nobody was talking about Korea's external debt problem. Due to high economic growth and export expansion, Korea's external debt in relation to its economic size had declined sharply. This is often attributed to the shift to an export-oriented development strategy in Korea.

Financial flows to the East Asian countries in 1980 and 1991 are shown in Tables 2.14 and 2.15. Panel A shows the absolute value of the selected categories of external financing, and Panel B compares the ratio of external financial flows to investment.

The financial flows/investment ratios of Singapore, Thailand, Indonesia, and the Philippines were higher than 10% in 1980. For Indonesia and Thailand, the official flows/investment ratios were higher than 10%. The financial flows/investment ratios of Hong Kong and ASEAN4 (Indonesia, Malaysia, Philippines and Thailand) were higher

Figure 2.4   Foreign Capital/GDFCF Ratio in Korea

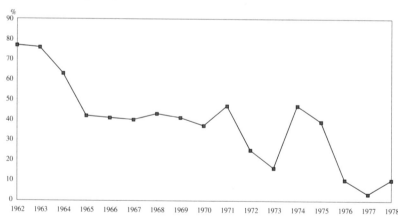

Source: Watanabe (1982), p.34.

Table 2.14 Financial Flows to East Asia (1980)

A. Amount ($ million)

	Total Receipt Net	ODA Net	ODA Gross	OOF Net	Total Official Gross	Private flows
Hong Kong	910.0	10.9	11.4	20.5	39.7	878.6
Korea	823.1	139.0	224.3	447.8	1,062.7	236.3
Singapore	752.4	14.0	21.4	29.3	93.3	709.1
Taiwan	438.9	-3.6	5.1	392.1	458.3	50.4
Indonesia	1,779.8	949.5	1,107.8	371.8	1,566.4	458.5
Malaysia	688.5	135.0	159.6	81.7	286.2	471.8
Philippines	975.2	303.6	325.0	230.0	669.6	441.6
Thailand	1,113.5	418.4	433.4	312.8	805.6	382.3

Note: Figures are net disbursement except ODA Gross and Total Official Gross.
Source: OECD, *Geographical Distrubution of Financial Flows to Developing Countries, 1979/1982.*

B. Amount (%, $ million)

	Total Receipt Net	ODA Net	ODA Gross	OOF Net	Total Official Gross	Private flows	Current Account
Hong Kong	9.9	0.1	0.1	0.2	0.4	9.5	na
Korea	4.1	0.7	1.1	2.2	5.3	1.2	-5,321
Singapore	15.8	0.3	0.4	0.6	2.0	14.9	-1,563
Taiwan	3.5	0.0	0.0	3.1	3.6	0.4	-913
Indonesia	11.8	6.3	7.3	2.5	10.4	3.0	3,011
Malaysia	9.0	1.8	2.1	1.1	3.8	6.2	-285
Philippines	11.0	3.4	3.7	2.6	7.6	5.0	-1,916
Thailand	13.8	5.2	5.4	3.9	10.0	4.7	-2,070

Note: Figures are net disbursement except ODA Gross and Total Official Gross.
Source: OECD, *Geographical Distrubution of Financial Flows to Developing Countries, 1979/1982.*
IMF-IFS, 1992 Yearbook; ADB, *Key Indicators,* 1992.

Table 2.15 Financial Flows to East Asia (1991)

A. Amount

($ million)

	Total Receipt Net	ODA Net	ODA Gross	OOF Net	Total Official Gross	Private flows
Hong Kong	2,860.1	36.1	39.0	-7.7	39.2	2,831.7
Korea	2,230.0	54.7	309.2	-440.6	517.5	2,615.9
Singapore	913.7	7.8	32.7	114.6	183.6	791.3
Taiwan	35.8	3.4	4.4	-2.1	4.6	34.5
Indonesia	5,225.9	1,877.3	2,499.8	2,129.8	5,706.1	1,218.8
Malaysia	1,910.1	289.0	433.2	163.9	819.8	1,457.2
Philippines	1,641.8	1,055.2	1,142.0	801.7	2,404.2	-215.1
Thailand	3,581.5	721.0	887.8	338.5	1,740.2	2,522.0
China	5,933.6	2,007.2	2,160.8	993.3	3,756.2	2,933.1
Vietnam	250.1	218.5	235.8	2.5	242.0	29.1

Note: Figures are net disbursement except ODA Gross and Total Official Gross.
Source: OECD, *Geographical Distribution of Financial Flows to Developing Countries, 1988/1991.*

B. Financial Flows/Investment Ratio

(%, $ million)

	Total Receipt Net	ODA Net	ODA Gross	OOF Net	Total Official Gross	Private flows	Current Account
Hong Kong	12.4	0.2	0.2	0.0	0.2	12.3	na
Korea	2.1	0.1	0.3	-0.4	0.5	2.4	-4,080
Singapore	5.7	0.0	0.2	0.7	1.2	5.0	4,208
Taiwan	0.1	0.0	0.0	0.0	0.0	0.1	10,769
Indonesia	12.8	4.6	6.1	5.2	14.0	3.0	-8,726
Malaysia	13.8	2.1	3.1	1.2	5.9	10.5	-4,530
Philippines	18.3	11.8	12.7	8.9	26.8	-2.4	-1,034
Thailand	12.6	2.5	3.1	1.2	6.1	8.9	-7,564
China	na	na	na	na	na	na	13,272
Vietnam	na	na	na	na	na	na	na

Note: Figures are net disbursement except ODA Gross and Total Official Gross.
Source: OECD, *Geographical Distribution of Financial Flows to Developing Countries, 1988/1991.*
IMF-IFS, April 1993; ADB, *Key Indicators, 1992.*

than 12% in 1991. As expected, the financial flows/investment ratios of ASEAN4 were higher than those of the Asian NIEs, except Hong Kong. Dependence on official flows increased in the 1980s for East Asian countries.

Financial flows to the East Asian countries in 1990 and 2001 are shown in Table 2.16. Due to the difference of data sources, figures in Table 2.16 are not completely comparable to the figures in Tables 2.14

Table 2.16 Financial Flows to East Asia (1990 and 2001) ($million)

	ODA(net)		Net private capital flows (NPCF)		Foreign direct investment (FDI)		Gross capital formation (GCF)	
	1990	2001	1990	2001	1990	2001	1990	2001
China	2,084	1,460	8,258	43,238	3,487	44,241	123,212	440,432
Hong Kong	38	4	na	na	na	22,834	20,476	45,474
Korea	52	–111	1,038	9,278	788	3,198	95,266	113,990
Singapore	–3	1	na	na	5,575	8,609	13,434	20,556
Cambodia	42	409	0	113	0	113	92	613
Indonesia	1,742	1,501	3,386	–7,312	1,093	–3,278	35,093	24,702
Laos	150	243	24	24	24	24	na	na
Malaysia	469	27	908	855	2,332	554	14,185	25,532
Myanmar	163	127	153	145	161	206	na	na
Philippines	1,276	577	779	2,076	530	1,792	10,706	12,859
Thailand	797	281	4,371	–3,052	2,444	3,820	35,293	27,523
Vietnam	189	1,435	16	710	16	1,300	840	10,144

(%)

	ODA/GCF		NPCF/GCF		FDI/GCF	
	1990	2001	1990	2001	1990	2001
China	1.7	0.3	6.7	9.8	2.8	10.0
Hong Kong	0.2	0.0	na	na	na	50.2
Korea	0.1	–0.1	1.1	8.1	0.8	2.8
Singapore	0.0	0.0	na	na	41.5	41.9
Cambodia	45.4	66.8	0.0	18.4	0.0	18.4
Indonesia	5.0	6.1	9.6	–29.6	3.1	–13.3
Laos	na	na	na	na	na	na
Malaysia	3.3	0.1	6.4	3.3	16.4	2.2
Myanmar	na	na	na	na	na	na
Philippines	11.9	4.5	7.3	16.1	5.0	13.9
Thailand	2.3	1.0	12.4	–11.1	6.9	13.9
Vietnam	22.5	14.1	1.9	7.0	1.9	12.8

Source: WDI-2002, 2003.

and 2.15. Although the ratio of ODA to gross capital formation (GCF) is low for China, Hong Kong, and Singapore, the ratio is higher than 10% for the new ASEAN members, such as Cambodia and Vietnam. The ratio of foreign direct investment (FDI) to GCF is higher than 40% in Hong Kong and Singapore. In 2001, the ratio of FDI to GCF was higher than 10% in China, Cambodia, the Philippines, Thailand, and Vietnam.

3.3 Geographical Distribution of Japan's ODA

Some economists conducted a regression analysis in order to find the determinants behind Japan's bilateral ODA distribution. Teranishi (1983) investigated the determinants behind Japan's ODA distribution for 1975–79. He found that Japan's ODA distribution bears a strong relation to Japan's exports to and the per capita gross national product (GNP) of recipient countries. Okamoto and Yokota (1992) also empirically analyzed determinants behind Japan's bilateral ODA distribution for the period from 1975 to 1989 with five subperiods. They found that the coefficients of Japan's exports to, the income level of, and the population of recipient countries show a statistically significant correlation with expected signs for total ODA and grant distribution. But in the case of Japan's ODA loan share, no estimated coefficients of income level of recipient countries show a statistically significant correlation in the five subperiods.[8]

3.3.1 ODA Distribution in 1991

In order to investigate the determinants for Japan's bilateral ODA distribution, the average Japanese ODA shares to the 79 countries where data was available for the period 1990–92 were regressed on the following variables of recipient countries as they existed in 1991 in six different specifications.

(Spec.1) ODA share = const. + a N + b YN + c FR + d X
(Spec.2) ODA share = const. + a N + b YN + c X
(Spec.3) ODA share = const. + a N + b YN + c FR + d XM
(Spec.4) ODA share = const. + a N + b YN + c XM
(Spec.5) ODA share = const. + a N + b YN + c FR + d XM + e AD
(Spec.6) ODA share = const. + a N + b YN + c XM + d AD

ODA share: Gross disbursement of total ODA;
            net disbursement of total ODA
    N: Population (million)
   YN: Per capita GNP(US$)
   FR: Gross international reserves (months of import coverage)
    X: Japan's exports (US$ million)
   XM: Japan's exports to and imports from the recipient country
       (US$ million)

AD: Asian dummy (Asian developing countries = 1, other developing countries = 0)

Shares of Japan's ODA categories (gross disbursement of total ODA, net disbursement of total ODA; 1990–92 average) are regressed on the explanatory variables in 1991 by the six specifications shown above. Estimated results for all specifications are presented in Tables 2.17 and 2.18. Although all estimated coefficients of FR (gross international reserves) are not statistically significant, other variables are significant. Income levels are all significantly negative, and foreign trade variables are significantly positive. Japan's ODA shares are higher for lower income countries and for countries with closer foreign trade relations. All Asian dummies, except for technical assistance share, are significantly positive. Japan's ODA shares to Asian developing countries are higher than developing countries in the other regions when adjusted for population size, income level, and foreign trade transactions.

3.3.2 ODA Distribution in 2001

In order to investigate the changes in determinants for Japan's bilateral ODA distribution, Japanese ODA shares to 119 countries where data was available for 2001 were regressed on the following variables in 2001 in six specifications.[9]

(Spec.1) ODA share = const. + a N + b YN + c X
(Spec.2) ODA share = const. + a N + b YN + c X + d AD
(Spec.3) ODA share = const. + a N + b YN + c X + d EAD
(Spec.4) ODA share = const. + a N + b YN + c XM
(Spec.5) ODA share = const. + a N + b YN + c XM + d AD
(Spec.6) ODA share = const. + a N + b YN + c XM + d EAD

ODA share: Gross disbursement of total ODA;
        net disbursement of total ODA
    N: Population (million)
  YN: Per capita GNI(US$)
    X: Japan's exports (US$ million)
  XM: Japan's exports to and imports from the
        recipient country (US$ million)
  AD: Asian dummy (Asian developing countries = 1,
        other developing countries = 0)
EAD: East Asian dummy (East Asian developing countries = 1,
        other developing countries = 0)

Estimated results are shown in Tables 2.19 (gross disbursement of total ODA) and 2.20 (net disbursement of total ODA). All coefficients

Table 2.17 Determinants of Japan's ODA Distribution(1990–92): Gross Disbursement of Total ODA

Specification	constant	population (N)	per capita GNP (YN)	reserves (FR)	exports (X)	exports+ imports (XM)	Asian dummy (AD)	R^2 adjusted
Spec.1	0.89923** (2.6061)	0.00546*** (3.9083)	-0.00029*** (-3.0260)	0.02728 (0.3615)	0.00033*** (4.2551)			0.4059
Spec.2	0.98085*** (3.7807)	0.00558*** (4.1369)	-0.00028*** (-3.0366)		0.00033*** (4.2653)			0.4128
Spec.3	0.87732*** (2.7506)	0.00367*** (2.6560)	-0.00033*** (-3.7267)	0.03014 (0.4329)		0.00024*** (5.8167)		0.4925
Spec.4	0.96780*** (4.0289)	0.00381*** (2.8485)	-0.00032*** (-3.7386)			0.00023*** (5.8329)		0.4980
Spec.5	0.62788** (2.0731)	0.00271** (2.0749)	-0.00029*** (-3.5048)	0.04622 (0.7157)		0.00015*** (3.3323)	2.27308*** (3.6650)	0.5655
Spec.6	0.76927*** (3.3622)	0.00293** (2.3217)	-0.00027*** (-3.4423)			0.00015*** (3.3181)	2.24293*** (3.6368)	0.5684

Source: Ministry of Foreign Affairs of Japan, Japan's ODA (in Japanese), 1993.
World Bank, World Development Report, 1993.
IMF, Direction of Trade Statistics Yearbook, 1993.

Note: **: significant at the 5 % level.
***: significant at the 1 % level.
( ): t-value.
Japan's ODA shares to 79 countries(1990–92 average) are regressed on the independent variables in 1991.

Table 2.18 Determinants of Japan's ODA Distribution(1990–92): Net Disbursement of Total ODA

Specification	constant	population (N)	per capita GNP (YN)	reserves (FR)	exports (X)	exports+imports (XM)	Asian dummy (AD)	R^2 adjusted
Spec.1	0.84018** (2.4827)	0.00655*** (4.7759)	-0.00025** (-2.6296)	0.02865 (0.3871)	0.00022*** (2.9169)			0.3936
Spec.2	0.92590*** (3.6383)	0.00667*** (5.0412)	-0.00024** (-2.6223)		0.00022*** (2.9089)			0.4005
Spec.3	0.82069** (2.5791)	0.00501*** (3.6359)	-0.00029*** (-3.3437)	0.03355 (0.4830)		0.00018*** (4.3997)		0.4641
Spec.4	0.92140*** (3.8530)	0.00517*** (3.8720)	-0.00028*** (-3.3330)			0.00018*** (4.3965)		0.4695
Spec.5	0.61053* (1.9692)	0.00420*** (3.1451)	-0.00026*** (-3.0897)	0.0471 (0.7124)		0.00010** (2.2874)	1.91505*** (3.0163)	0.5169
Spec.6	0.75462*** (3.2220)	0.00443*** (3.4270)	-0.00025*** (-3.0183)			0.00010** (2.2692)	1.88433*** (2.9848)	0.5201

Source: Ministry of Foreign Affairs of Japan, Japan's ODA (in Japanese), 1993.
World Bank, World Development Report, 1993.
IMF, Direction of Trade Statistics Yearbook, 1993.

Note: *: significant at the 10 % level.
**: significant at the 5 % level.
***: significant at the 1 % level.
( ): t-value.
Japan's ODA shares to 79 countries(1990–92 average) are regressed on the independent variables in 1991.

Table 2.19 Determinants of Japan's ODA Distribution (2001): Gross Disbursement of Total ODA

Specification	constant	population (N)	per capita GNP (YN)	exports (X)	exports+ imports (XM)	Asian dummy (AD)	East Asian dummy (EAD)	R^2 adjusted
Spec.1	0.57945*** (4.2265)	0.00733*** (7.9479)	−0.00012*** (−3.3805)	0.00014*** (4.1210)				0.6071
Spec.2	0.363*** (2.639)	0.007*** (8.176)	−0.00012*** (−3.673)	0.00009*** (3.015)		1.143*** (4.301)		0.6590
Spec.3	0.542*** (3.922)	0.007*** (8.086)	−0.00011*** (−3.204)	0.00013*** (3.760)			0.194 (1.623)	0.6126
Spec.4	0.556*** (4.074)	0.007*** (6.263)	−0.00009*** (−2.902)		0.00009*** (4.080)			0.6061
Spec.5	0.34415** (2.5424)	0.00641*** (2.0749)	−0.0001*** (−3.13401)		0.00005*** (3.1340_)	1.1631*** (4.4305)		0.6610
Spec.6	0.519*** (3.784)	0.007*** (6.423)	−0.00009*** (−3.785)		0.00006*** (3.758)		0.204* (1.709)	0.6126

Source: MIDS 2003 CD-ROM; WDI-2003; Japan Ministry of Finance (www.mof.go.jp).
Note: *: significant at the 10 % level.
**: significant at the 5 % level.
***: significant at the 1 % level.
( ): t-value.
Japan's ODA shares to 119 countries are regressed on the independent variables in 2001.

Table 2.20 Determinants of Japan's ODA Distribution(2001): Net Disbursement of Total ODA

Specification	constant	population (N)	per capita GNP (YN)	exports (X)	exports+ imports (XM)	Asian dummy (AD)	East Asian dummy (EAD)	R^2 adjusted
Spec.1	0.586*** (3.641)	0.008*** (7.282)	-0.00009** (-2.190)	0.00006 (1.483)				0.4733
Spec.2	0.363** (2.209)	0.008*** (7.367)	-0.00009** (-2.346)	0.00002 (0.444)		1.175*** (3.699)		0.5256
Spec.3	0.538*** (3.327)	0.008*** (7.437)	-0.00008** (-2.003)	0.00004*** (1.133)			0.245* (1.744)	0.4824
Spec.4	0.585*** (3.681)	0.007*** (5.863)	-0.00009** (-2.329)		0.00004* (1.956)			0.4804
Spec.5	0.379** (2.345)	0.007*** (6.027)	-0.0001*** (-2.731)		0.00002 (1.076)	1.130*** (3.605)		0.5295
Spec.6	0.542*** (3.395)	0.007*** (6.016)	-0.00008** (-2.213)		0.00003 (1.650)		0.236* (1.698)	0.4888

Source: IDS 2003 CD-ROM; WDI-2003; Japan Ministry of Finance (www.mof.go.jp).
Note: *: significant at the 10 % level.
**: significant at the 5 % level.
***: significant at the 1 % level.
( ): t-value.
Japan's ODA shares to 119 countries are regressed on the independent variables in 2001.

of recipients' size variable (population) and income level are statistically significant and have the expected signs for both gross disbursement and net disbursement of Japan's total ODA distribution. Although economic relations variables (exports and total trade) are statistically significant and have the expected signs for the gross disbursement distribution functions, they are not very effective variables for the net disbursement distribution functions. Asian dummies are statistically significant and have the expected signs for both gross disbursement and net disbursement of Japan's total ODA distribution. East Asian dummies are positive, but they are not always statistically significant.

4. Japan's Aid Policy

4.1 Japanese View on Long-Term Economic Development[10]

Let me summarize my understanding of the Japanese image of economic development and the Japanese view on development policy.

While the typical Western view on economic development considers that more or less the same economic model applies to the growth of industrialized countries as well as to the development of developing countries, the Japanese tend to regard the development of developing countries as something qualitatively different from the growth of industrialized countries. In the neoclassical growth model often utilized by Western economists, the market is assumed to allocate resources efficiently, technology smoothly advances either exogenously or through the accumulation of knowledge or learning by doing, and prices represent all information needed for the maximizing behaviour of economic units. Many Japanese economists consider that the development process of developing countries has qualitatively different dimensions from this model.

First, since the growth of developing countries occurs through borrowed technology, the formation of learning capability comprises an essential prerequisite for the initiation of the successful accumulation of knowledge or learning by doing. Ohkawa and Rosovsky (1973) have emphasized the importance of learning capability by the broad term of 'social capability'. Stiglitz (1987) has shed new light on this issue by introducing the concept of learning to learn. From this viewpoint, the enhancement of dynamic efficiency as compared with static efficiency comprises the essential part of development policy (Myint 1987 and Sachs 1987). The increase of total factor productivity does not occur automatically as a result of the accumulation of experience but must be pursued both by means of making the effort to accumulate social capability in the private sector and via policies aimed at fostering learning capabilities. Since the economic horizon of entrepreneurs needs to be longer than otherwise in order to take into account the time required for the formation of this capability, the provision of a stable and competitive environment suitable for long-term entrepreneurial behaviour is essentially important for successful development. Therefore, the supply of long-term funds or proper signalling by the government, as well as the provision of stable and easily foreseeable macroeconomic conditions, are considered to play an essential role in the development process.

Second, in the developing countries, various markets are considered to be underdeveloped due to significant informational asymmetry and monopoly in various markets. Moreover, since the accumulation of information and the establishment of an institutional framework for processing and disseminating information develop gradually, the development of markets takes a long time. Although effective in wiping out excess profits and, consequently, alleviating rent-seeking activities, liberalization measures are not sufficient in this regard. When the working of markets is insufficient and slow to improve, the role of organizations as compared to the market becomes all the more important in the allocation of resources as well as in the enhancement of economic efficiency. Examples are abundant with respect to the importance of the utilization of institutions. The maintenance of institutional efficiency is most important for the successful accomplishment of stabilization with growth (Teranishi 1991). Reliance on an intra-firm labour market could be justified for the accumulation of firm-specific skills. The utilization of a non-market allocation mechanism, such as equity issue within relatives and family, is not necessarily irrational when the equity market is underdeveloped.

It is also quite difficult to eradicate monopolistic moneylenders in the rural and urban informal sectors or monopsony in bank credits and the equity market by large family groups. In such a situation, it is necessary either to let the monopoly face international competition by means of liberalization on international fronts or to establish countervailing power in the sense of John Kenneth Galbraith, such as state-owned (but privately managed) enterprises, development banks, or national mutual funds.

In sum, the Japanese view of economic development has two traits: perception of the slow accumulation of learning capabilities with a consequent emphasis on dynamic efficiency as compared with static efficiency, and the notion of the slow development of the market with a consequent emphasis on organizational efficiency and countervailing power as compared to competitive market efficiency. We do not deny the importance of static efficiency, nor the role of markets, but only suggest that because the instantaneous realization of efficient markets and accumulation of learning capability is difficult, development policy should take into account these constraints. At the same time, it must be strongly cautioned that non-market and 'long-term' solutions are sometimes liable to induce rent-seeking activities and serious moral hazards.

4.2 Japan's ODA Charter

It is often claimed that Japan's aid policy lacks clearly defined principles and is implemented on an ad hoc basis. It is true that officially stated principles have undergone substantial changes over time depending on the economic status and conditions of Japan. The Japanese government announced only the two aid principles of 'humanitarian consideration' and 'recognition of interdependence' until it issued the ODA Charter in June 1992 (Japan's ODA 1990, pp.25–27).

The two aid principles of 'humanitarian consideration' and 'recognition of interdependence' are apparently too broad, and almost tantamount to no principle at all. Moreover, it seems true that Japan's aid is not always derived from a stated principle and implemented in a deductive fashion from it, but often blamed as a compromise through complicated power politics among various bureaucratic systems and political factions. This may be a very Japanese way of policymaking, but we need to make an effort to get other donors to understand this point.

Despite the vagueness of aid principles, however, it is important to note that Japan's aid has been consistently conducted in line with a strong, though implicit, motive.

The basic motive behind Japan's aid policy is as follows: Aid should be conducive to the long-term economic development of recipient countries in light of the Japanese view on development policy based on Japan's own development experience. Although never stated explicitly, this motive of contributing to the recipient's long-term development has comprised the background of Japan's policy formation and seems to have been broadly accepted. Japan's aid policy strongly reflects this motive.

At the beginning of the 1990s, there existed a movement in the ruling Liberal Democratic Party (LDP) and the Ministry of Foreign Affairs to increase the 'strategic considerations' in Japanese ODA.[11] In a Diet debate, Mr. Toshiki Kaifu, then Prime Minister of Japan, announced the ODA policy considerations relating to strategic factors, such as military expenditures in recipient countries, on 10 April 1991. This is not a new policy that replaces the two basic principles mentioned above – humanitarian considerations and recognition of interdependence. The following four points were the new considerations to implement Japan's bilateral ODA that Mr. Kaifu announced in April 1991. The Japanese government takes the following into consideration in providing bilateral ODA:

(i) military expenditures in recipient countries;
(ii) development and production of arms in recipient countries;
(iii) export and import of arms in recipient countries;
(iv) trend of democratization, introduction of market-oriented economic system, basic human rights, and freedom in recipient countries.

Based on these four points, the Official Development Assistance Charter was adopted by the cabinet on 30 June 1992.[12] It is desirable to implement development aid based on an explicit policy. However, once the policy is announced, we should not have many exceptions.[13]

4.3 Relationship of Japan's ODA and Development Policy

Let us consider the three basic characteristics of Japan's ODA:

(i) low share of grants;
(ii) emphasis on project financing, although the share of policy-based lending (PBL) is increasing in cooperation with the World Bank adjustment lending;
(iii) request principle, or the principle of extending aid on a request basis.

Needless to say, it is important to note that these characteristics stand in close relation with the Japanese view on economic development policy described in the previous section and, in a sense, could be regarded as logical consequences of it. The relationship is most clear with the emphasis on the request principle. Since the degree of underdevelopment of markets and the accumulation of learning capability differs among countries, and depends on the phase of development, Japan's aid policy puts special emphasis on a differentiated approach for each recipient country. Not only avoiding the application of uniform development strategy, it recommends a recipient country to devise its own methods of coping with the obstacles to development. Consequently, the emphasis on 'self-help' or 'ownership' constitutes another characteristic of Japanese aid, and, as for the choice of objectives of aid, the basic stance is passively reacting to a request emanating from the recipient's own initiatives.

In this regard, Japanese aid is expected to support the developing countries' initiatives for development. Japanese aid is based on the understanding that economic development should be promoted by 'self-help' efforts. Therefore, it is an implicit but common understanding of technocrats in Japan that it is not desirable to force policy reforms in exchange for providing monetary aid. I am not saying that policy reforms are not necessary but just want to emphasize the importance of the recipient's own initiatives in promoting development and reforms of its own economy.

Second, the Japanese preference for project aid and reluctance toward policy-based lending also reflect the Japanese view on development policy. From the viewpoint of organizational efficiency, project aid seems to be the most suitable instrument for effective implementation of aid, since it contributes directly to the enhancement of individual organizations or production units either by means of technology transfer or breaking particular bottlenecks. As Yanagihara (1998) points out, it could be argued that the Japanese government has adopted an 'ingredient' approach in this regard. If the policy reform programme is consistent with Japan's 'ingredients', which contrast with the 'framework approach', it is possible to expand PBLs.

Third, the high share of ODA loans in Japanese aid is also considered to claim special merits in light of the development policy held by the Japanese.[14] Although the private international capital market is a major source of developing countries' funds for development in the future as well as in the past, its basic drawback, instability, is well known; a massive inflow and an abrupt curtailment based on a bandwagon effect. Therefore, the complementary role of official credit is important. From the viewpoint of development policy described above, official credits have the following desirable properties: By smoothing out the resource transfer to developing countries, the pursuit of stable macroeconomic policy is made easier; this enables entrepreneurs to have a longer-term economic horizon, which is an essential prerequisite for successful development. By the same token, stable and easily foreseeable capital inflow could induce a higher rate of investment, since its macroeconomic consequences could be easily incorporated in the entrepreneur's expectations.

Moreover, in view of the underdevelopment of money markets in developing countries, the supply of long-term funds from donor countries – an international financial intermediation – is essential for active investment activities. Since learning and the formation of learning capability in developing countries suffer seriously not only from externalities of learning but also from the underdevelopment of financial markets, the supply of long-term funds through ODA seems to be especially beneficial in this regard.

From this viewpoint, the low share of grants in Japanese aid should not be viewed negatively; it has its own positive property in offsetting the shortcomings of the private capital market.

5. East Asian Dynamism and Development Cooperation

Many East Asian countries are recovering from the economic crisis at the end of the 1990s, but some of them have various difficulties. Some East Asian developing countries, such as China and Vietnam, are still in a state of transition to market economies.

East Asia is the most dynamic region in the world. Maintaining the East Asian dynamism is crucially important not only for the region but also for the world economy. I understand that the most important factor to explain the high growth of East Asian countries is that they are very clever followers. They utilize the diffusion of dynamism – from Japan to the Asian NIEs, from the NIEs to the ASEAN countries, then from the ASEAN countries to China. They correctly understand the mechanism to promote development and the role of government. In spite of a common misunderstanding of Japan's industrial policy, technocrats in East Asian countries understand that the crucial point is to utilize private dynamism. The role of government is not to intervene in the market directly; its role is to maintain a competitive economic environment and provide basic infrastructure. Furthermore, in East Asia, competition among countries is quite fierce. When one country announces a deregulation policy for foreign direct investment, neighbouring countries try to deregulate their foreign investment policy too. This competition among neighbouring countries is aimed at encouraging foreign companies to invest in the region.

Foreign direct investment has played a crucial role for the diffusion of dynamism and multilayered production networks (Yusuf 2003, Chapter 7). Many companies from Japan, Korea, Taiwan, and other more developed countries are rushing to China and Southeast Asian countries. Relatively open trade and foreign investment policies are common in East Asian countries. Basic economic infrastructure supply, such as electricity and port facilities, is a necessary condition for inviting foreign companies.

Generally speaking, the contribution of aid toward economic development in developing countries is limited, but aid contribution for development is not so small in some cases. Table 2.21 shows the contribution of Japan's ODA loans to selected economic infrastructures in East Asia. For example, in Thailand 20% of total electricity supply and 29% of irrigation facilities were financed by Japan's ODA loans.[15] Although it is difficult to verify the contribution of aid with a rigorous quantitative model, the figures in Table 2.21 are good illustrations to understand the positive role of aid in the economic development of East Asia.

Table 2.21   Contribution of Japan's ODA Loans to Economic Infrastructure in East Asia (%)

	China	Korea	Indonesia	Malaysia	Philippines	Thailand
Electricity	4		31	51	5	20
Rural electrification						21
Telephone	10					
Rural telephone network					11	
Railway	8		12	20		
Port	5					
Freeway			18			100*
Dam		82				
Rural water supply					13	
Irrigation			4			29
Pumping station					70**	

Source: OECF (1992).
Note: Contribution of Japan's ODA loans to total supply of infrastructure service.
   * Freeway in Bangkok.
   ** Pumping station for flood control in Manila.

Notes

[1] For the development of Japan's steel industry, see Yonekura (1994).

[2] For social capability, see Ohkawa and Kohama (1989, Chapter 6), and Koo and Perkins (1995).

[3] IMF conditionality gradually becomes realistic after the Asian economic crisis at the end of the 1990.

[4] MITI was reorganized to METI (Ministry of Economy, Trade and Industry) in 2001.

[5] OECD (2002). 11 countries are, Bangladesh, Dominica, Gambia, Ghana, India, Kyrgyz, Mauritania, Nicaragua, Palestine, and Saint Christfer and Nevis.

[6] We observe the rise in the share in 1998 and 1999. This is because of the sharp increase of ODA loans to the crisis countries in Asia.

[7] Japan's share of ODA loans was 30.3% in total bilateral ODA in 2000 (net disbursement basis). But the DAC average share of ODA loans was 5.6% in 2000.

[8] This paragraph and the following estimations of Japan's ODA distribution function in the beginning of the 1990s are drawn from Kohama (1995).

[9] Part II countries of DAC List of aid recipients are included in the 119 countries. All the parameters for "Foreign reserves" are not statistically significant for 1991, thus "Foreign reserves" is excluded for the estimation of 2001 distribution function.

[10] This section is drawn from Kohama and Teranishi (1992).

[11] As mentioned above, my view is that Japan's ODA should be mainly an aid to promote economic development.

[12] The revised Official Development Assistance Charter was announced in August 2003.

[13] China is one of the largest Japan's ODA recipients in spite of its military presence. It not easy to explain Japan's aid to China when we consider the basic points of the ODA Charter.

[14] A high share of ODA loans in Japan's ODAis partly due to the sources of budget. Japan's ODA loans are financed by both general budget and FILP (Fiscal Investment and Loans Program).

[15] Figures in this table could be overestimation.

References

IDS 2003. <CD-ROM> OECD. *International Development Statistics 2003 CD-ROM*. Paris: OECD, 2003.

JBIC (Japan Bank for International Cooperation). *Kokusai Kyoryoku Binran* (Handbook of International Cooperation). Tokyo: JBIC, annual.

Japan's ODA. Ministry of Foreign Affairs (Japan). *Seifu Kaihatsu Enjo Hakusho* (White Paper on Japan's ODA).

Kohama, Hirohisa and Juro Teranishi. "Japan's ODA Policy and Economic Development of Recipient Countries". A revised version of the paper presented at a conference on "Development Cooperation Policies of Japan, the United States, and Europe" (Tokyo: Institute of Developing Economies, January 29–30, 1992).

Kohama, Hirohisa. "Japan's Development Cooperation and the Economic Development in East Asia". In Takatoshi Ito and Anne O. Krueger (eds.), *Growth Theories in Light of East Asian Experience*, Chicago: University of Chicago Press, 1995.

Koo, Ban Ho, and Dwight H. Perkins (eds.). *Social Capability and Long-Term Economic Growth*. New York: St. Martin, 1995.

Ministry of Foreign Affairs (Japan). *Seifu Kaihatsu Enjo Hakusho* (White Paper on Japan's ODA). Tokyo: National Printing Bureau, annual. Japan's ODA.

Myint, Hla. "The Neoclassical Resurgence in Development Economics: Its Strength and Limitations." In Gerald M. Meier (ed.), *Pioneers in Development (Second Series)*. Oxford: Oxford University Press, 1987.

OECD. *Geographical Distribution of Financial Flows to Aid Recipients 1996–2000.* Paris: OECD, 2002.

OECD. *International Development Statistics 2003 CD-ROM.* Paris: OECD, 2003. IDS 2003 CD-ROM.

OECF (Overseas Economic Cooperation Fund). *Kaigai Keizai Kyoryoku Binran* (Handbook of Overseas Economic Cooperation). Tokyo: OECF, annual.

OECF (Overseas Economic Cooperation Fund). 1992. *ODA Loans Today* (in Japanese).

Ohkawa, Kazushi and Henry Rosovsky. *Japanese Economic Growth.* Stanford: Stanford University Press, 1973.

Ohkawa, Kazushi and Hirohisa Kohama. *Lectures on Developing Economies – Japan's Experience and its Relevance.* Tokyo: University of Tokyo Press, 1989.

Okamoto, Yumiko and Kazuhiko Yokota. "Nihon no Enjo Seisaku no Suryo Bunseki" (Empirical Analysis of Japan's Aid Policy), *Kokusai Kaihatsu Kenkyu* (The Japan Society for International Development). June 1992.

Sachs, Jeffrey. "Trade and Exchange Rate Policies in Growth-Oriented Adjustment Programs." In Vittorio Corbo, Morris Goldstein and Mohsin Khan (eds.), *Growth-Oriented Adjustment Programs.* Washington, D.C.: International Monetary Fund and the World Bank, 1987.

Stiglitz, Joseph E. "Learning to Learn, Localized Learning and Technological Progress." In P. Dasgupta and P. Stoneman (eds.), *Economic Policy and Technological Performance.* Cambridge: Cambridge University Press, 1987.

Teranishi, Juro. "Wagakuni no Seifu Kaihatsu Enjo (ODA) Seisaku ni tsuite" (On Japan's ODA Policy), *Keizai Kenkyu* (Institute of Economic Research, Hitotsubashi University, Tokyo). April 1983.

Teranishi, Juro. "Inflation Stabilization with Growth – Experience of Japan during 1945–1950." Discussion Paper Series A No. 243, Institute of Economic Research, Hitotsubashi University, Tokyo, 1991.

Watanabe, Toshio. *Gendai Kankoku Keizai Bunseki* (Korea's Economic Development). Tokyo: Keiso Shobo, 1982.

WDI World Bank. *World Development Indicators.*

World Bank/Tokyo Office. 1991. *Segin Shakkan Kaiso* (World Bank Loans to Japan). Tokyo: World Bank/Tokyo Office.

World Bank. *World Development Indicators.* various years. WDI.

Yanagihara, Toru. "Development and Dynamic Efficiency: 'framework approach' versus 'ingredient approach'." In Kenichi Ohno and Izumi Ohno (eds.), *Japanese Views on Economic Development: Diverse Paths to the Market.* London: Routledge, 1998.

Yonekura, Seiichiro. *The Japanese Iron and Steel Industry, 1850–1990.* London: Macmillan, 1994.

Yusuf, Shahid et al. *Innovative East Asia: The Future of Growth.* New York: Oxford University Press, 2003.

3
Japan's ODA and Poverty Reduction: A Cross-Donor Comparison and a Case Study of Malaysia

Yasuyuki Sawada and Hiroyuki Yamada

1. Introduction

Since the mid-1990s, the international community's development objectives seem to have converged on poverty reduction. The current policy statements of multilateral institutions and aid donor countries are stressing explicitly the importance of poverty reduction at the global level. Particularly, the international community is supporting the initiatives in order to achieve the Millennium Development Goals (MDGs). The MDGs, which were adopted by the United Nations Millennium Summit held in September 2000, defined specific targets and a time frame for reducing poverty in the world. The first goal of the MDGs is to eradicate extreme poverty and hunger in the world by the year 2015. The explicit indicators employed in measuring this goal are the proportion of population living on less than one dollar per day and the poverty gap ratio.

2. Review of the Related Literature

In this chapter, we investigate the effectiveness of Japan's ODA in reducing the recipients' poverty from two different aspects. First, we do so by employing the poverty targeting framework of Besley and Kanbur (1988) based on the Foster-Greer-Thorbecke (1984) poverty measure, we compare the effectiveness of eleven donor countries, i.e., France, Germany, Japan, the Netherlands, the United Kingdom, the United States, Canada, Italy, Finland, Norway, and Sweden. Second, by using a detailed case study of Malaysia, we investigate the effectiveness of Japan's ODA over a period of 30 years. Two main empirical results emerged. First, in the late 1990s, grant allocations of Japan, the Netherlands, United Kingdom, Canada, Norway, and Sweden were consistent with the theory of poverty targeting. Secondly, while Japan's bilateral ODA allocations to Malaysia have concentrated on economic infrastructure, our quantitative assessment suggests that they have also significantly contributed to poverty reduction in Malaysia.

The remainder of this chapter is organized as follows. After reviewing the literature in Section 2, Section 3 presents theoretical and econometric frameworks to evaluate the aid allocation. Then these empirical results are reported and discussed. Section 4 analyzes the case of Japan's ODA provisions to Malaysia over 30 years. The final section summarizes the analyses.

It would be useful to review the literature on the effectiveness of international aid. The existing studies on the role of international aid can be divided into two groups, according to their focus on recipients or donors (Alesina and Dollar 2000). First, there are studies on the policy response of recipients to aid provisions (Boone 1996; Burnside and Dollar 2000; Collier and Dollar 2002; World Bank 1998). For example, a very influential study by Burnside and Dollar (2000) found that the impact of aid on growth of recipients is positive with good fiscal, monetary and trade policies but has little effect for recipients with poor policies. Yet, they found no evidence that aid has systematically affected policies of recipients. This finding is in line with the findings of Boone (1996) who found that while aid does increase the size of government, it has no effect on investment and human development indicators. A number of other studies such as Alesina and Weder (2002) also concluded that the aid quantity does not alter the quality of policies of recipient countries. Rather, as Alesina and Weder (2000) found, an increase in aid is likely to increase corruption, probably because an unexpected transfer will induce rent seeking activities.

Second, several researchers have examined the motivations and the determinants of donors' aid allocation. In fact, there is substantial controversy over the motivation behind aid provisions. Aid donor countries may be concerned with diverse factors such as mutual or individual benefits through international trade or political relationships, poverty reduction and equity of recipients, and international security.

For example, a welfare function estimation suggests that donors as a whole have significant inequality aversion in the international distribution of aid (Behrman and Sah 1984). Based on a rigorous theoretical model of ODA, Trumbull and Wall (1994) found that foreign aid allocations are determined by the needs of the recipients represented by infant mortality and political/civil rights. Yet, according to the recent studies, donor countries largely seem to be motivated by strategic considerations rather than altruism or the real needs of the recipient countries (Alesina and Dollar 2000; Maizels and Nissanke 1984). Collier and Dollar (2002) also support this view by finding that the actual aid allocation is far from efficient in terms of poverty reduction. Moreover, Alesina and Weder (2002) document that there is no evidence that donors allocate more aid to less corrupt governments. A possible interpretation of this observation can be found in the work by Lahiri and Raimondos-Moller (2000), which, interestingly, argues that lobbying by ethnic groups in the donor country enhances aid provisions to its country of origin.

On the other hand, motivation for multilateral aid can be said to be more transparent. Multilateral agencies are largely apolitical and more exclusively concerned with development and/or poverty reduction (Cassen et al. 1986, p. 281; Maizels and Nissanke 1984; Frey and Schneider 1986; Sawada 1996).

In sum, in order to reduce global poverty, the existing studies suggest that there are two requirements of aid to be effective in reducing such poverty. First, the aid should be allocated towards the countries where poverty is an important issue and not to the relatively developed countries. This is the first requirement for effective aid allocations that should be imposed by the aid donors. Second, external assistance should be more tightly combined with the recipients' efforts. In countries where policies are inconsistent with efforts to reduce poverty, foreign aid will achieve far less. This is partly due to the fungibility with which it is difficult for donors to target particular groups. Therefore, in order to reduce poverty effectively, the recipients' policy should be appropriate. These are the two requirements for effective aid which should be satisfied by the aid recipients.

By investigating these two requirements through econometric analysis and a case study, this chapter will evaluate whether aid allocations by Japan have contributed to the recipients' poverty reduction. The chapter is composed of two parts, which approximately correspond to the above-mentioned two requirements. First, we conduct a cross-donor comparison to evaluate whether donors' aid allocations were designed to reduce poverty in the late 1990s. To accomplish this, we have constructed a global poverty indicator which formalizes the first goal of the MDGs. Then, by employing cross country data, we tested, statistically, whether aid allocation of donor countries and international institutions were consistent with the poverty reduction criteria. Specifically, we have extended Besley and Kanbur's (1988) model of targeting food subsidies in international aid provisions.

The above analysis is based on a reduced-form framework, focusing on the targeting condition which should be satisfied by the donors. At the same time, the conditions of efforts by the recipients to reduce poverty should be met, too. Both of these conditions are required, since foreign aid will be less effective when recipient countries employ policies which are inconsistent with the efforts to reduce poverty. In order to evaluate this second requirement, we conduct a detailed case study of the Japan's aid allocations to Malaysia over 30 years. In other words, we examine the intervening structure through which international aid will reduce poverty. We believe that by conducting a case study, we can test the structure through which Japan's aid provisions contribute to reducing poverty in Malaysia.

3. A Cross-Donor Comparison

In order to quantitatively evaluate the effectiveness of aid in terms of poverty reduction, we need to define an indicator of poverty. Suppose that the world's income distribution function is represented by $f(y)$. Then by using the Foster-Greer-Thorbecke (FGT) poverty index by Foster et al. (1984), we can define an index for global poverty $G(\alpha)$:

(1)
$$G(\alpha) \equiv \int_0^z [(y - \alpha)/z]^\alpha f(y) dy,_1$$

where z and y represent a person-specific poverty line and an income level after receiving aid, respectively. According to the nice properties of the FGT poverty index, the global poverty index in equation (1) can be decomposed into an additive form of each recipient's poverty index $G^r(\alpha)$:

(2)
$$G(\alpha) \equiv \sum_r \omega^r G^r(\alpha)$$

where r is an index for aid recipient countries and w^r represents the proportion of world population in the recipient country r. In equations (1) and (2), income after aid can be decomposed into pre-aid income y^b_r and an additional income component generated by aid y^a_r, where the latter is a function of $m_{d,r,i.e.,}$ international aid per recipient's population provided by donors indexed by d:

(3)
$$y_r = y^a_r(m_{1,r}, m_{2,r}, \dots m_{d,r}, \dots m_{N,r}) + y^b_r.$$

Then, applying Besley and Kanbur's (1988) formula, we can derive the global poverty reduction effect of donor d's additional aid provision to a recipient r:

(4)
$$\frac{\partial G(\alpha)}{\partial m_{d,r}} = \left(-\frac{\alpha}{z} \right) P_{dr} G^r \, (\alpha = 1)$$

where partial derivatives of equation (3) for recipient r, i.e.,

(5)
$$P_{d,r} = \frac{\partial y^\alpha_r}{\partial m_{d,r}}$$

summarize the extent to which disbursed aid by the donor d finally reaches people of the recipient r^2. The overall political rights in the recipient country should be reflected in the partial derivative (5), since political rights enable people to participate freely in the political process, including enjoying the right to vote for public offices and to elect representatives who have a decisive vote on public policies. Particularly, resources provided through foreign aid are typically fungible, which implies that aid is financing the whole public sector. Hence, the overall political rights in the recipient country is the key for foreign aid to reach the correct people and to eventually reduce poverty. Such aspects are summarized by the variable P in equation (5).

Combining equations (1) and (3), we can see that this index captures a potential effect of aid to increase the recipients' personal income. Then what equations (4) and (5) indicate is that if a donor's objective is to minimize the global poverty, $G(d)$, then the recipient with the better policy environment P and a higher poverty index $G'(\alpha\text{-}1)$ should be targeted at the margin. This theoretical result gives us a testable hypothesis of targeting through foreign aid provision.

3.1 Econometric Framework and Data

Suppose that the global poverty index in equation (1) is defined as the squared poverty gap index, i.e., $\alpha=2$. In this case, based on equation (5), the optimal policy for a donor to minimize global poverty is to target countries with a high poverty gap index and good policies. Accordingly, we can set up an econometric model to investigate whether aid allocations of donor countries and international institutions are consistent with the poverty reduction criteria. We regress bilateral and multilateral donors' aid allocations on poverty gap index $G'(1)$, a proxy variable for the political rights P_r, log of total population POP_r, and other control variables X:

(6) $\log(1+m_{d,r}) = \alpha_{d,r} + \alpha_1 G^r(1) + \alpha_2 \log(P_r) + \alpha_3 \log(POP_r) + X_r \beta + u_{d,r}$

If a donor's aid allocation is consistent with poverty reduction, we should observe that $\alpha_1 > 0$. Moreover, the hypothesis that political rights are reflected in aid allocation is represented by a restriction of $\alpha_2 > 0$.

Note that there are many 'zeros' for the dependent variables in equation (6), since donors do not give aid to some potential recipient countries. If such aid provision decisions are correlated with unobserved factors affecting the aid amount, OLS estimation of equation (6) will suffer from a standard sample selection bias. Accordingly, we run Amemiya's (1985) type I Tobit regression to estimate (6) to eliminate the selection bias.

3.2 Data

We employ data from 11 donor countries (France, Germany, Japan, the Netherlands, United Kingdom, the United States, Canada, Italy, Finland, Norway, and Sweden). Our data comes from 83 aid recipient countries, covering 87.4% of the total population of all aid recipient countries in 1999. Out of the total grant provisions of each donor, our data set covers 53.2% for France, 73.4% for Germany, 76.9% for Japan, 62% of the Netherlands, 75.4% for the United Kingdom, 65% for the United States, 76.6% for Canada, 31.4% for Italy, 69.1% for Finland, 54.6% for Norway, and 64.9% for Sweden.[3]

3.3 Dependent Variables

The OECD defines Official Development Assistance (ODA) as a net sum of grants, including funds tied to technical assistance and highly concessional loans with grant elements of at least 25%. Yet, Chang, Fernandez-Arias, and Serven (1998) pointed out that the net flow nature of net ODA underestimates the aid content of disbursed flows by netting out amortization payments. Also, 25%-grant elements for concessionality of loan over-represent loans with high concessionality and under-represent loans with low concessionality. In order to cope with these data problems, we employ gross ODA/OA grant flows, distinguishing them from loans.

Accordingly, we employ logged values of per capita gross grant as our dependent variable, which is the total ODA/OA grant from OECD (2001b) averaged over 1996–1999. We deflated this variable by using a donor country's deflator in OECD (2001a) to make a rough adjustment for exchange rate and price changes. With respect to the multinational institutions data, note that the amount of total official gross disbursement is equivalent to the total official gross amount including OOF for IBRD, gross ODA loan for IDA, and ODA grant for UNDP, UNFPA, UNHCR, and UNDP. These multinational institution data are deflated by applying a deflator of combined DAC countries in the OECD (2001a).

3.4 Independent Variables

We extract 1995 data of the following independent variables. Firstly, the poverty gap index is taken from the World Bank (2002) data file, which is available for 82 countries. Although the survey year of the poverty gap index varies by country to some extent, we adopt the index closest to 1995 by assuming the situation of poverty does not change so rapidly. The poverty index for Israel is calculated from its income statistics (Central Bureau of Statistics 1995).

Table 3.1   List of Variables

Variable Description	Data Source
ODA/OA grant per recipients' population average 1996–1999	OECD (2001a) World Bank (2001)
Log of poverty gap at $1	World Bank (2002) Central Bureau of Statistics (1995)
Log of political rights index in 1995	Freedom House http://www.freedomhouse.org/
Log of population in 1995	World Bank (2001)

Table 3.2   Descriptive Statistics

Variable	Sample mean	Sample std. dev.	No. of samples left censored
ODA/OA Grant (per recipients' population, average over '96 to '99, US$)			
France	2.119	4.091	0
Germany	2.357	3.148	0
Japan	2.339	3.659	0
Netherlands	0.892	1.331	3
U.K.	0.899	1.578	2
U.S.A.	3.724	11.728	0
Canada	0.395	0.583	2
Italy	0.222	0.459	6
Finland	0.216	0.731	22
Norway	0.494	0.997	8
Sweden	0.732	1.447	3
Independent Variables			
Poverty Gap at $1 a day (%)	7.287	10.307	
Population (million, 1995)	50.800	166.385	
Political Rights Index (1995)	3.687	1.834	
Sample Size		83	

Secondly, in order to capture the political rights, we employ the Freedom House's political rights index of 1995. The Freedom House does not rate governments per se, but rather the rights and freedoms enjoyed by individuals in each country or territory. The index considers not only the political conditions in a country or territory such as the prevalence of terrorism or war, but also the effect that these conditions have on freedom. Note that the political rights index ranges from 1 (best) to 7 (worst).

Thirdly, to control the scale of recipients, we have included recipients' population in 1995 as an independent variable, which is taken from World Bank (2001). This term is expected to capture non-linearity between per capita aid provisions and population size of recipients.

3.5 Estimation results

According to Table 3.3 and Figure 3.1, grant allocations of Japan, Netherlands, United Kingdom, Canada, Norway, and Sweden, i.e., in six out of eleven donor countries, have positive and statistically significant coefficients on the poverty gap indicator. These results are consistent with the theory of poverty targeting, i.e., these six donor countries provide more grants to recipient countries where poverty is severe.[4] Particularly, the elasticity of aid supply of Japan with respect to the poverty gap measured is the second largest among the donors investigated.

Figure 3.1   The Relationship between Population-Adjusted Japan's Grant Disbursements and the Recipient's Poverty Gap

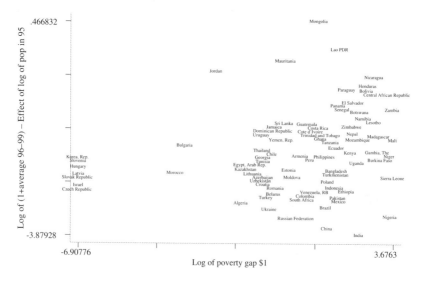

Table 3.3 General Results, ODA/OA Grant of Bilateral Donors
Dependent Variable: log(1+ODA/OA Grant per capita) for each country (avg. 1996-99)
Estimation Method: Tobit

	(1) France	(2) Germany	(3) Japan	(4) Netherlands	(5) U.K.	(6) U.S.A.	(7) Canada	(8) Italy	(9) Finland	(10) Norway	(11) Sweden
Poverty Gap	0.038 (1.21)	0.029 (1.40)	0.087 (3.29)**	0.091 (4.71)**	0.059 (2.64)*	0.014 (0.41)	0.046 (3.60)**	0.021 (1.89)	0.028 (1.62)	0.069 (3.93)**	0.052 (2.52)*
Political Rights	0.079 (0.51)	-0.072 (0.72)	0.032 (0.25)	-0.082 (0.86)	-0.025 (0.23)	-0.034 (0.20)	-0.119 (1.94)*	0.018 (0.33)	-0.066 (0.82)	-0.034 (0.41)	-0.113 (1.12)
Population	-0.148 (2.53)*	-0.233 (6.18)**	-0.190 (3.92)**	-0.107 (3.01)**	-0.111 (2.75)**	-0.197 (3.14)**	-0.033 (1.45)	-0.027 (1.34)	-0.033 (1.11)	-0.099 (3.22)**	-0.135 (3.59)**
Constant	3.041 (3.26)**	4.883 (8.11)**	3.936 (5.09)**	2.282 (4.01)**	2.257 (3.51)**	4.222 (4.23)**	0.936 (2.55)*	0.567 (1.74)	0.661 (1.37)	1.892 (3.85)**	2.682 (4.45)**
# of Obs	83	83	83	83	83	83	83	83	83	83	83

Note: Absolute value of t-statistics in parentheses.
* significant at 5%;
** significant at 1%.

On the other hand, no donor country is sensitive to democracy when it allocates grants, except Canada, whose coefficient is significantly negative, indicating that Canada allocates more aid to countries with better political rights.

With respect to the population variable, we find that coefficients are negative and statistically significant for eight out of eleven donor countries. This suggests that there is a negative scale effect for aid allocations, i.e., when a country's population is large, donors will allocate less aid per capita.

4. A Case Study: The Effectiveness of Japan's ODA to Malaysia

Since the 1970s, foreign aid has been one of Japan's leading foreign policy tools. Nowadays, Japan is one of the major actors in the international aid arena and is currently making a tremendous contribution to international development assistance. There are two notable characteristics in Japan's ODA. Firstly, Japan has provided a high percentage of loans and aid for economic infrastructure. Secondly, unlike other leading donors, Japan has chosen not to give much aid to military allies or former colonies as formally tested by Sawada and Yamada (2003). Moreover, as we have seen already, grant allocations of Japan were consistent with the theory of poverty targeting in the late 1990s.

The structure of Japan's foreign bilateral aid can be divided into two parts: Grants and technical assistance disbursed by the Japan International Cooperation Agency (JICA) and loans provided by the Japan Bank for International Cooperation (JBIC). For grants, actual policy decisions are facilitated mainly by the Economic Cooperation Bureau of the Ministry of Foreign Affairs (MOFA). Three ministries, MOFA the Ministry of Finance (MOF), and the Ministry of Economics, Trade and Industry (METI) are responsible for directing loan disbursements.

As such, the Japanese aid programme involves a complex decision making process. The responsibilities for aid administration are divided among the above-mentioned three main ministries (MOFA, MOF, and METI) plus other ministries and agencies concerned with particular types of projects such as health-related projects implemented through consultation with the Ministry of Health, Labour and Welfare. Conflict between these responsible ministries and agencies have confused the purpose of Japan's aid and obstructed effective direction of the programme (Yasutomo 1986; Orr 1990; Rix 1990). Aid by the Japanese government is given mainly as an international obligation, both to assist world peace and prosperity, and as a foreign policy mechanism to preserve Japan's peace and prosperity. In a publication, 'Philosophies of Economic

Cooperation: Why Official Development Assistance?' issued in 1980, the Ministry of Foreign Affairs stated that, officially, Japan's economic cooperation is guided by two rationales: 'humanitarian and moral considerations' and 'the recognition of interdependence among nations' (Ministry of Foreign Affairs 1994). On 30 June 1992, the Japanese Cabinet adopted Japan's Official Development Assistance Charter (ODA Charter), in which its philosophies and objectives are expanded. With regard to the basic philosophies of Japan's ODA, the Charter lists: (i) humanitarian considerations; (ii) recognition of interdependence among nations of the international community; (iii) environmental consideration; and (iv) support for self-help efforts of recipient countries (Ministry of Foreign Affairs 1994).

4.1 Growth and Poverty in Malaysia

Before looking into the role of Japan's ODA to Malaysia in reducing poverty, we review the nexus between economic growth and poverty reduction in Malaysia. Recent cross-country studies such as Ravallion (2001) and Dollar and Kraay (2001) find a significant negative relationship between economic growth and incidence of poverty. Such a relationship across countries can also be found in the time series data of Malaysia. In spite of temporal disruptions in 1975, 1985, and 1997, on a per capita basis, the economy grew at a high and sustainable rate of 4.1% per annum over 30 years (Figure 3.2).[5] Along with this striking trend in economic growth, the overall incidence of poverty based on the national poverty line was reduced between 1970 and 2000 from around half of the population to 5.5%.[6] The contribution of economic growth to poverty reduction could be verified by matching both trends. Accordingly, there is a consensus that growth was the primary means of reducing the incidence of poverty in Malaysia.

In order to quantify further the time series pattern of the poverty reduction with economic growth, we can employ the elasticity formula developed by Kakwani (1993). Let μ represent the mean per capita income of country r. Utilizing the Kakwani (1993) framework, we can obtain the elasticity of the FGT measure $G^r(\alpha)$ with respect to μ as

$$(7) \qquad \frac{\partial G^r(\alpha)}{\partial \mu} \frac{\mu}{G^r(\alpha)} = \frac{\alpha[G^r(\alpha-1) - G^r(\alpha)]}{G^r(\alpha)}.$$

In the case of the poverty gap measure, i.e., the case of $\alpha=1$, we can compute easily elasticities of the poverty measure with respect to the mean income by using the head count index and poverty gap index. Table 3.4 summarizes the calculated elasticity by using the one-dollar-a-day

Figure 3.2   Economic Growth in Malaysia

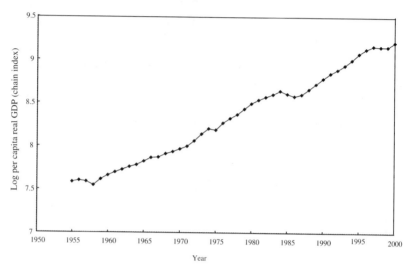

Source: Penn World Tables Mark 6.1, University of Pennsylvania.

Table 3.4   Elasticities of Poverty Gap Measures with Respect to Mean Income in Malaysia

Head Count Index G(0) in %	1970	1985	1995
Head Count Index G(0) in %	17.4	10.8	4.3
Poverty Gap G(1) in %	5.4	2.5	1.0
Elasticity	−2.22	−3.32	−3.3

Source: World Bank (http://www.worldbank.org/eapsocial/sector/poverty/povcwp2.htm)
Note: All numbers are based on the international poverty line of US$1 per person per day at 1985 prices.

international poverty line. The absolute magnitude of poverty elasticity with respect to mean income is much greater than one for all periods. Hence, poverty is significantly sensitive to economic growth. These results suggest that poverty should decrease faster than the rate of income growth under an assumption that the growth process does not lead to an increase in income inequality.[7] However, if the income inequality deteriorates during the course of a country's economic growth, poverty may even increase because the poverty measures are considerably more elastic for changes in inequality. By inspecting the Gini coefficients over time, we can plausibly conclude that economic growth has reduced income inequality in Malaysia since the mid-1970s (Table 3.5). Therefore, for the last 25 years, we can evaluate positively the role of economic growth as an effective poverty alleviation device under the elastic nature of poverty with respect to growth.

The above analysis also suggests that in the event of negative economic growth, the increase in poverty will be quite substantial. Particularly, this framework predicts that the financial crisis in 1997 and 1998 would have created a non-negligible negative social impact in Malaysia. This prediction seems to be supported by data. For example, during the 1997–98 financial crisis, GDP growth rates of Malaysia fell from 7.7% in 1997 to –7.6% in 1998. Incidentally, the poverty head count ratio increased significantly from 8.2% in 1997 to 10.4 % in 1998 (Fallon and Lucas 2002).

Table 3.5   Incidence of Poverty and Gini coefficient in Malaysia, 1970-2000

	1970	75	80	85	90	95	2000
Incidence of Poverty(%)	49.3	43.9	29.2	20.7	17.1	8.9	5.5
Gini coefficient(%)	50	53[a]	51[b]	48[c]	48.35[d]	N.A.	N.A.

Source: Various Five-Year Development Plans, OECF (1997); Deininger and Squire (1996).
[a] Figure in 1976;
[b] Figure in 1979;
[c] Figure in 1984; d) Figure in 1989.

4.2 Direct Poverty Targeting

Although there is no doubt that growth was the primary means of reducing the incidence of poverty in Malaysia, the Malaysian government has been committed to reducing overall poverty since the 1960s through direct poverty targeting policies. In 1959, Malaysia established a cross-sectoral ministry, the Ministry of Rural Development, for poverty reduction in the rural areas. Since the Second Malaysian Plan (1971–75), there have been clear government statements of poverty reduction and income equalization across ethnic groups and regions. In 1970, the government launched a programme called the New Economic Policy (NEP), an affirmative action plan designed to support poor Malays through a series of government regulations, quotas, scholarships, and other privileges. Through the NEP, from 1971 through 1990, the government successfully redistributed wealth to Malays who used to be the poorest group in Malaysia. Rapid and sustained economic growth along with proactive redistribution strategies contributed significantly towards the reduction of overall poverty (Siwar 2002).

Under the impressive economic growth record of Malaysia, as can be seen from Figure 3.2, it would be quite natural to expect the share of federal government development expenditure for poverty reduction to decline over time. However, the proportion of poverty reduction expenditure still forms a substantial portion of overall development expenditure, e.g., 23.8% for the Seventh Malaysian Plan over 1996–2000 (Chamhuri 2002).

The government continues to exert its effort to reduce poverty in the country further by eradicating ultra-poverty, particularly in Terengganu, Kelantan and Sabah states. The approaches of the government to target the hard-core poor include provisions of better infrastructure such as accessibility to paved roads, piped water, and electricity, as well as formal education and the implementation of social safety net programmes, such as provision of free housing and food supplements, child nutritional and scholarship programmes, and micro-credit programmes. Accordingly, even in the relatively backward areas of Malaysia, the incidence of poverty continues to decline significantly.

4.3 Japan's Co-operation with Malaysia

Since 1973, Japan has been the largest bilateral aid donor to Malaysia in terms of gross ODA disbursements (Figure 3.3). Yet, in general, the effectiveness of Japanese foreign aid has been widely disputed. Some argue that Japan's economic aid is only beneficial to the Japanese economy and that there has never been a highly moralistic rationale for aid in Japan, while others maintain that Japanese aid has been directed towards practical, even pragmatic, ends (Rix 1990). That a higher proportion of Japan's total ODA is in the form of loans, while a lesser proportion of ODA is through grants, has often been criticized since Japan's ODA may be provided in the hard and non-humanitarian end of the ODA spectrum, and most other DAC donors have an aid programme softer on the recipient (Rix 1990).

Japan's ODA to Malaysia is not an exception. It has been characterized by a high percentage of loans and aid for economic infrastructure, which is consistent with the overall ODA composition of the Japanese government (Figure 3.4). It is notable that Japan provided substantial amounts of aid to Malaysia for economic infrastructure, especially between 1975 and 1984, when Malaysia experienced rapid economic growth and a significant decline in the incidence of poverty.

Amazingly, contributions of Japanese ODA loans to Malaysia's total supply of electricity, railway, and highway infrastructure are 51%, 21%, and 19% respectively (Kohama 1995, 1998). Moreover, our evaluation results in Section 2 indicate that the criticisms of Japan's aid are basically inaccurate, a finding which is consistent with the official emphasis of Japan's aid on humanitarian considerations. Our next task is to investigate the poverty reduction effect of Japan's ODA flows to the infrastructure sector in Malaysia.

Figure 3.3   Gross ODA Disbursements to Malaysia

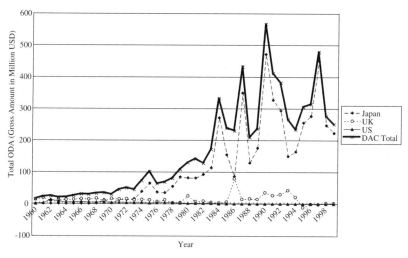

Source: OECD (2001a).

Figure 3.4   Japan's Bilateral ODA Commitments to Malaysia by Purpose

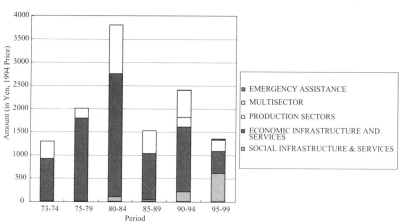

Source: OECD (2001a).

It is widely recognized that physical infrastructure plays an important role in the process of economic development. Since the classic works of development theory such as Hirschman (1958), development economists have considered infrastructure an indispensable precondition of industrialization. However, identifying the contribution of physical infrastructure to poverty reduction is not straightforward. As Lipton and Ravallion (1995, p. 263) and Jimenez (1995, p. 2788) have pointed out, there have been few rigorous empirical studies that systematically evaluates the role of infrastructure in reducing poverty empirically. Indeed, until very recently, the role of infrastructure was not recognized as an effective poverty reduction device. An exception is Datt and Ravallion's (1998) analysis using state-level poverty data from India for the period 1957–91. It concluded that state-level differences in poverty reduction can be attributed to differences in initial conditions, especially physical infrastructure and human resources. Particularly, a 20% higher initial irrigation rate augmented the annual rate of poverty reduction by 0.1 percentage points over 34 years. The data limitation inhibits us from conducting a similar evaluation study for Malaysia. However, as we have seen already from both cross-country studies and data from Malaysia, growth is an important means of reducing the incidence of poverty (Ravallion 2001; Dollar and Kraay 2001). Hence, our remaining task is to show whether physical infrastructure will contribute to economic growth. If the answer is yes, we may conclude that infrastructure will also reduce the incidence of poverty through enhancing economic growth.

Cross-country studies by Canning and Bennathan (2000) and Canning (1999) indicate that infrastructure, particularly telecommunications infrastructure, significantly increases economic growth. We investigate the nexus between economic growth and infrastructure in Malaysia by using the following two-step procedure. Firstly, we utilize a simple production function to calculate the Solow residual by eliminating the labour and capital accumulation components. Secondly, by regressing the residual on human capital and physical infrastructure, we will test whether infrastructure will contribute to economic growth.

4.4 Empirical Framework to Evaluate the Role of Infrastructure

Suppose the aggregate output of an economy Y is characterized by a constant return to scale Cobb-Douglas function of labour and capital inputs, L and K, respectively: $Y_t = A_t L_t^{1-\alpha} K_t^{\alpha}$ where A is the total factor productivity (TFP). Then, we can compute the TFP by using the formula:

$$(8) \qquad \log A_t = \log Y_t - \alpha \log K_t - (1 - \alpha) \log L_t.$$

The capital share is calculated by dividing the product of the interest rate and capital stock by GDP. Data on capital stock is extracted from Easterly (2001) and the interest rate is set at 20%. Then the estimated average capital share is around 0.2. By using equation (8) with α=0.2, we can calculate the TFP. The growth rates of TFP are summarized in Table 3.6. According to Table 3.6, the TFP growth rate increased until the mid-1970s and then declined continuously.

Table 3.6   Growth Rate of the Total Factor Productivity

Year	Growth rate of the TFP (%)
1960-64	2.91
1965-69	2.28
1970-74	3.01
1975-79	1.94
1980-84	1.84
1985-89	0.55

Source: Author's calculation

For the second stage estimation, we regress the TFP per worker on variables such as human capital and physical infrastructure and time trend variables:

$$(8) \qquad \log\left(\frac{A_t}{L_t}\right) = X_t\beta + u_t$$

where X include years of schooling, kilowatts of electricity-generating capacity, kilometres of paved roads, kilometers of railway lines, and number of telephones as well as time trend and squared time trend, and u is a well-behaved error term.

The summary statistics of variables used in equation (8) and its estimation results are represented in Table 3.7. According to Table 3.7, the TFP in Malaysia has been positively affected by years of schooling, kilometres of railway lines, and number of telephones. Hence, we may conclude that Malaysia has improved its macro-level productivity by accumulating human capital and developing infrastructure, especially transportation and telephone networks. This finding is consistent with Canning (1999) who, using a cross-country data set, found that investment in telephones is productive since there may be large externalities to telephones.

Accordingly, the implications derived from these existing studies provide supportive evidence that Japan's bilateral ODA allocations to Malaysia, which emphasized economic infrastructure, have positively contributed to the poverty reduction trend of Malaysia, given that infrastructure development sufficiently enhanced Malaysia's economic

Table 3.7   Determinants of the Total Factor Productivity Dependent Variable: Log of the Total Factor Productivity per Worker

Variable names	Descriptive Statistics (standard error)	Estimated Parameters (t-statistics)
Dependent Variable		
Log of Total Factor Productivity per Worker	−1.04 (.128)	
Independent Variables		
Log of years of schooling	1.30 (.276)	1.12 (2.63)**
Log of kilowatts of electricity generating capacity	−1.18 (.594)	−0.08 (1.28)
Log of kilometers of paved roads	1.33 (.129)	0.02 (0.24)
Log of kilometers of railway lines	−0.747 (.299)	0.97 (2.14)**
Log of number of telephones	4.31 (.780)	0.17 (1.83)*
Time		−0.01 (0.66)
Time squared		−0.0005 (2.91)***
Constant		−2.32 (4.88)***
R^2		0.967
Sample size	31	31

*** significant at 1% level, ** significant at 5% level, : * significant at 10% level.

growth. In addition, Japan has also recently increased its ODA proportion to social development projects such as human resource development, poverty eradication and small and medium-scale industry promotion. For example, technical cooperation of JICA with Malaysia has emphasized inequality reduction and capacity building of women in villages.

5. Conclusion

In this chapter, we have investigated how Japan's aid provisions have contributed to poverty reduction of recipients in the late 1990s. Two main empirical results have emerged. Firstly, in the late 1990s, grant allocations of Japan, the Netherlands, United Kingdom, Canada, Norway, and Sweden were consistent with the theory of poverty targeting. On the other hand, no donor country was sensitive to democracy when it allocated grants, except Canada, which allocated more aid to countries with better political rights.

Secondly, Japan's bilateral ODA allocations to Malaysia have concentrated on economic infrastructure. Since we have found that infrastructure development sufficiently enhanced Malaysia's economic growth, it is likely that Japan's ODA has contributed significantly to the economic growth of Malaysia. We have also found that economic growth was the primary means of reducing poverty in Malaysia. Accordingly, our empirical results support the view that Japan's bilateral ODA to Malaysia has contributed to the poverty reduction trend of Malaysia.

Notes

The authors would like to thank Professor Chamhuri Siwar of the National University of Malaysia, Mr. Harumi Ao of the JBIC Malaysia office, and Mr. Toshio Hida, Mr. Juichiro Sasaki, Ms. Reiko Akezumi, and Mr. Kenichiro Kasahara of the JICA Malaysia office for the first author's field survey in Malaysia. They would like to acknowledge useful comments and suggestions provided by the study group members and Andy Ragatz.

[1] This measure satisfies several desirable properties such as the Sen's (1976) monotonicity axioms, additive decomposability with population-share weights, and inclusion of a relative deprivation concept of poverty. The Transfer and Transfer Sensitivity Axioms are satisfied with $\alpha > 1$ and $\alpha > 2$, respectively.

[2] If aid is a direct income transfer, then the partial derivative (3) equals one. For simplicity, we assume that the partial derivative is constant across income.

[3] When we calculate coverage by amount, we exclude the "unallocated" amount of from loans, grants, and total official gross ODA. This is because the 'unallocated' amount includes administrative costs mainly incurred in the territory of the donor country, research performed in the donor country and so on. See page 9 of OECD (2001b).

[4] In order to avoid potential bias due to an omission of important variables, Sawada and Yamada (2003) include colonial past variables, which are defined as number of years as a colony of the donor, number of years as a colony of any country other than the donor since 1900, and a UN-voting similarity variable. The results indicate that even after including colonial variables and voting variables, Japan and the Netherlands are still targeting countries

with large poverty gap ratios. On the other hand, France and the UK have provided foreign aid exclusively to their previous colonies. Sawada and Yamada (2003) also show that IDA and UN agencies such as UNDP and UNICEF have consistent fund allocation patterns with the theory of poverty targeting.

[5] Note that the slope of log per capita GDP data in Figure 3.2 represents per capita GDP growth rate approximately. For a proof of this argument, see for example, Jones (2002), pp.201–202.

[6] When the poverty line income is defined, the minimum caloric requirement for the food component was estimated by the Institute of Medical Research (IMR) based on a daily requirement of 2,530 calories for an adult male. Then the minimum requirements for clothing, footwear, and other non-food items, which are based on standards set by the Department of Social Welfare and on the Household Expenditure Survey, are added as the non-food component.

[7] With internationally comparable poverty data, we can compute the elasticity for different countries. Using the point estimates of Ravallion, Datt, and van de Walle (1991), the poverty reduction elasticity for the whole world in 1985 with the international poverty line is around 2.23. Kakwani's (1993) results indicate the elasticity for Côte D'Ivoire in 1985 is between 1.97 and 2.86, depending on the poverty line used. The poverty elasticities in Malaysia are basically larger than these estimates, suggesting that economic growth in Malaysia has been pro-poor.

References

Alesina, A. and D. Dollar. 2000. "Who Gives Foreign Aid to Whom and Why?" *Journal of Economic Growth* Vol. 5, 33–64 March.

Alesina, A. and B. Weder. 2002. "Do Corrupt Governments Receive less Foreign Aid?" *American Economic Review* 92(4), 1126–1137.

Amemiya, Takeshi. 1985. *Advanced Econometrics*, Harvard University.

Besley, T. and R. Kanbur. 1988. "Food subsidies and poverty alleviation," *Economic Journal* Vol. 98, 701–719.

Boone, P. 1996. "Politics and the effectiveness of foreign aid," *European Economic Review* 40: 289–329.

Burnside, C. and D. Dollar. 2000. "Aid, Policies, and Growth," *American Economic Review* Vol.90, 847–868.

Burnside, C. and D. Dollar. 1998. "Aid, the Incentive Regime, and Poverty Reduction," *Policy Research Working Paper* 1937. World Bank, Development Research Group, Washington, D.C.

Canning, David. 1999. "Infrastructure's Contribution to Aggregate Output," *Policy Research Working Paper* #2246, DECRG, World Bank.

Canning, David and Esra Bennathan. 2000. "The Social Rate of Return to Infrastructure Investments", *Policy Research Working Paper* #2390, DECRG, World Bank.

Central Bureau of Statistics. 1995. *Statistical Abstract of Israel.*

Central Intelligence Agency. 1998. *The World Factbook.* Brassey's.

Chamhuri, Siwar. 2002. "Urban Poverty Alleviation and the Financial Crisis: Issues, Problems, Prospects and Challenges," in *Cities in the 21st Century: Urban Issues and Challenges,* edited by Sharifah Norazizan Abd Rasid, Asishah Edris, and Nobaya Ahmad. Penerbit Universiti Putra Malaysia.

Chang, Charles C., Eduardo Fernandez-Arias, and Luis Serven. 1998. "Measuring Aid Flows: A New Approach," *Policy Research Working Paper* #2050, DECRG, World Bank.

Collier, P. and D. Dollar. 2002. "Aid Allocation and Poverty Reduction," *European Economic Review* 46, 1475–1500.

Datt, Gaurav and Martin Ravallion. 1998. "Why Have Some Indian States Done Better than Others at Reducing Rural Poverty?". *Economica* 65, 17–38.

Deininger, Klaus and Lyn Squire. 1996. "A New Data Set Measuring Income Inequality". *World Bank Economic Review* 10 (3): 565–591.

Dollar, David and Aart Kraay. 2000. "Growth is Good for the Poor," mimeographed, DECRG, World Bank.

Dowling, J.M. and U. Heimenz. 1985. "Biases in the allocation of foreign aid: some new evidence," *World Development* Vol. 13: 535–541.

Dudley, L. and C. Montmarquette. 1976. "A model of the supply of bilateral foreign aid," *American Economic Review* Vol. 66: 132–142.

Easterly, William. 2001. "The Lost Decades: Developing Countries' Stagnation in Spite of Policy Reform 1980-1998," *Journal of Economic Growth* 6 (2), 135–57.

Foster, J., J. Greer, and E. Thorbecke. 1984. "A class of decomposable poverty measures". *Econometrica* Vol. 52, 761–766, 1984.

Freedom House. 2000. "Annual Survey of Freedom Country Ratings 1972–73 to 1999-00". (http://www.freedomhouse.org/).

Hirshman, Albert O. 1958. *The Strategy of Economic Development,* Yale University Press.

Jimenez, Emmanuel Y. 1995. "Human and Physical Infrastructure," in *Handbook of Development Economics,* Volume 3B, edited by Jere Behrman and T. N. Srinivasan. Elsevier Science, North Holland, 2773–2843.

Jones, Charles I. 2002. *Introduction to Economic Growth,* second edition, Norton.

Kakwani, Nanak. 1993. "Poverty and Economic Growth with Application to Côte D'Ivoire," *Review of Income and Wealth* 39 (2), 121–139.

Kohama, H. 1995. "Japan's Development Cooperation and Economic Development in Asia". in *Growth Theories in Light of the East Asian*

Experience, edited by Takatoshi Ito and A. O. Krueger. University of Chicago Press, 201–226.

Kohama, H. 1998. *Economics of Development Cooperation* (in Japanese). Nihon Hyoron Sha.

Lahiri, Sajal and Pascalis Raimondos-Møller. 2000. "Lobbying by Ethnic Groups and Aid Allocation". *Economic Journal* 110, 62–79.

Lipton, M. and M. Ravallion. 1995. "Poverty and Policy," in *Handbook of Development Economics*, Volume 3B, edited by Jere Behrman and T. N. Srinivasan. Elsevier Science, North Holland, 2551–2657.

Maizels, A. and M. Nissanke. 1984. "Motivations for Aid to Developing Countries," M. Nissanke. 1984. *World Development* 12: 879–900.

Ministry of Foreign Affairs. 1994. *Japan's ODA: Annual Report 1994*. Economic Cooperation Bureau, Ministry of Foreign Affairs, Government of Japan.

Organisation for Economic Co-operation and Development (OECD). 2001a. *International Development Statistics* (CD-ROM).

———. 2001b. *Geographical Distribution of Financial Flows to Aid Recipients 1995–1999*.

Overseas Economic Cooperation Fund (OECF). 1997. "Rural Development Administration for Poverty Eradication in Malaysia: Focusing on Coordination Mechanisms," *OECF Research Papers* No. 17, Research Institute of Development Assistance (RIDA), The Overseas Economic Cooperation Fund (OECF).

Orr, R. M., Jr. 1990. *The Emergence of Japan's Foreign Aid Power*, Columbia University Press, New York.

Ravallion, Martin. 2001. "Growth, Inequality, and Poverty: Looking Beyond Averages," *World Development* 29 (11), 1803–1815.

Ravallion, Martin, Gaurav Datt, and Dominique van de Walle. 1991. "Quantifying Absolute Poverty in the Developing World," *Review of Income and Wealth* 37 (4), 345–361.

Rix, A. 1990. "Japan's Aid Program: A New Global Agenda," *International Development Issues* No. 12, Australian International Development Assistance Bureau.

Sawada, Y. 1996. "Aid and Poverty Alleviation: An International Comparison," *IDS Bulletin* 27, January 100–108.

Sawada, Y. and H. Yamada. 2003. "Is Aid Allocation Consistent with Poverty Indicators? A Cross-Donor Comparison," Mimeograph. Faculty of Economics, University of Tokyo.

Stein, H. 1998. "Japanese Aid to Africa: Patterns, Motivation and the Role of Structural Adjustment," *Journal of Development Studies* Vol. 35, No. 2: 27–53.

Trumbull, W. N. and H. J. Wall. 1994. "Estimating Aid-Allocation Criteria with Panel Data". *Economic Journal* 104: 876–882.

Wall, H. J. 1995. "The Allocation of Official Development Assistance," *Journal of Policy Modeling* 17(3): 307–314.

World Bank 1996. *Annual Report*, World Bank.

World Bank 1998. *Assessing Aid: What Works, What Doesn't, and Why*, World Bank.

World Bank 2001. *World Development Indicators 2001* (CD-ROM).

World Bank 2002. *Global Poverty Monitoring*, (http://www.worldbank.org/research/povmonitor/).

Yasutomo, D. T. 1986. *The Manner of Giving: Strategic Aid and Japanese Foreign Policy*, Lexington Books, Massachusetts.

4

Upgrading Technology in ASEAN Countries and Japan's ODA

Shujiro Urata

1. Introduction

Upgrading technology plays a very important role in promoting economic development. Even with the same amount of factors inputs such as labour, capital, and land, improvement in technological level would result in an increase in the output level. Indeed, many episodes of economic development and economic growth have been accompanied by technological progress. A World Bank (1993) study found that the remarkable economic growth of East Asian countries in the post–WWII period was attributable to rapid technological progress.

Various factors influence technological progress. For developing countries, indigenous technological capability and the inflow of foreign technology from developed countries, particularly their combination, play important roles in promoting technological progress. Indigenous technological capability depends on education, training, and research and development (R&D) among others, while inflow of foreign technology, which may take the forms of foreign direct investment (FDI), imports of technology, capital goods, technical experts, and others, depends on the policies and strategies of developing countries, foreign firms and the governments of developed countries.

The purpose of this paper is two-fold. On one hand it serves to analyze the levels of technology and the factors affecting them for ASEAN countries, in order to find the ways to improve technological levels for these countries. On the other hand, it serves to examine the contribution of Japan's official development assistance (ODA) to upgrading technological capability for ASEAN countries. We first examine the technological levels of ASEAN countries in Section 2, in order to set the stage for the later analysis. Section 3 investigates the factors that determine technological levels of ASEAN countries by making an international comparison. Specifically, we shed light on the levels of ASEAN vis-à-vis other countries in terms of indigenous technological factors and inflows of foreign technology. Section 4 analyzes the contribution of Japan in transferring technology to ASEAN countries via ODA by reviewing selected past technical assistance programmes. Some concluding comments are given in Section 5.

2. Technological Level of ASEAN Countries

The technological level of a country can be measured by various indicators. Recognizing the importance of technology in determining economic performance, one can assume per capita GDP to reflect the technological level. A more direct indicator of technological level is productivity. Among various measures of productivity, total factor productivity (TFP), which explains the component of economic growth not captured by the increase in factor inputs such as labour and capital, is considered to be most appropriate. Another indicator may be the composition of exports. A country with a high technological level is expected to export the products, which require extensive and intensive use of technological skills. We examine the technological level of ASEAN4 countries (Indonesia, Malaysia, Philippines and Thailand) by examining these three indicators.

ASEAN countries achieved rapid economic growth in the pre-financial crisis period. Indeed, the average annual growth rate of ASEAN4 countries from 1980 to 1997 was 4.1%, significantly higher compared to 1.5% recorded for developing countries (Table 4.1).[1] Although ASEAN4 countries achieved higher growth rates than other developing countries, NIEs and China performed more favourably as their respective annual average growth rates for the 1980–97 period were 6.1% and 8.6%.

Among ASEAN4 countries some variations in their economic growth are observed. Thailand maintained high economic growth rates from 1980 to 1997, while Indonesia and Malaysia increased their respective growth rates from the 1980s to 1990s. In contrast to these countries, the Philippines experienced poor economic performance during the period. Indeed, it recorded negative growth rate in the 1980s.

The level of economic development, expressed in terms of per capita GDP, rose for ASEAN4 as a result of rapid economic growth. The average per capita GDP for ASEAN4 countries almost doubled in 17 years from $2,389 in 1980 to $4,728 in 1997. Despite this rapid increase, the gap in the level of per capita GDP vis-à-vis the NIEs widened as the average per capita GDP for the NIEs increased 2.7 times during the same period from $5,891 to $16,044. It should also be noted the gap vis-à-vis China narrowed because China increased its per capita GDP more than four times during the period to a record $2,801 in 1997. Wide variations are

Table 4.1 Per Capita GDP and TFP Levels

	Per capita GDP Level (1992 US$, PPP)				TFP Level (US1980=1.0)			
	1970	1980	1990	1997	1970	1980	1990	1997
Developed countries	13,267	16,679	20,510	22,988	0.83	0.87	0.97	1.02
Developing countries	4,201	5,588	5,804	7,185	0.44	0.47	0.48	0.54
1. East Asia & the Pacific	1,998	3,622	6,611	9,703	0.29	0.36	0.47	0.55
(1) ASEAN4	1,547	2,389	3,378	4,728	0.22	0.28	0.32	0.35
Indonesia	764	1,291	1,993	2,917	0.15	0.23	0.27	0.34
Malaysia	2,527	4,235	5,707	8,486	0.26	0.34	0.36	0.43
Philippines	2,629	3,629	3,311	3,493	0.28	0.35	0.33	0.33
Thailand	1,545	2,294	4,104	5,914	0.26	0.28	0.36	0.37
(2) NIES	3,071	5,891	11,126	16,044	0.39	0.48	0.70	0.79
Hong Kong	5,438	10,324	17,205	21,540	0.45	0.64	1.02	1.06
Korea	2,509	4,367	9,240	13,831	0.43	0.47	0.70	0.75
Singapore	4,498	8,722	14,873	23,296	0.48	0.64	0.79	1.00
Taiwan	2,724	5,691	10,668	15,578	0.32	0.43	0.59	0.71
(3) China	493	690	1,437	2,801	0.18	0.21	0.21	0.31
2. South Asia	962	1,030	1,454	1,845	0.24	0.22	0.28	0.32
3. Latin America and the Caribbean	4,626	6,515	5,966	6,971	0.61	0.62	0.53	0.58
4. Europe and Central Asia	3,664	4,933	5,844	6,835	0.42	0.55	0.49	0.56
5. Middle East and North Africa	11,482	12,804	7,709	7,496	0.49	0.65	0.66	0.76
6. Sub-Saharan Africa	4,258	4,733	4,307	4,182	0.35	0.42	0.33	0.32

Source: Kawai and Urata (2003).

observed for the level of per capita GDP among the ASEAN4 countries. In 1997, Malaysia had the highest per capita GDP amounting to $8,486, and it is followed by Thailand at $5,914. Indonesia and the Philippines trailed far behind as their respective per capita GDP were $2,917 and $2,801.

Turning to the level of TFP, one finds ASEAN4 countries falling behind other developing countries. Setting the TFP level of the United States in the 1980 unity as a reference, the average TFP level of ASEAN4 in 1997 was 0.35, significantly lower than the average for developing countries at 0.54. The low technological level of ASEAN4 can be shown even more clearly when compared to the high technological level achieved by the NIEs at 0.79. Having noted the low technological level of ASEAN4 countries, one can make several important observations. First, the technological level of ASEAN4 countries increased continuously from 1970 to 1997. Second, although catching up very fast, China's TFP level is still lower compared to that of ASEAN4. Third, wide variations in the TFP levels are observed for ASEAN4. Similar to the pattern observed for per capita GDP, Malaysia had the highest TFP level among the ASEAN4 countries. Behind Malaysia was Thailand, followed by the Philippines and Indonesia.

The technological level of a country can also be measured by its pattern of comparative advantage. A country with high technological capability can export high technology products such as office processing/ telecommunications equipment and pharmaceutical products, while a country without high technological capability exports low technology products such as textiles and clothing. Table 4.2 shows the patterns of comparative advantage for East Asian countries including those of ASEAN. The indicator used for the analysis is 'Revealed Comparative Advantage (RCA)'. RCA is defined as the share of country's exports of a particular product divided by the share of its total exports in world exports, and thus RCA exceeding unity for a product indicates that the country has a revealed comparative advantage in that product. According to the figures in Table 4.2, RCAs for medium technology and high technology products for ASEAN4 countries increased from 1985 to 1998, largely reflecting the improvement in technological level of ASEAN4 countries. It is surprising to find that RCAs in high technology products for ASEAN4 countries in 1998 were quite high, when compared to those for the NIEs. In particular, the Philippines recorded as high as 3.042, which is higher than RCAs for any NIEs. High RCAs in high technology products for the ASEAN4 countries are largely attributable to processing and assembling, which are labour-intensive activities for high technology products, particularly electronics products. This point can be seen by the RCA figures of less than unity for high technology products excluding electronic products.

Table 4.2 Revealed Comparative Advantage for East Asian Economies by Technology Category

	1985					1998				
	Resource	Low Tech	Mid Tech	High Tech	High Tech+	Resource	Low Tech	Mid Tech	High Tech	High Tech+
Indonesia	0.893	0.234	0.044	0.050	0.042	1.470	1.148	0.311	0.252	0.079
Malaysia	1.695	0.322	0.208	1.195	0.224	1.032	0.625	0.557	2.217	0.482
Philippines	1.695	0.930	0.157	0.467	0.048	0.471	0.873	0.317	3.042	0.169
Thailand	1.124	1.336	0.378	0.197	0.080	1.080	1.302	0.508	1.339	0.311
Hong Kong	0.174	4.415	0.609	1.146	0.275	0.291	3.352	0.378	1.158	0.766
Korea	0.471	2.890	1.183	0.986	0.318	0.671	1.210	1.073	1.288	0.418
Singapore	2.070	0.523	0.645	1.644	0.750	0.912	0.417	0.537	2.683	0.414
Taiwan	0.539	3.657	0.663	1.237	0.205	0.362	1.829	0.804	1.654	0.208
China	0.525	0.751	0.096	0.099	0.248	0.619	2.883	0.563	0.862	0.455

Notes: *Resource:* resource based manufactures include agroforest based products and other resource based products.
  Low tech: low technology manufacturers include textile/fashion cluster and other low technology products.
  Mid tech: medium technology manufacturers include automotive products, medium technology process, and medium technology engineering .
  High tech: high technology manufacturers include electronics and electrical, and other high technology.
  High tech+: other high technology.

Source: Lall (2003).

An examination of the technological levels of ASEAN4 countries in terms of per capita GDP, TFP levels, and the patterns of comparative advantage shows that technological levels of ASEAN4 improved significantly in recent years. However, it also revealed that their technological levels lag behind those of the NIEs, while China is rapidly catching up with ASEAN4.

3. The Determinants of Technological Levels[2]

In the previous section we found that technological levels of ASEAN4 countries were lower when compared to the NIEs. It is of interest to identify the factors that explain these differences. A number of studies have attempted to examine the determinants of technological levels, in many cases the rate of change in technological levels, or the rate of technological progress, among different countries. For example, the World Bank (1993) found that openness had a statistically positive impact on TFP growth in its study of 51 countries for the 1960–89 period. It also found in some cases that a high share of manufactured exports in total exports (high manufactured export ratio) tends to result in high TFP growth. Furthermore, it was found that a high manufactured export ratio contributed significantly to TFP growth when it was interacted with a high educational attainment level. This finding was interpreted to indicate that manufactured export orientation and high labour force skills interact to facilitate the acquisition and mastery of technology with attendant spillovers. In their analysis of the determinants of per capita GDP growth and TFP growth, Kawai and Urata (2003) found that domestic technological capability and availability of foreign technology play important roles. Domestic technological capability is a crucial factor in determining the technological level of a country because it not only contributes to the creation of new ideas but also facilitates assimilation of foreign technology. In light of the determinants of technological levels of different countries observed by the previous studies, this section investigates the factors that may explain the low technological levels of ASEAN4 countries.

3.1 Domestic Technological Capability

Educated and well–trained workers can contribute to the growth of technological levels as they can not only use machines and equipment productively but also make improvements in the production processes. Research and development activity plays an important role in improving technological capability of a country by producing new technology, new production processes, and new products. In light of these observations, this section examines education and R&D activities in ASEAN4.

3.1.1 Education

Education is an important factor for determining technological capability. Although formal education may not be a source of technological capability without technical training or experience, it serves as a base, upon which technical skills are developed.[3] A number of studies have found that education has a positive impact on economic growth, supporting the argument that education plays an important role for promoting economic growth. For example, the World Bank (1993) found that education, particularly primary education, contributes significantly to the increase in per capita GDP in its study of 113 countries for the 1960-1985 period. Specifically, it was found that a 10% increase in the school enrolment ratio in primary and secondary education would lead to a 0.3% increase in the growth rate of per capita GDP.

Let us examine the educational levels of ASEAN4 countries. To measure the educational level, we use the indicator on educational attainment that is estimated by Barro and Lee (2000). The Barro and Lee data set has at least one observation on school attainment, the highest educational level attained for the population aged 15 or over and for the population aged 25 or over, for 142 economies, of which 107 have complete information at five-year intervals from 1960 to 2000. The data for the period up to 1995 is an estimate and that for 2000 is a projection. In our analysis, we interpolated the data to obtain the values for in-between years.

Table 4.3 shows educational attainment along with the average year of schooling for developed countries and developing countries including ASEAN4 and other East Asian countries. The figures indicate the proportion of population aged 25 or over that attained a secondary and higher level of education. According to the figures in the table, ASEAN4 countries performed less favourably in all three categories, average years of schooling, educational attainment for secondary and higher levels, compared to the NIEs. Moreover, ASEAN4 members fared less favourably than other developing countries including China in the average years of school and educational attainment for secondary levels. Concerning educational attainment for higher levels, the average level for ASEAN4 is higher compared to other developing countries including China. Favourable performance of ASEAN4 countries in this category is attributable to the Philippines, which had a very high educational attainment for higher levels. Indeed, 21.3% of the population in the Philippines aged 25 or over achieved a higher level of education, which surpassed Hong Kong, Singapore and Taiwan. In contrast to the high achievement in the Philippines, the corresponding level for Indonesia was low at 4.3%. As to educational attainment at secondary level, one finds that Thailand registered a very low figure at 9.1% when compared

Table 4.3 Educational Attainment

	Average Years of School					Highest Educational Attainment (Secondary)					Highest Educational Attainment (Higher)				
	1960	1970	1980	1990	1997	1960	1970	1980	1990	1997	1960	1970	1980	1990	1997
Developed countries	7.24	7.82	9.00	9.53	9.97	34.0	36.1	45.2	42.1	41.7	8.4	10.9	17.3	24.9	28.7
Developing countries	1.71	2.37	3.15	4.28	4.90	5.3	9.6	14.9	21.2	23.5	0.9	1.5	2.4	4.1	5.2
1. East Asia & the Pacific	1.75	2.84	3.73	5.16	5.67	6.1	15.0	19.8	31.1	32.4	1.3	1.5	2.0	3.4	4.6
(1) ASEAN4	2.12	3.05	3.88	4.54	5.46	4.5	7.0	11.6	17.9	21.7	1.5	2.5	4.1	6.6	8.9
Indonesia	1.11	2.29	3.09	3.30	4.37	1.9	5.1	9.6	16.8	20.5	0.1	0.5	0.8	2.3	4.3
Malaysia	2.35	3.05	4.49	5.54	7.76	7.2	9.4	19.9	27.1	42.9	1.5	1.5	1.4	2.8	7.2
Philippines	3.77	4.81	6.06	7.07	7.48	10.6	14.2	18.9	27.2	30.2	6.2	9.6	15.2	18.7	21.3
Thailand	3.45	3.54	3.77	5.35	5.91	4.9	4.4	6.8	8.0	9.1	0.6	1.1	2.9	7.8	10.4
(2) NIEs	3.37	4.64	6.56	8.52	9.55	11.9	20.8	31.7	47.6	47.5	3.1	5.2	8.7	12.5	20.5
Hong Kong	4.74	5.11	6.73	8.37	9.40	17.4	22.3	30.5	43.3	47.3	4.7	3.1	7.1	10.6	14.9
Korea	3.23	4.76	6.81	9.25	10.27	10.9	21.8	36.9	53.9	50.7	2.6	5.6	8.9	13.4	23.5
Singapore	3.14	3.74	3.65	5.52	7.97	23.4	20.9	14.6	31.3	49.5	0.0	2.0	3.4	4.7	9.1
Taiwan	3.32	4.39	6.37	7.44	8.28	11.0	18.1	23.3	37.7	40.7	4.2	5.4	9.3	12.2	17.3
(3) China	1.58	2.75	3.61	5.23	5.61	6.2	17.2	21.7	34.4	35.2	1.1	1.0	1.0	2.0	2.5
2. South Asia	1.31	1.77	2.52	3.37	4.03	3.2	4.6	13.3	14.3	16.1	0.1	1.3	2.3	3.7	4.2
3. Latin America and the Caribbean	2.95	3.32	3.97	4.93	5.53	9.4	10.4	12.7	16.5	19.1	1.9	2.5	5.4	8.9	11.1
4. Europe and Central Asia	4.27	4.75	5.62	6.57	7.00	9.9	12.2	19.7	27.1	29.3	1.9	3.4	4.9	6.9	9.0
5. Middle East and North Africa	0.76	1.06	2.00	3.36	4.39	2.3	4.1	7.8	14.8	19.7	0.6	1.2	3.0	5.0	7.2
6. Sub-Saharan Africa	1.18	1.32	1.90	2.78	3.50	3.9	4.4	6.1	10.3	15.3	0.3	0.6	0.6	1.8	2.5

Sources: 1. Barro RJ and Lee JW (2000), "International Data on Educational Attainment Updates and Implications", NBER Working Paper No.7911.
2. Data for 1997 is interpolated from those on 1995 and 1999.

to other countries. This observation is consistent with the allegation that Thailand needs to increase secondary education enrolment as well as completion rate. Having pointed out the relatively low educational level of ASEAN4 countries, it should be stressed that it is improving over time, although they need to speed up the rate of improvement.

3.1.2 Research and Development

The number of researchers in the population should be a good indicator of technological capability. This is because researchers are generally engaged in developing new technology, new products, or ways to modify existing technologies, which in turn would contribute to the improvement of technological capability.

Table 4.4 shows the number of researchers per million population for ASEAN4 and other East Asian countries along with other developing regions. The number of researchers per million population for ASEAN4 is 162 in 1997, significantly lower than that for the NIEs at 2,613. The figure for ASEAN4 countries is much lower compared to China at 454. Compared to the gap between ASEAN4 countries and the NIEs, the variations in the figures among ASEAN4 countries appear relatively small. What is remarkable about the performance of the NIEs is the rapid increase in the number of researchers. In 1970, the average number of researchers per million population for the NIEs was 198, or approximately 10% of the corresponding value for the developed countries. The number increased to 2,613 in 1997, reaching as much as 80% of the value for developed countries. Compared to the NIEs, the increase in the number of researchers for ASEAN4 countries was much lower, resulting in an increased gap between the NIEs and the ASEAN4 countries in this indicator.

Research and development activity can be considered as an input for developing and improving technological capability. The ratios of R&D to GDP for the ASEAN4 and other developing countries are shown in Table 4.4. The picture emerging from R&D/GDP ratios is generally similar to the picture that emerges from the number of researchers per million population. Specifically, ASEAN4 countries performed less favourably than the NIEs or China. In 1997, ASEAN4 countries spent a meager 0.14% of GDP for R&D, while the corresponding ratios for the NIEs and China are higher at 2.27 and 0.66, respectively. What is alarming is the situation in ASEAN4 countries, because the ratios for many ASEAN4 countries are declining over time.

The preceding examination of the domestic technological capability for the ASEAN4 countries revealed that they have fared less favourably compared to the NIEs in both educational attainment and R&D activities. ASEAN4 countries also performed less favourably when compared to

Table 4.4 Researchers and R&D

	Reseachers per million population				R&D/GDP (%)			
	1970	1980	1990	1997	1970	1980	1990	1997
Developed countries	1798	2201	3107	3161	1.99	2.01	2.43	2.39
Developing countries	157	208	278	334	0.31	0.43	0.71	0.79
1. East Asia & the Pacific	178	226	373	486	0.33	0.48	1.04	1.27
(1) ASEAN4	86	104	164	162	0.33	0.35	0.20	0.14
Indonesia	85	102	189	191	0.35	0.35	0.15	0.07
Malaysia	137	165	208	93	0.33	0.34	0.41	0.24
Philippines	93	112	141	153	0.15	0.26	0.20	0.22
Thailand	66	79	94	103	0.39	0.39	0.18	0.13
(2) NIEs	198	523	1826	2613	0.42	0.62	1.71	2.27
Hong Kong	na	na	na	na	na	na	na	na
Korea	176	484	1645	2195	0.38	0.57	1.88	2.82
Singapore	326	417	1426	2323	0.21	0.27	0.94	1.13
Taiwan	226	620	2260	3530	0.50	0.72	1.66	1.88
(3) China	203	243	348	454	0.19	0.37	0.68	0.66
2. South Asia	71	85	132	132	0.32	0.53	0.74	0.69
3. Latin America and the Caribbean	134	203	252	222	0.17	0.27	0.47	0.56
4. Europe and Central Asia	968	1378	798	792	0.71	0.95	0.84	0.56
5. Middle East and North Africa	154	212	296	377	0.24	0.19	0.28	0.32
6. Sub-Saharan Africa	70	109	141	235	0.57	0.56	0.56	0.47

Sources: UNESCO, Statistical Yearbook
World Bank, World Development Indicators, 2000
Republic of China, Taiwan Statistical Data Book

China in R&D and educational attainment except for higher education. These findings appear to indicate that the low technological level for ASEAN4 countries is partly attributable to low educational attainment and inactive R&D activities.

3.2 Inflow of Foreign Technology

Turning to the external sources of technology for upgrading technological capability, one identifies several channels including the importation of technology, capital goods, human resources, FDI, and others. We will examine foreign direct investment, foreign trade, and technology imports in this section, and importation of human resources in the next section by focusing on inflows of exports from Japan under the ODA programmes.

3.2.1 Foreign Direct Investment

In recent years, FDI has become an important means of importing technology for developing countries. Several reasons can be presented to explain the increasing importance of FDI. First, FDI has been increasing rapidly, as we will see later, to increase recipients' importance in international economic activities. Second, multinational enterprises (MNEs), which are major economic players in international economic activity, prefer to use FDI as a way of using their technology in foreign countries. One reason behind such behaviour is the difficulty in monitoring the use or abuse of technology if they sell technology to other firms. Third, as technology has become sophisticated, selling technology to other firms at appropriate prices has become difficult, because the potential buyers may not be able to evaluate the value of the technology properly.

Transfer of technology and managerial know-how from MNEs to the recipient or host country may take two different forms. One is intra-firm technology transfer in that technology is transferred from a parent company of an MNC to its foreign affiliate, and the other is technology spillover in that technology is transferred from a foreign affiliate to domestic firms.

Intra-firm technology transfer takes the forms of on-the-job training, training at parent companies, and others. Technology spillover is realized through various means. For example, technology spillover takes place when local workers, who acquired technology and managerial know-how by working at foreign affiliates, use these skills at domestic companies. Technology spillover may also be realized when local firms imitate technology and managerial know-how used at foreign affiliates. It should be pointed out that FDI inflow also leads to the improvement in technical efficiency of local firms because of competitive pressures imposed on them by foreign firms.

Intra-firm technology transfer has been identified by several studies. Using the results of a survey conducted on the East Asian affiliates of Japanese firms, Urata (1999) finds that relatively simple technologies such as maintenance and repair of production lines have been transferred from parent companies to foreign affiliates. He also finds that relatively sophisticated technologies such as development of new technologies and new products have not been transferred. Analyzing the determinants of the extent of intra-firm technology transfer achieved by Japanese multinationals, Urata and Kawai (2000) find the capability of absorbing technologies reflected in educational level in host countries plays a key role for successful intra-firm technology transfer. Their study also points out the fact that intra-firm technology transfer takes time and experience, suggesting the importance of maintaining a stable economic environment in the host country, so that multinational firms may stay there for a long period.

The results of the analyses on the presence of technology spillover are mixed. Using industry-level data, Caves (1974) found the presence of technology spillover in his study of the Australian manufacturing sector but not in his study of Canadian manufacturing. Using similar methodology, Globerman (1979) finds the presence of the spillover effect of FDI in the Canadian manufacturing sector. Blomstrom and Persson (1983) and Blomstrom and Wolff (1989) also detect technology spillover in their studies of the Mexican manufacturing sector. Unlike the studies that identified technology spillover by foreign firms, Haddad and Harrison (1993), and Aitken and Harrison (1994) do not find spillover in their respective studies of Morocco and Venezuela by using firm-level data. One possible reason for not detecting technology spillover in these studies is the limited presence of foreign firms in these countries.

Turning to the impact of FDI inflow on economic growth, one finds that only few studies on the subject have been conducted by using macroeconomic indicators. Borensztein, de Gregorio, and Lee (1998) find that FDI has a marginally positive impact on economic growth, but it has a significantly positive impact when FDI is interacted with educational levels of host countries.[4] Their finding may be interpreted to mean that education becomes more effective when it is associated with foreign knowledge. Recognizing that educational levels in East Asia are high for developing economies, it is reasonable to assert that substantial FDI inflow contributed to economic growth in East Asia.

Foreign direct investment has been growing rapidly in recent years. World FDI inflows increased more than threefold in eight years from $203 billion in 1990 to $680 billion in 1998.[5] Rapid increase in FDI is attributable to several factors. Technological progress and deregulation in communication services have reduced the cost of international communication, facilitating MNEs to conduct international business through FDI. Liberalization of FDI policies by many countries also contributed to the expansion of FDI. Among different regions, East Asia has been experiencing a remarkably rapid expansion of FDI inflows. One factor leading to the rapid expansion in FDI inflows by East Asian economies is substantial liberalization in FDI policies.[6] Indeed, a number of East Asian economies have provided various incentives such as preferential tax treatment to attract FDI, especially the type of FDI that generates exports. To take advantage of the favourable investment environment, a number of foreign firms interested in exporting undertook FDI in East Asia. Another factor that promoted FDI inflows to East Asia is favourable future prospects of the Asian markets, which was formed on the basis of the earlier performance. A number of foreign firms set up their subsidiaries to capture the local markets.

One notable development concerning FDI in Asia in recent years is the rapid increase in cross-border M&A (mergers and acquisitions). The share of M&A in FDI inflows for South, East and Southeast Asia increased rapidly from around 3% in 1995 to 16% in 1998.[7] Among Asian countries, which Korea and Thailand which were hit hard by the Asian crisis experienced a rapid increase in M&A. The increase in M&A in FDI implies the greater importance of the capability on the part of recipient countries to assimilate technology, in order to reap benefits from FDI inflows. This is because M&A do not expand physical capacity and therefore an improvement in technological capability through successful technology transfer is a major source of benefits.

Table 4.5 shows the importance of FDI inflows for East Asian and other economies. The importance of FDI inflows in East Asian economies increased steadily over time. The proportion of FDI inflows to GDP increased from 1.1% in 1970 to 2.8% in 1997. In 1997, East Asia was behind Latin America in terms of the FDI inflows to GDP ratio, which registered 3.3%. The importance of FDI inflows in economic activity differs substantially among East Asian economies. Singapore had by far the greatest exposure to foreign investors, as the ratio of FDI inflows in its GDP was as high as 10% in 1997, even after a notable decline from 14.4% in 1990. Malaysia had the second highest ratio at 5.1%, and China was third at 4.9% in 1997. The increase in the share of FDI inflows in GDP for China was spectacular, since the corresponding ratio for 1990 was as low as 0.98%. Hong Kong also recorded a relatively high ratio of 3.5%. In contrast to these countries with high FDI inflows-GDP ratios, Korea and Taiwan had substantially low ratios around 0.6–0.8% in 1997. It is interesting to note that the ratio for Taiwan declined over time, while that for Korea increased steadily from the very low ratio.

Table 4.5 FDI Inflows (Gross): Percent of GDP

	1970	1980	1990	1997
Developed countries	0.46	0.52	1.06	1.27
Developing countries	0.75	0.78	0.85	2.32
1. East Asia & the Pacific	1.10	1.07	1.59	2.76
(1) ASEAN4	0.80	0.91	2.23	2.60
Indonesia	0.86	0.23	0.96	2.17
Malaysia	2.24	3.52	5.45	5.10
Philippines	0.17	0.79	1.20	1.49
Thailand	0.61	0.57	2.86	2.50
(2) NIEs	1.72	1.59	1.59	1.60
Hong Kong	na	na	2.31	3.46
Korea	na	0.01	0.28	0.60
Singapore	5.53	14.00	14.36	10.21
Taiwan	2.45	1.13	0.83	0.79
(3) China	na	na	0.98	4.92
2. South Asia	0.08	0.08	0.13	0.83
3. Latin America and the Caribbean	0.82	0.78	0.68	3.25
4. Europe and Central Asia	0.21	0.09	0.85	1.73
5. Middle East and North Africa	0.64	1.15	0.55	1.00
6. Sub-Saharan Africa	0.56	0.41	0.28	1.79

Source: IMF, Balance of Payment Statistics
World Bank, World Development Indicators, 2000
Republic of China, Taiwan Statistical Data Book

3.2.2 Imports of Capital Goods

Foreign trade has also been an important source for obtaining foreign technologies for developing countries. Through importation of intermediate and investment goods that are embodied with technology, an importing country can potentially obtain technology. Reverse engineering is one effective way of assimilating technology from the importation of intermediate and investment goods. Coe, Helpman, and Hoffmaister (1997) show that developing countries benefited from foreign R&D through importing capital goods in their study.

Table 4.6 shows the share of machinery imports in total imports.[8] When compared to other developing countries, East Asian economies exhibit a notable upward trend. The shares of machinery imports in total imports for East Asian economies increased from 0.30 in 1980 to 0.41 in 1997, while the corresponding share for developing countries increased more slowly from 0.31 to 0.35 during the same period. It is interesting to observe that ASEAN4 had a consistently higher share than the NIEs or China. In 1997, the share of machinery imports for ASEAN4

Table 4.6   Machinery Import Share of Total Imports

	1980	1990	1997
Developed countries	0.256	0.355	0.378
Developing countries	0.310	0.348	0.348
1. East Asia & the Pacific	0.297	0.344	0.406
(1) ASEAN4	0.325	0.421	0.501
Indonesia	0.376	0.411	0.425
Malaysia	0.370	0.525	0.616
Philippines	0.296	0.320	0.487
Thailand	0.260	0.428	0.473
(2) NIEs	0.254	0.383	0.438
Hong Kong	0.237	0.308	0.371
Korea	0.227	0.351	0.355
Singapore	0.281	0.441	0.553
Taiwan	0.273	0.434	0.474
(3) China	0.251	0.351	0.365
2. South Asia	0.257	0.244	0.254
3. Latin America and the Caribbean	0.295	0.339	0.373
4. Europe and Central Asia	0.274	0.320	0.364
5. Middle East and North Africa	0.323	0.341	0.335
6. Sub-Saharan Africa	0.330	0.373	0.325

Sources: World Bank, World Development Indicators, 2000
Republic of China, Taiwan Statistical Data Book

was 0.5, while the corresponding shares for the NIEs and China were 0.41 and 0.36. Among the East Asian economies, Singapore and Malaysia had particularly high shares with 0.553 and 0.616, respectively, in 1997. The high shares observed for these countries reflect the large number of foreign affiliates of manufacturing multinationals in these countries, which depend on imports for the supply of machinery used for manufacturing production.

An expansion in imports could also lead to an improvement in technical efficiency of domestic firms through different channels. One important channel is the increased competitive pressure that results from an increase in imports. In order to survive under competitive pressures, domestic firms have to improve their productivity by adopting various strategies such as the introduction of new technologies and new products. The positive impact of greater imports on productivity has been found in several studies. In their study of trade policy and its impact on productivity for Japan in the post–WWII period, Lawrence and Weinstein (2000) find that import expansion resulted in improving productivity in Japan.

So far we have discussed the impact of increased imports on productivity. We can also expect the increase in exports to have a positive impact on productivity. Export expansion may lead to greater productivity for a variety of reasons: greater capacity utilization in industries in which the minimum efficient scale (MES) of plant is large relative to domestic market; increasing familiarity with and absorption of new technologies; greater learning by doing insofar as this is a function of cumulative output, and the stimulative effects of the need to achieve internationally competitive prices and quality.[9] Several studies have shown that export expansion, particularly that of manufactured products, resulted in improving productivity. The World Bank (1993) finds that the high share of manufactured exports in total exports increased the growth rate of total factor productivity in its study of 69 countries for the 1960–89 period.[10] A case study of Korean firms by Rhee, Ross-Larson and Pursell (1984) finds that exporting firms achieved higher productivity by obtaining technologies through contact with foreign firms, supporting the assertion that exports increase productivity.

Table 4.7 indicates the importance of foreign trade for East Asian economies. From the figures in the table, which measure the ratio of

Table 4.7   Trade (Exports+Imports) : Percent of GDP

	1970	1980	1990	1997
Developed countries	28.8	39.2	38.3	42.5
Developing countries	37.4	52.1	53.2	60.8
1. East Asia & the Pacific	47.6	78.6	82.7	91.7
(1) ASEAN4	40.1	62.7	74.3	94.9
Indonesia	28.4	54.4	49.9	56.0
Malaysia	79.9	112.6	150.6	185.5
Philippines	42.6	52.0	60.8	108.5
Thailand	34.4	54.5	75.8	94.8
(2) NIEs	76.0	122.0	115.7	118.9
Hong Kong	181.5	180.6	260.1	264.2
Korea	37.5	74.4	59.4	70.5
Singapore	231.6	439.0	397.0	315.6
Taiwan	60.7	106.3	88.5	95.7
(3) China	3.8	15.5	31.9	41.6
2. South Asia	10.7	19.4	20.5	28.1
3. Latin America and the Caribbean	20.5	26.7	28.9	36.3
4. Europe and Central Asia	29.6	36.1	39.1	60.1
5. Middle East and North Africa	71.9	72.7	68.0	64.8
6. Sub-Saharan Africa	47.2	59.7	51.4	60.1

Sources: World Bank, World Development Indicators, 2000
Republic of China, Taiwan Statistical Data Book

total trade, that is exports and imports, to GDP (the trade-GDP ratio), one finds the increasing importance of foreign trade in economic activities for East Asian economies. Specifically, the trade-GDP ratio for East Asian economies increased sharply from 47.6% in 1970 to 91.7% in 1997. These values are significantly higher when compared with those for other developing regions or developed countries. The importance of foreign trade expressed by the trade-GDP ratios varies widely among East Asian economies. Singapore and Hong Kong register very high ratios of 250–300% in 1997, reflecting their roles as centres of entrepot trade and their open trade regimes. Malaysia also shows a high trade-GDP ratio of 190% in 1997, which results partly from the large presence of export-oriented MNEs. In contrast, China, Indonesia, and Korea register relatively low trade-GDP ratios. It should be noted that China experienced a significant increase in trade-GDP ratio, while Korea and Indonesia saw fluctuations in their trade-GDP ratios. Fluctuations in the trade-GDP ratios are also observed for Taiwan, although the ratios are somewhat higher than those for Korea. For the Philippines and Thailand, the trade-GDP ratios increased steadily, but the ratios in 1997 were around 100%, significantly smaller than those for Malaysia.

3.2.3 Technology Imports

Importation of technology in the form of patents is an important method to obtain foreign technology. In the past, technology trade was conducted largely through arms' length transactions, but in recent years intra-firm transactions have expanded rapidly. Specifically, technology trade between the MNE's parent company and its overseas affiliates has grown substantially. This pattern reflects at least two developments, which are related to each other. One is rapid FDI expansion, and the other is increased preference on the part of MNEs to use FDI as a means of using their technology in foreign countries, as we discussed above concerning recent developments of FDI.

Table 4.8 describes the patterns of technology trade in terms of ratio between payments of royalty and licence fees, and GDP (royalty payments-GDP ratio) for East Asian economies. One has to note that the information is available for a limited number of countries. Specifically, the information for Hong Kong, Singapore, Indonesia, and Malaysia are not available. Therefore, the term 'East Asia' in the discussions of technology trade has to be interpreted with a qualification. The royalty payments-GDP ratio for East Asia increased sharply from 0.075% in 1970 to 0.292% in 1997, compared with other regions including developed countries. Among the East Asian economies, the increase in the royalty payments-GDP ratio was particularly spectacular for Thailand, as it increased from 0.092% in 1980 to 0.539% in 1997. Albeit somewhat at a slower rate, the royalty

Table 4.8   Payments of Royalty: Percent of GDP

	1970	1980	1990	1997
Developed countries	0.124	0.124	0.178	0.231
Developing countries	0.112	0.086	0.137	0.172
1. East Asia & the Pacific	0.075	0.128	0.259	0.292
(1) ASEAN4	na	0.098	0.162	0.357
Indonesia	na	na	na	na
Malaysia	na	0.152	na	na
Philippines	na	0.058	0.086	0.192
Thailand	na	0.092	0.200	0.539
(2) NIEs	na	0.195	0.472	0.467
Hong Kong	na	na	na	na
Korea	na	0.195	0.540	0.507
Singapore	na	na	na	na
Taiwan	na	na	0.363	0.405
(3) China	na	na	na	0.060
2. South Asia	0.016	0.008	0.021	0.034
3. Latin America and the Caribbean	0.158	0.055	0.090	0.115
4. Europe and Central Asia	0.050	0.050	0.050	0.227
5. Middle East and North Africa	0.186	0.177	0.183	0.215
6. Sub-Saharan Africa	0.181	0.155	0.074	0.131

Sources: World Bank, World Development Indicators, 2000
     Republic of China, Taiwan Statistical Data Book

payments-GDP ratio for Korea increased notably. In 1997, the royalty payments-GDP ratios for Korea, Taiwan, and Thailand were more or less comparable around 0.4–0.5%, while the corresponding rates for the Philippines and China were significantly smaller, around 0.03–0.06%.

4. Technological Assistance through Japan's ODA Programmes

Technology can be transferred internationally via the movements of people or experts embodying technology. Such movement can take place by private initiatives and with the assistance of public support. For example, an MNC may send its technical staff to its overseas affiliates to transfer technology and know-how. It may also send its technical staff to other firms in a foreign country as part of a technology licensing agreement. Technological experts may also be sent to developing countries by donor governments as a part of economic assistance programmes, while workers and technicians from developing countries may be invited to acquire technical skills in developed countries. While very specific technology or skills such as those used for the production of patented products are transferred via private channels, basic and general-purpose skills such as moulding techniques tend to be transferred through public assistance. This section reviews the Japanese Government's technical assistance programmes in the form of ODA to ASEAN countries, in order to investigate their possible contribution to upgrading technological capability in ASEAN countries.

ODA takes two forms, bilateral and multilateral forms. While multilateral ODA is provided through multilateral development agencies such as the World Bank and the United Nations Development Program, bilateral ODA takes the form of provision of economic assistance given to a specific country. Bilateral ODA consists of grants and loans, and bilateral grants further consist of financial assistance and technical assistance. We focus on technical assistance in this section since our main interest in this paper is technological upgrading in ASEAN countries.

Before examining Japan's contribution to technical upgrading in ASEAN countries via movement of people, we examine the amount of financial resources expended on technical assistance in the form of ODA by the Japanese government. In 2001, the Japanese Government spent ¥341.5 billion (US$9.7 billion) on technical assistance, amounting to 29% of overall ODA. Technical assistance is provided by various government agencies including the Japan International Cooperation Agency (JICA), the Japan Foundation, the Japan External Trade Organization (JETRO), the Association for Overseas Technical Scholarship (AOTS), the Japan Overseas Development Corporation (JODC), and others. Among these agencies, JICA, AOTS, and JODC have programmes that specialize in technical assistance via movement of people. JICA undertakes programmes for mainly government officials, while AOTS and JODC conduct programmes for the private sector. AOTS specializes in inviting overseas participants to Japan, while JODC specializes in sending Japanese experts to foreign countries. Among these three agencies, JICA plays a core role in providing technical assistance for the Japanese Government. In 2001, JICA used 48.7% of government funds allocated to technical assistance. As to the invited overseas participants in technical seminars in Japan, dispatched Japanese experts abroad, and dispatched survey team members abroad, JICA accounts for 49.0%, 83.7%, and 91.8% of the total, respectively.

It may be useful to explain the activities of the Japan Foundation and JETRO before analyzing technical assistance programmes by JICA, AOTS, and JODC. The Japan Foundation provides programmes with the objectives to deepen mutual understanding through international exchange, such as the introduction of Japanese culture to foreign countries. JETRO was set up to provide assistance to Japanese firms in expanding their exports, but as Japan's trade surplus increased over time its mission changed to expand imports. In addition to these trade related programmes, JETRO has programmes that promote structural adjustment and technical progress in developing countries.

Table 4.9 shows JICA's activities in ASEAN and other East Asian countries from 1954 to 2001. The figures indicate the importance of ASEAN4 countries for JICA's technical assistance, as they account for approximately 25%–30% of JICA's programmes. Among ASEAN4 countries, Indonesia has been given the greatest importance, while Thailand is second after Indonesia. Although not shown in the table, the importance of ASEAN4 countries has been declining slightly over time. This is largely due to ASEAN4 countries' successful economic development compared to other developing countries, whose need for technical and other assistance have increased. Similarly to ASEAN4 countries, the NIEs lost their position in JICA's programme because of their declining importance as recipients of technical assistance. It should be noted that the importance of China has been increasing in recent years.

JICA invited 77,579 participants from ASEAN4 countries to technical seminars in Japan from 1954 to 2001, amounting to 33% of a total of 239,493 participants. Among ASEAN4 countries, Indonesia ranks first in terms of the number of participants given technical training in Japan, as it sent as many as 27,852 participants. Thailand comes in second, and it is followed by the Philippines and Malaysia. China comes after the Philippines and before Malaysia, as it has sent 12,654 participants to Japan. As to Japanese experts and survey team members dispatched overseas, ASEAN4 countries received 21,456 experts and 45,551 members from 1954 to 2001. Similar to the case for the programmes for overseas participants, Indonesia and Thailand have been given a lot of importance in these programmes.

AOTS was established in 1959, and its objective was to invite technical personnel from developing countries to Japan and other countries for approximately three to four months, in order to improve their technical skills. Technical training is provided by recipient private firms and AOTS makes necessary arrangements as well as provides classes on Japanese language, society, culture and others, to facilitate overseas participants' adjustment to Japan. The AOTS programmes are financed partly by ODA and partly by the firms involved in the programmes. Technical skills provided by the programmes include managerial skills, and production and quality control skills. It should be noted that a number of alumni associations have been established in many countries and some of them have been very active in disseminating and improving skills they acquired in Japan. Table 4.10 presents the number of overseas participants in AOTS programmes by country and by industry from 1961

Table 4.9 Technical Assistance by JICA: 1954–2001

	Absolute values					Regional and country shares (%)				
	Technical cooperation	Overseas participants	Japanese experts	Survey team members	Overseas cooperation volunteers	Technical cooperation	Overseas participants	Japanese experts	Survey team members	Overseas cooperation volunteers
ASEAN4	668	77,579	21,456	45,551	3,082	25.08	32.39	32.95	27.35	13.41
Indonesia	239	27,852	8,192	16,496	381	8.97	11.63	12.58	9.90	1.66
Malaysia	95	11,643	2,214	5,821	1,109	3.57	4.86	3.40	3.49	4.82
Philippines	152	14,230	4,008	11,333	1,172	5.71	5.94	6.15	6.80	5.10
Thailand	182	23,854	7,042	11,901	420	6.83	9.96	10.81	7.14	1.83
NIEs	45	10,946	2,808	1,782	0	1.69	4.57	4.31	1.07	0.00
Korea	24	6,176	1,626	1,040	0	0.90	2.58	2.50	0.62	0.00
Singapore	21	4,770	1,182	742	0	0.79	1.99	1.82	0.45	0.00
China	132	12,654	4,654	11,631	466	4.96	5.28	7.15	6.98	2.03
World	2,663	239,493	65,123	166,578	22,985	100.00	100.00	100.00	100.00	100.00

Notes: The figures are cumulative from 1954 to 2001. Technical cooperation is measures in terms of billion Yen, while the figures for other categories are measured in terms of persons.

Table 4.10 Technical Training of Foreign Participants in Japan by AOTS (The Association for Overseas Technical Scholarship) (The cumulative number of participants for 1961–2001)

Absolute values (persons)

	Total	Agriculture fishery	Mining	Food	Textiles	Petro-chemicals	Metals and products	General machinery	Electric machinery	Transport machinery	Precision machinery	Other manufacturing	Construction	Others
Asia	74,871	345	61	959	2,707	2,518	3,694	9,220	16,415	13,985	1,131	3,881	3,292	16,663
ASEAN4	33,122	58	21	434	1,843	1,131	1,762	4,096	7,179	7,538	383	2,098	1,533	5,046
Indonesia	10,824	27	4	104	977	607	786	1,742	1,727	2,186	33	907	420	1,304
Malaysia	6,990	14	3	105	136	92	396	708	1,659	1,635	86	416	300	1,440
Philippines	4,939	9	13	74	42	106	201	433	1,573	908	111	228	396	845
Thailand	10,369	8	1	151	688	326	379	1,213	2,220	2,809	153	547	417	1,457
NIEs	11,325	159	23	115	202	512	635	2,411	3,041	1,639	270	557	446	1,288
Hong Kong	903	2	0	3	18	8	5	202	259	228	8	22	36	112
Korea	6,639	156	3	84	88	255	484	1,405	1,796	754	176	312	236	873
Singapore	2,657	0	0	0	5	32	126	558	715	540	56	121	33	276
Taiwan	1,126	1	20	28	91	217	20	246	271	117	30	102	141	27
China	17,944	83	8	269	434	584	952	1,798	4,111	1,739	390	721	820	6,048
east	2,981	22	0	23	9	196	154	239	473	1,120	27	103	130	485
Africa	3,957	6	3	14	165	44	90	210	372	1,691	20	77	40	1,225
Latin America	7,722	32	4	61	224	77	214	417	1,705	1,496	66	55	211	3,160
Oceania	520	4	0	2	0	0	1	26	37	393	2	21	12	22
Europe	2,249	4	1	3	7	14	5	138	171	525	2	115	15	1,249
World	92,300	413	69	1,062	3,112	2,849	4,158	10,250	19,173	19,210	1,248	4,252	3,700	22,804

Country and Regional Composition (%)

	Total	Agriculture fishery	Mining	Food	Textiles	Petro-chemicals	Metals and products	General machinery	Electric machinery	Transport machinery	Precision machinery	Other manufacturing	Construction	Others
Asia	81.1	83.5	88.4	90.3	87.0	88.4	88.8	90.0	85.6	72.8	90.6	91.3	89.0	73.1
ASEAN4	35.9	14.0	30.4	40.9	59.2	39.7	42.4	40.0	37.4	39.2	30.7	49.3	41.4	22.1
Indonesia	11.7	6.5	5.8	9.8	31.4	21.3	18.9	17.0	9.0	11.4	2.6	21.3	11.4	5.7
Malaysia	7.6	3.4	4.3	9.9	4.4	3.2	9.5	6.9	8.7	8.5	6.9	9.8	8.1	6.3
Philippines	5.4	2.2	18.8	7.0	1.3	3.7	4.8	4.2	8.2	4.7	8.9	5.4	10.7	3.7
Thailand	11.2	1.9	1.4	14.2	22.1	11.4	9.1	11.8	11.6	14.6	12.3	12.9	11.3	6.4
NIEs	12.3	38.5	33.3	10.8	6.5	18.0	15.3	23.5	15.9	8.5	21.6	13.1	12.1	5.6
Hong Kong	1.0	0.5	0.0	0.3	0.6	0.3	0.1	2.0	1.4	1.2	0.6	0.5	1.0	0.5
Korea	7.2	37.8	4.3	7.9	2.8	9.0	11.6	13.7	9.4	3.9	14.1	7.3	6.4	3.8
Singapore	2.9	0.0	0.0	0.0	0.2	7.6	3.0	5.4	3.7	2.8	4.5	2.8	0.9	1.2
Taiwan	1.2	0.2	29.0	2.6	2.9	1.1	0.5	2.4	1.4	0.6	2.4	2.4	3.8	0.1
China	19.4	20.1	11.6	25.3	13.9	20.5	22.9	17.5	21.4	9.1	31.3	17.0	22.2	26.5
east	3.2	5.3	0.0	2.2	0.3	6.9	3.7	2.3	2.5	5.8	2.2	2.4	3.5	2.1
Africa	4.3	1.5	4.3	1.3	5.3	1.5	2.2	2.0	1.9	8.8	1.6	1.8	1.1	5.4
Latin America	8.4	7.7	5.8	5.7	7.2	2.7	5.1	4.1	8.9	7.8	5.3	1.3	5.7	13.9
Oceania	0.6	1.0	0.0	0.2	0.0	0.0	0.0	0.3	0.2	2.0	0.2	0.5	0.3	0.1
Europe	2.4	1.0	1.4	0.3	0.2	0.5	0.1	1.3	0.9	2.7	0.2	2.7	0.4	5.5
World	100	100	100	100	100	100	100	100	100	100	100	100	100	100

Source: AOTS website

to 2001. ASEAN4 countries sent 33,122 participants to Japan, accounting for 36% of all participants for the period. Among ASEAN4 countries, Indonesia and Thailand are the two countries with a large number of participants. It should be noted, however, as of the end of 2001 China is the largest country in terms of the cumulative number of participants in AOTS programmes, as its importance has been increasing rapidly in recent years. Among different sectors, large numbers of participants are enrolled in the programs in machinery, especially electric and transport machinery, in the case of ASEAN4 countries. This reflects not only the increasing importance of these sectors in ASEAN4 but also the active performance of Japanese firms in these countries. Indeed, in many cases, participants are recommended by Japanese firms operating in ASEAN4 countries, as Japanese firms find the need for local technicians to improve their skills.

JODC was established in 1970 to promote industrialization in developing countries. JODC sends Japanese experts to private companies in developing countries at the request of private companies in foreign countries. JODC's programmes are financed by ODA and participating private companies. As many requests'come from overseas affiliates of Japanese firms, JODC's programmes may be considered mainly to provide technical assistance to Japanese firms. However, it is important to note that when the beneficiaries from the program are Japanese firms, they are required to provide technical assistance to local firms as well. As such, JODC's programmes have been set up to contribute to the improvement in technical capability in LDCs. According to Table 4.11, where geographical and sectoral distribution of Japanese experts participating in the programme are shown, ASEAN4 accounts for 57.4% of total Japanese experts sent overseas from 1979 to 2002. As was the case for JICA and AOTS programmes, Indonesia and Thailand are the two most important recipients of JODC programmes. China is the third largest recipient of JODC programmes, similar to the pattern found in other programmes. Unlike the case for AOTS programmes, the textile industry has the largest number of participants in the JODC programmes, largely reflecting the large number of Japanese textile firms undertaking investment in foreign countries, especially in Asia. After textiles, machinery and material producing sectors such as iron and steel, metal products, and plastic products account for a large number of participants in the JODC programme.

Several interesting common characteristics of these programmes should be noted. First, as was noted above, ASEAN has been a central focus of Japan's technical assistance programmes involving JICA, AOTS, JODC and other agencies. At least two factors may be noted to explain the focus on ASEAN. One is Japan's strong interest in ASEAN's economic development for the social and political stability in East Asia, which

Table 4.11 Technical Assistance by Japan Overseas Development Corporation JODC (1979–2002)

		ASEAN4	Indonesia	Malaysia	Philippines	Thailand	NIES	Korea	Singapore	China	Asia	M. East and Africa	Latin America	Oceania	Europe	Total
Absolute number (persons)																
Minig		43	0	0	41	2	0	0	0	8	52	2	2	1	0	57
Construction		91	52	8	14	17	2	2	0	5	105	0	2	0	1	108
Manufacturing	total	2,077	921	221	242	693	186	168	18	729	3,405	81	97	0	22	3,605
Textiles		715	436	12	64	203	21	18	3	165	1,059	21	5	0	7	1,092
Genearal machinery		107	54	6	11	36	46	45	1	112	304	7	8	0	1	320
Transport machinery		220	62	32	33	93	2	2	0	63	320	5	4	0	1	330
Ship building		17	4	0	5	8	0	0	0	12	30	4	2	0	0	36
Electric machinery		113	31	43	22	17	19	17	2	102	255	0	16	0	3	274
Precision instruments		24	4	4	6	10	10	9	1	20	56	0	0	0	0	56
Iron and steel		157	46	19	22	70	3	2	2	28	223	19	3	0	0	245
Metal products		161	68	21	13	59	4	9	1	26	208	2	3	0	0	213
Non-ferrous metal products		22	10	1	1	10	9	0	0	11	45	0	18	0	6	69
Petroleum products		3	2	0	0	1	0	0	0	3	6	8	0	0	2	16
Chimical products		67	25	7	9	26	21	21	0	41	150	1	8	0	0	159
Rubber products		34	14	1	1	18	2	2	0	2	39	1	0	0	0	40
Plastic products		113	21	30	17	45	8	5	3	21	146	0	6	0	0	152
Ceramics		68	17	15	8	28	21	21	0	31	151	6	7	0	0	164
Pulp, paper products		11	0	2	0	9	5	3	2	11	30	1	0	0	0	31
Publishing and printing		5	2	0	2	1	0	0	0	5	17	0	0	0	0	17
Wood, wood products		145	106	18	9	12	3	0	3	25	190	0	1	0	0	191
Food products		75	16	7	15	37	7	7	0	41	129	5	13	0	2	149
Other manufacturing		20	3	3	4	10	5	5	0	10	47	1	3	0	0	51
Services	total	325	70	31	26	198	30	16	14	90	593	20	33	1	3	650
Financial services		32	3	0	1	28	1	1	0	0	33	0	2	0	0	35
Information technology		22	4	1	8	9	11	4	7	33	92	2	1	0	1	96
Enteprise services		67	21	20	7	19	1	0	1	13	106	4	1	0	0	111
Professional services		159	26	4	9	120	16	10	6	23	274	6	28	0	0	308
Other servies		45	16	6	1	22	1	1	0	21	88	8	1	1	2	100
Total		2,536	1,043	260	323	910	218	186	32	832	4,155	103	134	2	26	4,420

Table 4.11 Technical Assistance by Japan Overseas Development Corporation JODC (1979–2002) (continued)

Country and regional composition (%)

		ASEAN4	Indonesia	Malaysia	Philippines	Thailand	NIES	Korea	Singapore	China	Asia	M. East and Africa	Latin America	Oceania	Europe	Total
Mining		75.4	0.0	0.0	71.9	3.5	0.0	0.0	0.0	14.0	91.2	3.5	3.5	1.8	0.0	100.0
Construction		84.3	48.1	7.4	13.0	15.7	1.9	1.9	0.0	4.6	97.2	0.0	1.9	0.0	0.9	100.0
Manufacturing	total	57.6	25.5	6.1	6.7	19.2	5.2	4.7	0.5	20.2	94.5	2.2	2.7	0.0	0.6	100.0
Textiles		65.5	39.9	1.1	5.9	18.6	1.9	1.6	0.3	15.1	97.0	1.9	0.5	0.0	0.6	100.0
Genearal machinery		33.4	16.9	1.9	3.4	11.3	14.4	14.1	0.3	35.0	95.0	2.2	2.5	0.0	0.3	100.0
Transport machinery		66.7	18.8	9.7	10.0	28.2	0.6	0.6	0.0	19.1	97.0	1.5	1.2	0.0	0.3	100.0
Ship building		47.2	11.1	0.0	13.9	22.2	0.0	0.0	0.7	33.3	83.3	11.1	5.6	0.0	0.0	100.0
Electric machinery		41.2	11.3	15.7	8.0	6.2	6.9	6.2	0.7	37.2	93.1	0.0	5.8	0.0	1.1	100.0
Precision instruments		42.9	7.1	7.1	10.7	17.9	17.9	16.1	1.8	35.7	100.0	0.0	0.0	0.0	0.0	100.0
Iron and steel		64.1	18.8	7.8	9.0	28.6	1.2	0.8	0.4	11.4	91.0	7.8	1.2	0.0	0.0	100.0
Metal products		75.6	31.9	9.9	6.1	27.7	1.9	0.9	0.9	12.2	97.7	0.9	1.4	0.0	0.0	100.0
Non-ferrous metal products		31.9	14.5	1.4	1.4	14.5	13.0	13.0	0.0	15.9	65.2	0.0	26.1	0.0	8.7	100.0
Petroleum products		18.8	12.5	0.0	0.0	6.3	0.0	0.0	0.0	18.8	37.5	50.0	0.0	0.0	12.5	100.0
Chimical products		42.1	15.7	4.4	5.7	16.4	13.2	13.2	0.0	25.8	94.3	0.6	5.0	0.0	0.0	100.0
Rubber products		85.0	35.0	2.5	2.5	45.0	5.0	5.0	0.0	5.0	97.5	2.5	0.0	0.0	0.0	100.0
Plastic products		74.3	13.8	19.7	11.2	29.6	5.3	3.3	2.0	13.8	96.1	0.0	3.9	0.0	0.0	100.0
Ceramics		41.5	10.4	9.1	4.9	17.1	12.8	12.8	0.0	18.9	92.1	3.7	4.3	0.0	0.0	100.0
Pulp, paper products		35.5	0.0	6.5	0.0	29.0	16.1	9.7	6.5	35.5	96.8	3.2	0.0	0.0	0.0	100.0
Publishing and printing		29.4	11.8	0.0	11.8	5.9	0.0	0.0	0.0	29.4	100.0	0.0	0.0	0.0	0.0	100.0
Wood, wood products		75.9	55.5	9.4	4.7	6.3	1.6	0.0	1.6	13.1	99.5	0.0	0.5	0.0	0.0	100.0
Food products		50.3	10.7	4.7	10.1	24.8	4.7	4.7	0.0	27.5	86.6	3.4	8.7	0.0	1.3	100.0
Other manufacturing		39.2	5.9	5.9	7.8	19.6	9.8	9.8	0.0	19.6	92.2	2.0	5.9	0.0	0.0	100.0
Services	total	50.0	10.8	4.8	4.0	30.5	4.6	2.5	2.2	13.8	91.2	3.1	5.1	0.2	0.5	100.0
Financial services		91.4	8.6	0.0	2.9	80.0	2.9	2.9	0.0	0.0	94.3	0.0	5.7	0.0	0.0	100.0
Information technology		22.9	4.2	1.0	8.3	9.4	11.5	4.2	7.3	34.4	95.8	2.1	1.0	0.0	1.0	100.0
Enteprise services		60.4	18.9	18.0	6.3	17.1	0.9	0.0	0.9	11.7	95.5	3.6	0.9	0.0	0.0	100.0
Professional services		51.6	8.4	1.3	2.9	39.0	5.2	3.2	1.9	7.5	89.0	1.9	9.1	0.0	0.0	100.0
Other servies		45.0	16.0	6.0	1.0	22.0	1.0	1.0	0.0	21.0	88.0	8.0	1.0	1.0	2.0	100.0
Total		57.4	23.6	5.9	7.3	20.6	4.9	4.2	0.7	18.8	94.0	2.3	3.0	0.0	0.6	100.0

Note: The figures in the table refer to the cumulative value for 1979–2002. NIES include Korea and Singapore only.
Source: JODC database.

would in turn benefit Japan. Successful economic development of ASEAN countries would be a balancing element in the region, in the face of China's rapid emergence as an economic and political power. The other factor is the beneficial impact of successful technological upgrading of the ASEAN countries on Japanese firms operating in ASEAN countries. Many Japanese firms are faced with problem of low technological capability of ASEAN workers at their ASEAN affiliates, making it difficult for Japanese firms to compete effectively in the world market. To alleviate this problem faced by Japanese firms, Japanese government has been actively engaged in technical assistance programmes in ASEAN countries.

The second common characteristic of technical assistance programmes pursued by several Japanese agencies is their involvement of both public and private sectors. In light of a large number of private companies that are in need of technical assistance, assistance provided only by the public sector cannot be sufficient; private sector involvement is required for making ODA programmes effective. Third, an increasing number of technical assistance programmes take the form of institution building such as the establishment of human resource development centres. Despite the importance of "grass roots" technical assistance at the firm level, the problem of low technical skills and management know-how may be tackled more effectively from a broader perspective. Specifically, establishment of technical centres and human resource development centres can be effective in improving technical skills and the quality of human resources, since they provide training not only to persons in need of such training but also to prospective teachers and trainers, who in turn provide technical assistance to persons in need of upgrading skills. Fourth, many programmes are jointly pursued by several organizations, including JICA, AOTS, JODC and others. Joint programmes can prove very effective for a large-scale project, one of which will be discussed below, as they can avoid unnecessary overlaps, which may be created if the programmes are carried out independently.

Among many technical assistance projects extended to ASEAN countries by the Japanese government, let me introduce a small and medium-enterprise (SME) promotion project in Indonesia, in which I participated, to illustrate a new type of technical assistance project pursued by the Japanese government recently. The SME promotion project for Indonesia started at the request of then President Wahid of Indonesia in November 1999. After becoming the president, President Wahid realized the need to strengthen SMEs not only to promote economic growth but also to improve the living standard of many Indonesian workers working at SMEs. By responding to the request, a Japanese team of experts consisting of government officials, private sector personnel, and academics was formed in January 2000 with an objective of making recommendations to President Wahid on SME promotion policies for Indonesia. In this project, the Ministry of Foreign Affairs, Ministry of Economy, Trade and Industry, and Ministry of Finance were involved, while semi-government agencies including JICA, JETRO, JODC, the Japan Bank for International Cooperation (JBIC), and others were also involved.

The team visited Indonesia at least once a month for six months to study the situation intensively and discuss it with their Indonesian counterparts, and then presented their report and recommendations to President Wahid in July 2000. The recommendations included various subjects ranging from technical assistance to financial assistance and also covered the issues of institution building in the government and private sectors. One area that was given focus was technical assistance. One common characteristic of SMEs is a lack of technical and managerial skills. In order for SMEs to compete effectively, SMEs need to improve their technical and managerial skills. Faced with limited financial and human resources, SMEs are forced to rely on external assistance, which may come from other private companies or from public sources such as government and international organizations. The recommendations noted the importance of these two sources of assistance, particularly that from public sources, as it could play a catalyst role, which would lead to the establishment of supporting linkages with private companies. Specifically, the recommendations pointed to the need to improve the quality of existing institutions for providing technical and managerial assistance and to setting up new institutions. The Indonesian government adopted many of the recommendations and it has already begun working on technical and management centers.

Evaluation of the technical assistance programmes is very difficult, as quantification of their achievement is not easy. Based on anecdotal evidence, evaluation of the specific programmes is mixed, although overall assessment of the programmes by the participants is reported to be reasonably good. Having noted the general impressions of the technical programmes by the participants, it is important to devise a good evaluation method in order to improve technical assistance programmes.

5. Conclusion

Technology, not only in the form of engineering technology but also management know-how, plays a very important role in achieving economic development. For developing countries, technology is generally obtained from developed countries, in various forms including technology licensing, foreign direct investment, importation of capital goods, importation of technical experts, and others. Regardless of the form of acquisition of technology, domestic technological capability plays a crucial role in the success or failure of absorption of imported technology. Without good local technological capability, even high-quality technology cannot be used effectively to contribute to economic growth.

Our analysis has found that ASEAN countries are lagging behind the developed countries and the NIEs in technological capability. Recognizing the importance of good technological capability in achieving economic development, ASEAN countries as well as donors of economic assistance to these countries have made efforts to upgrade their technological capability. As a country keenly aware of the importance of economic development of ASEAN countries, Japan has provided them with economic assistance, including technical assistance, extensively over the years. Although it is difficult to quantify the contribution of such technical assistance to upgrading technological capability, anecdotal evidence appears to show that it has had favourable impacts.

Building and improving technological capability is a long process, therefore, it is important to continue technology upgrading programmes for a sufficient amount of time. It is also important to formulate and implement effective programmes by making effective coordination between public and private sectors, between donor agencies and between donor countries. Finally, one cannot emphasize enough the importance of good institutions and good governance in implementing technical assistance programmes effectively.

Notes

[1] Economic growth rates are computed by GDP expressed by purchasing power parity (PPP) 1992 US dollars.

[2] This section draws on Kawai and Urata (2003).

[3] Lall (2000) provides a detailed discussion of human capital in East Asian economies.

[4] United Nations (1999) presents similar findings.

[5] United Nations (1996, 2000).

[6] Yamazawa and Urata (2001) discuss FDI and trade liberalization by APEC economies.

[7] UN, *World Investment Report 1999*, pp.56-58.

[8] Machinery imports here are defined as those imports included in SITC 7.

[9] Pack (1988) presents a good survey of the impact of foreign trade on economic growth and development.

[10] A number of studies have found positive contribution of outward-oriented trade regime on improving productivity. See Pack (1988) for a survey of such studies.

References

Barro, Robert J. and Jong-Wha Lee. 2000. "International Data on Educational Attainment Updates and Implications". Working Paper 7911, NBER, Cambridge.

Aitken, Brian and Ann Harrison. 1994. "Do Domestic Firms Benefit from Foreign Direct Investment? Evidence from Panel Data". Policy Research Working Paper 1248, Policy Research Department, World Bank, Washington, D.C.

Blomstrom, Magnus and Hakan Persson. 1983. "Foreign Investment and Spillover Efficiency in an Underdeveloped Economy: Evidence from the Mexican Manufacturing Industry". *World Development* 11 (6), 493–501.

Bloomstrom, Magnus and E. Wolf. 1994. "Multinational Corporations and Productivity Convergence in Mexico". In Convergence of Productivity: Cross-national Studies and Historical Evidence, edited by William Baumol, Richard Nelson, and E. Wolf. Oxford University Press, New York.

Borensztein, Eduardo, Jose de Gregorio, and Jong-Wha Lee. 1998. "How Does Foreign Direct Investment Affect Economic Growth?". *Journal of International Economics* 45, 115–135.

Caves, Richard E. 1974. "Multinational Firms, Competition, and Productivity in Host-Country Industries". *Economica* 41 (May)

Coe, David T., Elhaman Helpman, and Alexander W. Hoffmaister. 1997. "North-South Spillovers". *The Economic Journal* 107 (January), pp. 134–149.

Globerman, Steven. 1979. "Foreign Direct Investment and 'Spillover' Efficiency Benefits in Canadian Manufacturing Industries". *Canadian Journal of Economics*, 12 (1), pp. 42–56.

Kawai, Hiroki and Shujiro Urata. 2003. "Competitiveness and Technology: An International Comparison". In *Competitiveness, FDI and Technological Activity in East Asia*. Edited by Sanjaya Lall and Shujiro Urata. Edgar-Elga, London.

Lall, Sanjaya. 2000. "Technological Change and Industrialization in the Asian Newly Industrializing Economies: Achievements and Challenges". In *Technology, Learning and Innovation*. Edited by Linsu Kim and Richard R.Nelson. Cambridge University Press, Cambridge and New York.

Lall, Sanjaya. 2003. "Foreign Direct Investment, Technology Development and Competitiveness: Issues and Evidence". *Competitiveness, FDI and Technological Activity in East Asia*, Edited by Sanjaya Lall and Shujiro Urata. Edgar-Elga, London.

Lawrence, Robert Z. and David E. Weinstein. 2000. "Trade and Growth: Import-Led or Export-Led? Evidence from Japan and Korea". Paper prepared for the World Bank project titled "Rethinking the Asian Miracle".

Navaretti, Giorgio Barba and David G. Tarr. 2000. "International Knowledge Flows and Economic Performance: A Review of the Evidence". *World Bank Economic Review*, vol. 14, no. 1, pp. 1–15.

Rhee, Y.W., Bruce Ross-Larson, and Gary Pursell. 1984. *Korea's Competitive Edge: Managing Entry to World Markets*. John Hopkins University Press, Baltimore.

United Nations. 1996. *World Investment Report 1996*. New York.

———. 1999. *World Investment Report 1999*. New York.

———. 2000. *World Investment Report 2000*. New York.

Urata, Shujiro. 1999. "Intrafirm Technology Transfer by Japanese Multinationals". In *Japanese Multinationals in Asia: Regional Operations in Comparative Perspective*. Edited by Dennis J. Encarnation. Oxford University Press, New York.

Urata, Shujiro and Hiroki Kawai. 2000. "Intra-Firm Technology Transfer by Japanese Manufacturing Firms in Asia". In *The Role of Foreign Direct Investment in Economic Development*. Edited by Takatoshi Ito and Anne O. Krueger. University of Chicago Press for NBER.

World Bank. 1993. *The East Asian Miracle: Economic Growth and Public Policy*. Oxford University Press.

5

The Significance of Japan's Official Development Assistance in Indonesia's Agricultural Development: The Case of Increased Rice Production

Masahiro Omura

1. Introduction

1.1 Awareness of the Issues

In the wake of the Asian economic crisis, sweeping changes have taken place in Indonesia's government and economy. Even considering the situation surrounding the example of food provision, problems are numerous. The amount of imported rice continued to reach new record highs in both 1998 and 1999. As a consequence of the then plummeting rupiah, costs expended on imported raw materials, such as fertilizer and agricultural chemicals, soared, and El Nino ravaged drought across the nation. Prices for both imported rice and domestically produced staple grains soared. It is said that this, coupled with increasing unemployment and poverty as a result of the economic crisis, led to civil unrest (JICA, Materials for the Reporting Session upon Return to Japan on the Interim Assessment of Umbrella Cooperation). Thereafter, the amount of imports decreased rapidly in 2000 and 2001. Since the 1980s, Indonesia's rice production per unit has continued to be one of the highest in Southeast Asia. However, growth has reached a standstill, and there is even a trend toward decline (ibid).

This chapter examines experiences in Indonesia's development focusing on the era of the Soeharto regime, examining in particular the significance of official development assistance (ODA) in agricultural development. This chapter is written in the hope that some inspiration can be gleaned from that experience, given the fact that the significance of ODA in development taking place in such countries as those in the sub-Saharan region of Africa is also being considered. As Robert Bates points out, a special feature in economic strategy within African nations following their independence was the element of preferential treatment accorded to urban cities over rural villages (Robert H. Bates 1981). The rationale behind this lay in the fact that developmental economic studies at the time regarded as a given that industrialization was brought about through the transfer of resources from the agricultural sector and in the fact that in terms of maintaining political power, the rural sector had little importance. The same policies were adopted in Indonesia too, in the era of the Sukarno government. However, the Soeharto government carried out policies attaching much importance to agriculture. I believe the key to Indonesia's economic growth is inherent in this point. If we tentatively take that as a fact, what kind of role did Japanese ODA play in the agricultural development of Indonesia? This issue is not simply an historical question. As I discussed in the foregoing, I believe it has a contemporary significance.

1.2 Prior Research

'The East Asian Miracle' by the World Bank focuses in particular on economic growth and the role of government and gives various assessments of policies in each of the East Asian countries (The World Bank [1993] 'The East Asian Miracle: Economic Growth and Public Policy' [Oxford University Press]). In this publication, references are made to the facts that each of the governments of the East Asian countries supported agricultural research and the spread of technology, that large-scale investment was carried out in regional infrastructure in such areas as irrigation, and that tax rates were lower in the agricultural sector. However, analysis of agricultural development is not treated as a central theme of the publication. In particular, one cannot find any analysis on the role that ODA played in this development.

As for research on the role Japanese ODA played in the development of Asia, in particular Thailand, Chuo University in Japan and Chulalongkorn University in Thailand have carried out joint research ('Comprehensive Research on Japanese ODA'). The International Development Center of Japan has carried out quantitative evaluations on the impact of Japanese ODA on the respective macroeconomies of Thailand, Indonesia, and Malaysia (International Development Center of Japan, Quantitative Evaluation of Japanese ODA in the Development of East Asian Economies, 1995).

In recent years, the Japan Institute of International Affairs has been involved with research on experiences in Asia's development. In one of the initial products of this research, namely a report titled 'Significance of ODA in ASEAN External Relations', Ryokichi Hirono states the following:

> In order to assist these developing countries in East Asia and in particular ASEAN to promote outward-oriented industrialization policies, Japan, far

more than any other industrial country, concentrated its official development assistance (ODA) in the region and steadfastly increased its aid programmes focused on the development and improvement of the economic infrastructures such as highways, ports, power generation and distribution and irrigation facilities as well as such social infrastructures as education, health and sanitation. The Japanese aid programmes thus contributed a great deal to the expansion and modernisation of productive capacity and including physical and human resource development and to constant rises in productivity of agricultural and industrial sectors in ASEAN countries. ('Changing Japanese Development Cooperation Policy Toward ASEAN in the Postwar Period', p 13).

As this example shows, the viewpoint that positively evaluates the role played by Japanese ODA in the development of East Asian economies has been strong in Japan.

2. The Significance of Agricultural Development and the Importance of Technological Advances

According to Hayami and Goudou (2002), agricultural issues run through a course of three stages in economic development. In other words, low-income countries face the issue of food security, middle-income countries face the issue of poverty, and high-income countries face the issue of agricultural adjustment. With respect to the food security issue, increases in population and income lead to an increased demand for food leading to price increases for food. This is linked to an increase in wages, which in turn restricts industrialization. The solution to this problem lies in reducing production costs. This can be realized through imports of agricultural products and development of agricultural technology. However, the former is problematic with respect to foreign exchange, and the policies of the government in question often prove a restrictive factor on the latter. By policies of the government in question we mean exploitation of the agricultural industry for the purpose of industrialization based on the preferential treatment of urban cities in revolt against the historical division of roles with suzerain states and to maintain support for the government, disregard development of agricultural technology, and insufficient investment in agricultural infrastructure. Accordingly, there is potential to overcome the food issue when there is no restriction on foreign exchange or when the government of the country in question lays emphasis on agriculture. Conversely, in the event of these conditions not being present, the food security problem will come to constitute a restriction on development (Hayami and Goudo 2002, pp 15–26).

Technological development and investment are crucial in solving the food security issue in low-income countries without having to resort to imports. Considered from the standpoint of agricultural demand, the rate of population increase is generally high in low-income countries, and there is a high degree of income elasticity in food demand. Accordingly, the rate of increasing demand for food is high. Whereas the rate of increase in agricultural production is higher in developing nations than in developed nations, this is principally based on increases to the element of production, and the rate of improvement in productivity is low. In particular, certain research indicates that in low-income countries, growth in total factor productivity is actually in negative figures. Taking this into consideration, total factor productivity – that is, technological advances – is crucial in solving the food problem in low-income countries. Development of new technology and how it is being put into common use are essential factors. According to Gerschenkron, the later a country commences its industrialization, the greater the leeway to use borrowed technology. The same situation may arise with respect to agriculture. There is a possibility for developing countries to solve their food security problem through the transfer of agricultural technology. However, given that restrictions stemming from nature are greater in agriculture than in industry, the likelihood of the technology of developed countries being transferred without adaptation is low, and hence applied research is crucial. Furthermore, it is essential that improvement on a land basis be made to improve the environments in developing countries to the equivalent level existing in developed countries (Hayami and Goudo 2002, pp 3–10, 116–127).

The course of agricultural growth changes depending on the relative scarcity of land or population in a country at a given time. Generally speaking, land in the developing countries in Asia is relatively scarce compared to population. Given the low incomes, the rate of population growth is high, the nonagricultural sector is undeveloped, and its ability to absorb labour is minimal. Thus, the agricultural labour force increases, and there is a trend toward a declining ratio of land equipped by labour (land/labour). Accordingly, increased labour productivity (production/labour) through increases in land productivity (production/land) is sought. Improved land productivity through land-saving technological innovation is sought. Specifically, improvement in the use of fertilizers, improved breeding, irrigation, and drainage is essential (Hayami and Goudo, 2002, pp 82–94).

3. Indonesia and Rice

3.1 Importance of Rice in the Indonesian Economy

The importance of rice in the Indonesian economy is multifaceted. Motooka (1975) cites the following nine factors in the background to the

Soeharto government's adoption of its increased rice production policy. As a direct factor, the stability of the economy was of major importance. Stability in rice prices was sought on the grounds of overcoming the catastrophic inflation of the Sukarno era.

Second, rice was the nation's staple diet. For Indonesians, rice is the most important source of nutritional calories and protein. In keeping with increases in Indonesia's national income, it was forecast that rice consumption would replace corn and cassava consumption.

Third, rice was becoming a major headache in terms of Indonesia's international balance of payments. In Indonesia's trade of agricultural products, there was a trend toward a decreasing ratio of 'agricultural' exports over total exports, and, given that imports of rice and wheat were on the increase, import substitution had become a topic of concern. Equilibrium in the foreign exchange balance of payments was secured under the support of the group of Indonesian creditor nations. Due to the foreign exchange restrictions, increased rice production was an absolute necessity.

The fourth factor was the large percentage of gross national product that rice represented. This ratio was estimated at 20%–22% in the 1960s and was the largest individual item of production. Increased rice production was a vital and decisive factor in national income and economic growth.

The fifth factor was the share of employment relating to rice production in total employment. In a 1971 census, agricultural employment comprised 68% of total employment. The labour force employed in rice production in the agricultural sector was estimated at 70% of overall employment. Accordingly, rice-related employment stood at approximately 48% of the nation's total employment.

The sixth factor was the percentage that rice accounted for in total investment. Compared to the percentages for GNP and employment, the ratio of investment in the agricultural sector was low. By way of example, the agricultural sector percentage of the central government's development budget was approximately 23% in fiscal 1970–71, and the majority of this was destined for use in irrigation. Only several percent of foreign investment was destined for the agricultural sector.

The seventh factor was that rice was something indispensable to the stability of the nation's life. Rice accounted for 33% of the Indonesian cost of living index – in other words, one-third of costs. Accordingly, stability in the price of rice was closely linked to political stability.

The eighth factor was the percentage that rice accounted for in farmers' real incomes and in the determination of real wages. Rice production accounted for at least half of agricultural income. The greater part of urban workers' wages was spent on purchasing rice, and rice prices were the most vital and decisive factor in real wages in cities.

The ninth factor was that rice supported Indonesian agriculture as an agricultural resource. Amounts harvested per unit of area were high, the nutritional value was relatively balanced, and as long as water was present, production was simple. It was rice that made Java's population density feasible (Motooka 1975, pp 25–42).

3.2 Implementation of Policies for Increased Rice Production and Changes in Rice Production

3.2.1 Era of the Sukarno Government

Indonesia's rice imports rapidly increased in the latter half of the 1950s. In the period from 1938 to 1940, immediately preceding World War II, average rice imports amounted to approximately 240,000 tons. Imports remained at the same level for the first half of the 1950s, but from 1956 onward imports of between 500,000 tons and almost 1 million tons continued, and in the period from 1961 to1964 the figure was over 1 million tons. Per capita production in the post-war period fell to a level lower than that for the period preceding the war. Indonesia's combined production of wetland rice and dry-land rice was between 14 million and 16 million tons in the latter half of the 1950s and in the first half of the 1960s it was between 15 and 17 million tons. Per hectare yield throughout the latter half of the 1950s and the first half of the 1960s was around 2.1–2.3 tons. In Japanese terms, this was the level at around the turn of the nineteenth to the twentieth century (Motooka 1975, p 90, 116, 121–138; Hayami and Goudo 2002, p 114).

The development plans in the era of the Sukarno government, in other words, the First Five–Year Plan (1956–1960) and the Eight–Year Comprehensive Development Plan (1961–1968), especially the latter of these plans, laid emphasis on increased rice production. It was the Three–Year Plan for Increased Rice Production(1958–1960) and the Paddy Centers (1958–1964) that were established to bring these development plans into reality. The Three–Year Plan was split into a short-term plan for the intensive increased production of already cultivated land and a long-term plan for the expansion of the cultivated land area in the Outer Islands.

In order to carry out the short-term plan, Paddy Centers were established in various locations. In 1960–1961, these Paddy Centers were established in 250 locations and covered 1.5 million hectares – in other words, approximately a quarter of total paddy field area at the time. Paddy Centers would provide a fixed amount of seeds, fertilizer, and a predetermined level of cash, and farmers would return either cash or actual produce back to the Paddy Centers. In reality, the Paddy Centers lacked able staff, and they could not arrange for sufficient seed or fertilizer. Lending cash did not achieve its objectives, and repayments were late.

Because of the government's financial difficulties, the Paddy Centers were abolished in 1964. The actual results of the increased production plan are unclear. As outlined in the forgoing, amounts harvested per hectare were not improved during the period (Motooka 1975, p. 90, pp. 121–138).

The Bimas Programme (BIMAS meaning Bimbingan Massal Swa Sembada Bahan Makanan, or Mass Guidance to Become Self-Supporting in Food) commenced in 1963. The Demas Programme (DEMAS meaning Demonstrasi Massal), which was to become the forerunner to the Bimas Programme, was independently carried out by students at Bogor Agricultural University throughout 1963 and 1964. The Demas Programme commenced on a scale of 100 hectares in the Krawang prefecture of West Java and expanded in the following year to approximately 10,000 hectares. The following five principles relating to rice cultivation were put into practice by the farmers at that time:

(i)   Use of high yield seed varieties
(ii) Use of adequate fertilizers
(iii) Prevention and eradication of damage caused by blight and insects
(iv) Appropriate irrigation control
(v)   Other methods for the improvement of cultivation

Throughout 1964 and 1965, the Bimas Programme was put into action by the Department of Agriculture. The initial achievements remained at 9,000 hectares (Motooka 1975, p. 90, 121–138).

The period from 1965 to 1967 was one of transition from the Sukarno regime to the Soeharto regime. In connection with increased rice production, the Bimas Programme was being developed during this period. The achievements of the Bimas Programme shifted from 172,500 hectares in 1965–66 to 510,700 hectares in 1966–67 and 489,200 hectares in 1967–68 (ditto p. 141).

3.2.2 Agricultural Production in the Initial Stages of the Soeharto Era

In the early days following the inauguration of the Soeharto government, Indonesia was hit with a rice crisis. This must have had a significant impact on the same government's rice policies thereafter. The reasons for the crisis lay in the government's excessive optimism over increased domestic rice production and the lowering of its rice import targets in spite of the dry-season droughts. As a result, there was a widespread increase in rice prices (Motooka 1975, pp 148-153). It is said that Soeharto always emphasized the fact that he came from a farming background. In the beginning of his autobiography, Soeharto mentions that he was commended by the Food and Agriculture Organization (FAO) for his contribution to Indonesia's achievement of self-sufficiency in rice. The acceptance of his award in Rome must have been the ultimate achievement for the son of a farmer (Vatikiotis 1998, p. 9). After Soeharto initiated the development policies, promotion of the agricultural sector was always a central topic of development. The greatest effort was put into agriculture and irrigation facilities since the start of the First Development Plan (Kunio Igusa Translation 1987, p 23).

In the 1970s, the ratio of agriculture as part of GDP fell, but this does not mean that the rate of growth in the agricultural sector was very low. That is, the ratio of agriculture, forestry, and fisheries as a part of GDP fell from 47.2% to 24.8%, and edible crop production fell from 28.8% to 14.0%. But whereas the average annual rate of growth in real terms was 7.6% for GDP, it was 3.8% for the agricultural sector, so the rate of growth of the agricultural sector had climbed more than 1%, up from 2.7% in the 1960s. In particular, increased rice production was conspicuous. Comparing Java with the so-called Outer Islands, the harvested area in both regions increased by approximately 10%, but yield per unit area was 43% higher in Java and 31% higher in the Outer Islands (Kanou 1988, p 24-27).

The Indonesian government's Increased Food Production Programme was developed by way of two intensification programmes, namely the Bimas Programme and the Inmas Programme. Under the Bimas Programme, the government provided farmers with a package of investment in the form of new varieties of rice seed, chemical fertilizers, and agricultural chemicals in exchange for credit at government financial institutions. Farmers made repayments in the form of cash or actual produce. The Inmas Programme started after the Bimas Programme. The Bimas Programme had come to a standstill due to the decreasing rate of credit repayment, and the Inmas Programme came to surpass it in terms of the area over which it was implemented. Under the Inmas Plan, the acquisition of investment assets was left to the farmers, and the government carried out only technical guidance on agricultural management using new seed varieties. Through the 1970s, the percentage of land under an intensification programme out of total rice cropland expanded from 25.6% to 67.2%, and of this particular land the percentage of land using high-yield seed varieties expanded from 37.2% to 81.5%. At the end of the 1970s, more than 50% of total rice cropland area used high–yield seed varieties (Kanou 1988, p. 27–30).

In the 1970s, the amount of chemical fertilizer applied rapidly increased and the government's intervention also played a role in this. The total amount of chemical fertilizer applied to food crops increased from 197,000 tons in 1970 to 423,000 tons in 1975 and further to 1,012,000 tons in 1980. With the progress in transition from the Bimas Programme to the Inmas Programme, application of chemical fertilizer came to be left to the discretion of farmers. As a consequence, movements in the relative price between rice and fertilizer became of importance. This relative price shifted to the benefit of rice due to an official price system for fertilizer. Furthermore, the government contributed to increased food production through improving and expanding irrigation facilities as well. Improvement of both organization relating to water management and a system of agricultural guidance also took place (Kanou 1988, p 30-37).

4. The Significance of Japan's ODA in Indonesia's Agricultural Development: from the Viewpoint of Flow of Funds

In this section, the significance of Japan's ODA in Indonesia's agricultural development is examined from two angles, namely as the flow of funds and the transfer of technology and know-how. First, the aspect of transfer of resources is dealt with. To examine this aspect, the issue of fungibility has to be considered at the outset.

4.1 The Issue of Fungibility

According to the World Bank's Assessing Aid study, there is an issue in most aided nations involving the possible diversion of aid funds (fungibility) (The World Bank 1998). While the notion of fungibility has been known for some time, only recently has plentiful evidence for it emerged. In the absence of external restrictions, the governments of recipient countries can use increased resources as a result of foreign assistance as they please in the form of either increased financial expenditure, reduced taxes, or eliminating or decreasing financial debt. In the case of increased financial expenditure, either increased investment or increased consumption is possible. Viewed from another perspective, whether or not fungibility becomes an issue depends on whether or not the aid donor has the same objectives as the recipient country. Generally, it is said that one dollar of aid results in less than one dollar in increased government expenditure – on average, one dollar of aid generates an increase in public investment of 29 cents, with the remaining amount being used in government consumption. Supposing that fungibility exists in most cases, more important than a donor concentrating aid into a particular field is whether or not the government of the developing country in question regards that field as important. And, if aid funds are fungible, it is not sufficient to assess their effect only in aid projects themselves. If aid funds are fungible between fields, what the donor is specifically aiding is not the issue.

This argument is extremely important, because it exposes the possibility of the recipient country going against the donor's wishes. One can say it is an important point that clarifies the limits of the donor's power. It demands reviews in the evaluation of aid, especially project aid.

According to Pack & Pack (1990), however, there is no need to look at problems of fund diversion in Indonesia. In this research, analysis was carried out for the period from 1966 to 1986, and the following conclusions were arrived at:

(1) Overseas assistance did not replace Indonesian expenditure on development, rather it stimulated overall public expenditure (one rupiah of aid generated 1.58 rupiah of government expenditure).

(2) Sector-based aid, in most cases, was used by the recipient in line with the planned objective. Appropriation into other areas of development expenditure or diversion from development expenditure to ordinary expenditure was not observed. There were no decreases in domestic revenue as a result of the aid.

With regard to aid to Indonesia, premised on the foregoing, one can conclude that there is significance in debating the effectiveness of aid to a particular sector, such as agriculture.

4.2 The Track Record of Japanese Agricultural ODA in Indonesia

It is usual to discuss the track record of Japanese ODA in accordance with major types of aid. These types comprise technical cooperation, grant aid, and loan aid.

4.2.1 Technical Cooperation

As the largest implementing agency of Japan's technical cooperation, the Japan International Cooperation Agency (JICA) has been implementing a large number of projects in the Indonesian agricultural sector. JICA's track record of aid was formerly based on total numbers of dispatched and received personnel. It was toward the end of the 1980s that totals came to be prepared on how much had been spent on technical assistance costs broken down by sector in the recipient country. JICA's cooperation with the Indonesian agricultural sector is illustrated on a personnel basis in Table 5.1 and on a cost basis in Table 5.2.

4.2.2 Grant aid

The Japanese Ministry of Foreign Affairs implements grant aid, and facilitation is carried out by JICA. Instances of previous cooperation with the Indonesian agricultural sector are set out in Table 5.3. Food aid has been excluded from this table. The rationale behind this is that the present chapter is examining ODA in agricultural development, in particular its impact on increased rice production. The objective of food aid is not increased food production; it is an emergency measure provided in times of food crisis.

Table 5.1 JICA Cooperation in the Indonesian Agricultural Sector
(Personnel Based)

	Trainees	Experts	Survey	JOCV	Others	Agri T/C	Tatal T/C
1964							
1965							
1966							
1967							
1968							
1969							
1970							
1971							
1972							
1973							
1974	35	14	47			96	433
1975	40	18	52			110	536
1976	26	23	29			78	576
1977	35	17	34			86	698
1978	53	39	112			204	839
1979	43	39	62			144	776
1980	55	42	111			208	981
1981	53	61	190			304	1154
1982	67	50	127			244	1227
1983	37	58	38			133	1148
1984	44	47	61			152	1583
1985	43	41	98			182	1491
1986	47	39	82			168	1355
1987	50	40	102			192	1537
1988	48	60	98			206	1771
1989	62	43	100			205	1621
1990	68	69	106			243	1661
1991	73	54	117			244	1654
1992	67	51	78			196	1614
1993	55	46	74	3		178	1693
1994	50	57	110	2		219	1940
1995	59	56	70	7		192	1888
1996	70	40	64	3		177	1818
1997	59	48	87	9		203	1834
1998	98	45	18	5		166	3523
1999	159	48	33	3		243	4684
2000	80	28	50	6	2	166	4460
2001	379	22	44	2	5	452	5291

Source: JICA

Table 5.2 JICA Cooperation in the Indonesian Agricultural Sector (Costs Based) (million Yen)

	Total Agri Costs	Total T/C Costs
1964		70
1965		59
1966		68
1967		175
1968		255
1969		442
1970		
1971		836
1972		1439
1973		1540
1974		1728
1975		2373
1976		3014
1977		4030
1978		4303
1979		5096
1980		6042
1981		6082
1982		7621
1983		7286
1984		8359
1985		8513
1986		7228
1987		8037
1988	1607	10021
1989	1714	9637
1990	1841	11208
1991	2297	10377
1992	1889	11424
1993	1355	10346
1994	1746	12223
1995	1445	12031
1996	1546	11539
1997	1540	12309
1998	1267	10927
1999	1277	10178
2000	1133	10065
2001	908	11322

Source: JICA

Table 5.3   List of Japanese Grant Aid Projects Extended to the Indonesian Agricultural Sector

	Project Name	Amount	Year Total (Million Yen)
1964			
1965			
1966			
1967			
1968			0
1969			0
1970			0
1971			0
1972			0
1973			0
1974			0
1975			0
1976			0
1977	Central Agricultural Research Institute	102.6	222.6
	Local diffusion Centers	120	
1978	Aid for Increased Food Production	1300	1300
1979	Nutrition Improvement	250	1950
	Aid for Increased Food Production	1100	
	Aid for Increased Food Production	600	
1980	Aid for Increased Food Production	1700	3600
	Guidance and Service Center for Irrigation and Drainage	1500	
	Training Center for Middle Level Cultural Technicians	400	
1981	Aid for Increased Food Production	1900	2660
	Terminal Irrigation Facilities in Riam Kanan	760	
1982	Aid for Increased Food Production	2000	2000
1983	Aid for Increased Food Production	2200	2250
	Bogor Agricultural University	50	
1984	Aid for Increased Food Production	2200	4540
	Development of Bogor Agricultural University	2340	
	Aid for Increased Food Production	2200	5145
1985	Rice Pest Forecasting and Control	445	
	Aid for Increased Food Production	2500	
1986	Pest and Disease Forecasting and Control	2061	7440
	Center for Development of Appropriate Agricultural Engineering Tech	1749	
	Pest and Disease Forecasting and Control	1230	
	Aid for Increased Food Production	2400	
1987	Pest and Disease Forecasting and Control	1978	2365
	Facilities for Strengthening Pioneering Resarch for Palawija Crops	387	

Table 5.3 List of Japanese Grant Aid Projects Extended to the Indonesian Agricultural Sector (*continued*)

	Project Name	Amount	Year Total	(Million Yen)
1988	Aid for Increased Food Production	2300	5445	
	Facility for Integrated Improvement of Post Harvest & Quality of Rice	845		
	Aid for Increased Food Production	2300		
1989	Improvement of the Equipment for the Pemali Irrigation	389	389	
1990	Aid for Increased Food Production	1700	4491	
	Multiplication and Distribution of High Quality Seed Potato	941		
	Aid for Increased Food Production	1850		
1991	Remote Sensing Engineering Project on Site Selection System	425	2683	
	Pumping Station for Bengawan-Solo Lower Reaches	458		
	Aid for Increased Food Production	1800		
1992	Pumping Station for Bengawan-Solo Lower Reaches	328	2028	
	Aid for Increased Food Production	1700		
1993	Aid for Increased Food Production	1600	1600	
1994	Aid for Increased Food Production	1550	1550	
1995	Reservoir Development in East Nusa Tenggara	1418	5228	
	Reservoir Development in East Nusa Tenggara	46		
	Multiplication and Distribution of Improved Soybean Seed	980		
	Aid for Increased Food Production	1350		
	Reservoir Development in East Nusa Tenggara	1434		
1996	Aid for Increased Food Production	1350	1350	
1997	Supply of Equipment for Irrigation in Eastern Area	877	2543	
	Aid for Increased Food Production	1200		
	Supply of Equipment for Irrigation in Eastern Area	466		
1998	Resarch Institute for Water Resources Development	767	2217	
	Aid for Increased Food Production	1450		
1999	Irrigation Facilities in the Eastern Area	526	526	
2000			0	
2001	Aid for Increased Food Production	1400	1400	

Source: Ministry of Foreign Affairs

Table 5.4   List of Assistance Projects Extended to the Indonesian Agricultural
Sector by JBIC and OECF

PROJECT NAME	APPROVAL	AMOUNT OF APPROVAL (Millions; Yen)
EQUIPMENT SUPPLY FOR PRE AND POST HARVEST SERVICES	8/3/84	5800
RICE SEED PRODUCTION AND DISTRIBUTION PROJECT	15/2/85	3000
ASEAN-JAPAN DEVELOPMENT FUND CATEGORY B-KI PROGRAMME	7/11/89	16955
AGRICULTURAL DEVELOPMENT PROJECT	4/11/93	6718
AGRICULTURAL DEVELOPMENT PROJECT(II)	1/12/95	4065
INTEGRATED HORTICULTURAL DEVELOPMENT IN UPLAND AREAS	4/12/96	7769
KALI PORONG PROJECT	3/12/70	446
BRANTAS DELTA IRRIGATION REHABILITATION PROJECT	3/12/70	326
KALI PORONG PROJECT	21/9/71	534
BRANTAS DELTA IRRIGATION REHABILITATION PROJECT	21/9/71	142
ULAR RIVER FLOOD CONTROL PROJECT	22/11/71	468
WAY JEPARA IRRIGATION PROJECT	31/3/73	669
KARI SURABAYA RIVER IMPROVEMENT PROJECT	20/9/74	1399
C/S FOR WAY UMPU AND WAY PANGUBUAN IRRIGATION	27/12/74	375
PORONG RIVER IMPROVEMENT PROJECT	17/2/76	480
KALI SURABAYA RIVER IMPROVEMENT PROJECT	23/7/76	2681
WAY UMPU AND WAY PENGUBUAN IRRIGATION PROJECTS	23/7/76	1948
ENGINEERING SERVICES FOR THE WONOGIRI IRRIGATION PROJECT	31/3/77	513
E/S FOR WAY BUNG AND WAY RARE IRRIGATION	31/3/77	322
E/S FOR THE FLOOD CONTROL AND FLOOD MITIGATION OF BRANTAS	18/10/77	504
THE WONOGIRI IRRIGATION PROJECT	16/2/79	9800
WIDAS IRRIGATION PROJECT	15/3/79	1833
E/S ON THE ULAR RIVER FLOOD CONTROL AND IMPROVEMENT	15/3/79	420
BRANTAS MIDDLE REACHES RIVER IMPROVEMENT PROJECT	15/3/79	5718
WAY RAREM IRRIGATION	15/3/79	7365
ENGINEERING SERVICES FOR RIAM KANAN IRRIGATION PROJECT	31/3/80	450
ENGINEERING SERVICES FOR KRUEN ACEH FLOOD CONTROL	24/4/80	550

Table 5.4   List of Assistance Projects Extended to the Indonesian Agricultural Sector by JBIC and OECF   (*continued*)

PROJECT NAME	APPROVAL	AMOUNT OF APPROVAL (Millions; Yen)
WAY RAREM IRRIGATION PROJECT (SECOND STAGE)	2/5/80	10245
OVERALL ULAR RIVER IMPROVEMENT AND IRRIGATION PROJECT	29/5/81	8140
ENGINEERING SERVICES FOR JENEBERANG RIVER IMPROVEMENT	29/5/81	198
E/S FOR UPPER SOLO AND MADIUN RIVER URGENT FLOOD CONTROL	14/9/81	805
ENGINEERING SERVICES FOR KRUENG ACEH IRRIGATION PROJECT	30/4/82	380
ENGINEERING SERVICES FOR LANGKEME IRRIGATION PROJECT	30/4/82	320
ENGINEERING SERVICES FOR UPPER KOMERING IRRIGATION PROJECT	22/9/83	1180
KRUENG ACEH URGENT FLOOD CONTROL PROJECT	6/10/83	4659
MOUNT SEMERU URGENT REHABILITATION PROJECT	6/10/83	2808
WEST JAKARTA FLOOD CONTROL SYSTEM PROJECT	6/10/83	5275
KRUENG ACEH URGENT FLOOD CONTROL PROJECT STAGE 2 PHASE 1	13/6/84	8953
ENGINEERING SERVICES FOR BILA IRRIGATION PROJECT	13/6/84	550
RIAM KANAN IRRIGATION PROJECT	13/6/84	8636
WEST JAKARTA FLOOD CONTROL SYSTEM PROJECT (II)	13/6/84	5774
LOWER JENEBERANG RIVER URGENT FLOOD CONTROL PROJECT	15/2/85	5381
ENGINEERING SERVICES FOR PADANG AREA FLOOD CONTROL	15/2/85	580
BRANTAS RIVER MIDDLE REACHES IMPROVEMENT PROJECT (II)	15/2/85	6000
MADIUN RIVER URGENT FLOOD CONTROL PROJECT	15/2/85	6400
E/S FOR SURABAYA RIVER IMPROVEMENT PROJECT (STAGE II)	27/12/85	418
UPPER SOLO RIVER IMPROVEMENT PROJECT	27/12/85	4746
MT. MERAPI URGENT VOLCANIC DEBRIS CONTROL PROJECT	27/12/85	4672
LANGKEME IRRIGATION PROJECT	27/12/85	6951

Table 5.4   List of Assistance Projects Extended to the Indonesian Agricultural Sector by JBIC and OECF   (*continued*)

PROJECT NAME	APPROVAL	AMOUNT OF APPROVAL (Millions; Yen)
WAY UMPU AND WAY PENGUBUAN IRRIGATION REHABILITATION	13/1/87	1392
ENGINEERING SERVICES FOR LOWER ASAHAN RIVER FLOOD CONTROL	18/3/87	628
WAY RAREM IRRIGATION PROJECT (PACKAGE III)	8/12/87	3027
ENGINEERING SERVICES FOR EAST JAKARTA FLOOD CONTROL	8/12/87	1053
PORONG RIVER REHABILITATION PROJECT	5/7/88	1767
WAY JEPARA IRRIGATION SYSTEM REHABILITATION PROJECT	5/7/88	1082
PAMARAYAN-CIUJUNG IRRIGATION SYSTEM REHABILITATION	21/10/88	5667
THE SMALL SCALE IRRIGATION MANAGEMENT PROJECT	22/12/89	1896
REHABILITATION OF IRRIGATION SCHEMES AND FLOOD ALLEVIATION	22/12/89	21518
KRUENG ACEH IRRIGATION PROJECT	14/12/90	6333
SURABAYA RIVER IMPROVEMENT PROJECT (II-1)	14/12/90	4220
PADANG AREA FLOOD CONTROL PROJECT(I)	14/12/90	8063
BILA IRRIGATION PROJECT(I)	14/12/90	6460
ANCOL DRAINAGE IMPROVEMENT PROJECT	25/9/91	3128
ENGINEERING SERVICE FOR WONOREJO MULTIPURPOSE DAM	25/9/91	241
MOUNT KELUD URGENT VOLCANIC DISASTER MITIGATION	25/9/91	3246
ENGINEERING SERVICE FOR LOWER SOLO RIVER IMPROVEMENT	25/9/91	669
WAY CURUP IRRIGATION PROJECT	25/9/91	1422
WAY RAREM IRRIGATION PROJECT (IV)	25/9/91	1623
BILA IRRIGATION PROJECT (II)	8/10/92	3788
WAY SEKAMPUNG IRRIGATION PROJECT (I)	8/10/92	7653
SOUTH SUMATRA SWAMP IMPROVEMENT PROJECT	8/10/92	5577
UPPER CITARUM BASIN URGENT FLOOD CONTROL PROJECT (I)	4/11/93	3165
ENGINEERING SERVICES FOR BATANG HARI IRRIGATION PROJECT	4/11/93	676
WAY SEKAMPUNG IRRIGATION PROJECT (II)	29/11/94	16210
SMALL SCALE IRRIGATION MANAGEMENT PROJECT (II)	29/11/94	8135
KOMERING IRRIGATION PROJECT(II)	1/12/95	6544
LOWER SOLO RIVER IMPROVEMENT PROJECT (I)	1/12/95	10796

Table 5.4 List of Assistance Projects Extended to the Indonesian Agricultural
Sector by JBIC and OECF *(continued)*

PROJECT NAME	APPROVAL	AMOUNT OF APPROVAL (Millions; Yen)
PADANG AREA FLOOD CONTROL PROJECT (II)	1/12/95	4859
MT. MERAPI & MT. SEMERU VOLCANIC DISASTER COUNTERMEASURES (II)	1/12/95	4405
ENGINEERING SERVICES FOR BATANG KUMU IRRIGATION PROJECT	4/12/96	374
BATANG HARI IRRIGATION PROJECT	4/12/96	6050
BILI-BILI IRRIGATION PROJECT	4/12/96	5472
PROJECT TYPE SECTOR LOAN IN WATER RESOURCES DEVELOPMENT	4/12/96	11797
ENGINEERING SERVICES FOR GILIRANG IRRIGATION PROJECT	28/1/98	617
UPPER CITARUM BASIN URGENT FLOOD CONTROL PROJECT (II)	28/1/98	4722
CILIWUNG-CISADANE RIVER FLOOD CONTROL PROJECT (I)	28/1/98	17326
MEDAN FLOOD CONTROL PROJECT	28/1/98	9697
WAY SEKAPUNG IRRIGATION PROJECT (III)	28/1/98	9216
SMALL SCALE IRRIGATION MANAGEMENT PROJECT (III)	28/1/98	16701
BATANG HARI IRRIGATION PROJECT(PHASE.U)	5/7/01	7639
SECTOR LOAN FOR WATER RESOURCES DEVELOPMENT	5/7/01	18676
DECENTRALIZED IRRIGATION SYSTEM IMPROVEMENT IN EASTERN REGION	10/10/02	27035
WATER RESOURCES FACILITIES REHABILITATION & CAPACITY IMPROVEMENT	10/10/02	14696
		469582

Source: JBIC

4.2.3 *Loan Aid*

One of the characteristics of Japan's assistance lies in the fact that a considerable portion of it is earmarked for financial assistance through low-interest long-term financing. Other than Japan, Germany, Spain and the European Union have concessional financing schemes. However, Japan's concessional financing scheme in terms of percentage of total aid and in terms of total amount far surpasses the other bilateral loan aid institutions. The implementing agency is the Japan Bank for International Cooperation (JBIC). The JBIC carries out its activities, including non-ODA loans, on a scale equivalent to the World Bank and the European Investment Bank (EIB). The results of cooperation extended from the JBIC and its predecessor, the Overseas Economic Co-operation Fund (OECF), to Indonesia's agricultural sector are illustrated in Table 5.4.

4.3 Evaluation of Flow of Funds

The objective of the present section is to evaluate the role that ODA funds have played in Indonesia's agricultural development, in particular toward increased rice production. Examination is based on Indonesian government statistics (Statistik Indonesia for each year).

4.3.1 Variables Relating to Rice Production Totals

As potential variables relating to the rice production totals available from the Statistik Indonesia figures above, total rice production (for wetland and dry-land rice) and total rice yield per hectare are possibilities. Because this chapter is principally interested in increased production through intensification of rice production, the latter is analyzed as a primary variable here. Two types of figures are given in the Statistik Indonesia with respect to yield amounts per hectare. They are yield rate (YR) and production per hectare (PPHA). Of these, other than the lack of figures for up to 1974 and for 1997, there is no figure of the PPHA for 1976 consistent with the other figures, because the PPHA figure for that year is 24 times larger than that of the previous year. On the other hand, other than the availability of figures for the YR for each year from 1968 onward, there is little wide-scale movement in the figures. Thus, the figures for the YR shall take precedence over the PPHA figures. Changes to the series for the YR and PPHA are expressed in Figure 5.1. The YR from 1974 onward increases almost consistently throughout. The PPHA from 1980 onward similarly increases.

4.3.2 Rice Production Related Variables

Seeds, pesticides, and fertilizer make up the principal constituents of production input, and statistics relating to these are available. There are difficulties in financially assessing labour, and given that appropriate statistics are not available, it is not included as a valuable. In terms of government expenditure having a significant impact on rice production, totals are available for agriculture– and irrigation–related expenditure within government development expenditure, excluding project-type aid. Furthermore, with respect to the primary subject of this section, namely the flow of Japan's ODA funds, actual figures for bilateral

Figure 5.1 Changes to the YR and PPHA

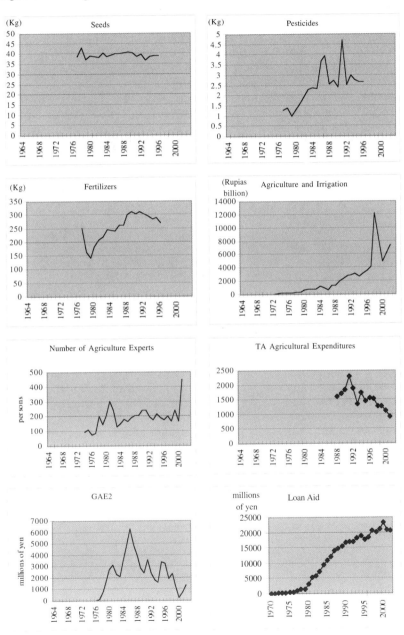

assistance schemes are considered broken down by the categories of technical cooperation, grant aid, and loan aid. A portion of Japan's'contributions to multilateral aid institutions has probably also contributed to agricultural development cooperation in Indonesia. Because it is difficult to determine actual figures, however, it is not examined here.

With respect to technical cooperation, as set out above, because the actual costs broken down by sector are not available for most of the 1970s and 1980s, which constitute the main subject of examination in this chapter (figures from 1988 onward are available), the actual numbers of technical cooperation personnel (the total of trainees, experts, survey team members, and volunteers) in the agricultural sector are used as a substitute index.

With regard to grant aid, it is assumed that the disbursements were made both in the year in which an official agreement between the governments was concluded and the following year.

With regard to loan aid, it is assumed that the disbursements were made over ten years, the ordinary period of deferment. Specifically, for each of the years starting from the year of the loan contract, I shall deem this as disbursements of 0%, 5%, 10%, 10%, 15%, 20%, 15%, 10%, 10%, and 5% in each year. Chronological changes to the above-mentioned seven variables are expressed in Figure 5.2.

4.3.3 Correlation between the Variables

The correlation between the yield from one hectare (expressed as the YR and PPHA) on the one hand and the seven separate variables of seeds, pesticides, fertilizer, government expenditure on agriculture and irrigation, numbers of technical cooperation personnel, grant aid disbursements, and loan aid disbursements on the other is expressed in Table 5.5 and Figure 5.3. Loan aid disbursements demonstrated the highest level of correlation with both the YR and PPHR. In particular,

Table 5.5 List of Correlative Indexes between YR & PPHR versus Seven Variables

	Yield Rate	Production per HA
Agriculture and Irrigation	0.602	0.4328
Seeds	0.3319	0.3515
Pesticides	0.7887	0.6056
Fertilizers	0.6358	0.5351
Number of Agricultural Experts	0.5036	0.0363
Grant Aid Disbursement	0.5596	0.0919
Loan Aid Disbursement	0.937	0.7705

Figure 5.2   Changes to Each of the Variables

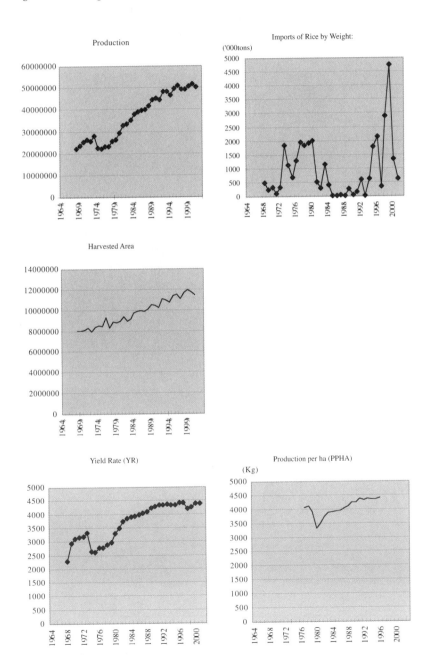

Figure 5.3   Correlation between Per Hectare Yield (YR and PPHR) on the One Hand and the Seven Variables of Seeds, Pesticides, Fertilizer, Government Expenditure on Agriculture and Irrigation, Technical Cooperation Personnel, Grant Aid Disbursements, and Loan Aid Disbursements on the Other

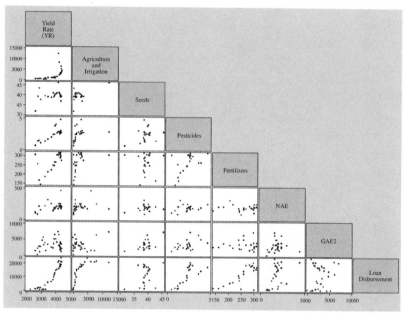

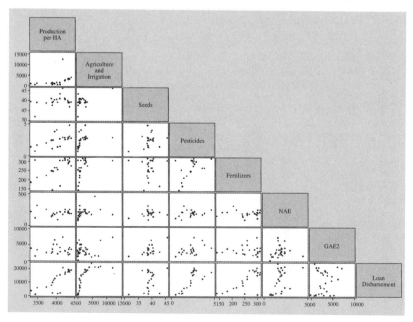

a high coefficient of 0.937 was obtained with the YR. With regard to the other variables, pesticides, fertilizer, and government expenditure on agriculture and irrigation demonstrated a relatively high correlation with the YR, and pesticides and fertilizer demonstrated a relatively high correlation with the PPHR. As for technical cooperation personnel and grant aid disbursements, there is a considerable correlation with the YR, but the correlation with the PPHR is quite low.

5. Significance of Japanese Agricultural ODA in Indonesia: Transfer of Knowledge and Know-how

When considering the significance of ODA, in addition to the flow of ODA funds, it is also necessary to examine the aspect of transfer of knowledge and know-how. In the definition of ODA according to the DAC, the flow of funds is the primary concern, because the original objective of collecting statistics on ODA was to expand the overall flow of funds. However, because the results generated through technical cooperation and financial cooperation closely associated with it manifest also in human resources development and institution building through the transfer of knowledge and know-how, it is insufficient to examine only the amounts of expenditure generated by the transfer of funds. Analysis relating to the content and effects of technology transfer is essential. This section examines the content and significance of agricultural technology transfer in Indonesia, in particular during the first and second so-called Umbrella Cooperation programmes that took place in the 1980s, making use of the analyses contained in the Evaluation Reports prepared by JICA together with Indonesian counterparts. JICA played a central role in the implementation of agricultural cooperation between Japan and Indonesia.

5.1 Technological Issues in Increased Rice Production in Indonesia

Technological issues arising in the intensification of rice production in Indonesia that initially began in the first half of the 1970s are, according to Motooka (1975), as set out below.

The first issue is the spread of new seed varieties. The production of high-yield seed varieties started at the Bogor Central Agricultural Research Center in 1966, and production and propagation rapidly increased throughout each of the regions thereafter. However, the system for testing and certification of seeds was defective. The production of superior seed varieties was an important topic.

The second issue was the use of fertilizer. The use of chemical fertilizers at the time was on the increase. The impact of chemical fertilizers on increased production, in particular the impact on high-yield seed varieties, was demonstrated at test sites.

The third issue was irrigation. Essentially, irrigation facilities in Indonesia, in particular in Java and Bali, were the most developed and integrated in Southeast Asia. But since many of the irrigation facilities established in the era of Dutch colonization were ruined after being abandoned for a long time following the end of World War II, their restoration was the most pressing issue at the time.

The fourth issue was the eradication of damage caused through blight and insects. Problems in this connection were numerous. There was a lack of experts, and there was a need to change from pesticides harmful to human beings to safe agricultural chemicals. No method of effective dispersion of agricultural chemicals existed. There was also no organized research conducted on strategies to counter rats.

The fifth issue was agricultural equipment. This did not have an important role in traditional rice production methods and at the time was not accorded due emphasis. Hand-dusters of agricultural chemicals were of importance at the time.

5.2 First Half of the Era of the Soeharto Government (1960s–1970s)

Even prior to the start of the Umbrella Cooperation, Japan's technical cooperation to the Indonesian agricultural sector had been extended in an organized manner. A list of Japanese project-type technical cooperation carried out in the Indonesian agricultural sector is set out in Table 5.6. The West Java Food Production Increase Project was representative of the period up to the 1970s.

This project was carried out over an eight-year period from 1968 to 1976. The objectives of the project were to increase food production and improve the lives of farmers, and guidance and training were carried out to ensure the spread of agricultural technology. Emphasis was placed on four important areas: namely, the popularization of production of superior seed varieties, training in connection with agricultural mechanization, promotion of model zone villages, and farmers' organizational training, together with the popularization of technology for rice production. Seven prefectures in West Java constituted the geographical subject area of the project. This was on a much smaller scale than the development under the Umbrella Cooperation of the 1980s, which took place on a nationwide scale. Costs totalled ¥351,972,000 (FY 1967–1973) and in terms of nominal value constituted only 1/100 of the First Umbrella Cooperation (JICA Agricultural Development Cooperation Department [1975] Report on the Evaluation Survey of West Java Food Production Increase Project).

Table 5.6 List of Japanese Project-Type Technical Cooperation to the Indonesian Agricultural Sector

Project Name	Cooperation Period
Maize Project in East Java	67.12~74.7
Food Increase Project in West Java	68.5~76.5
Strengthening of Legumes in relation to Cropping System Research Project	70.10~85.10
Lumpung Agricultural Development Project	72.11~82.11
Southeast Sulawesi Regional Agricultural Development Planning	76.5~82.6
The Agricultural Products Processing Pilot Plant Project	77.10~84.10
The Middle Level Agricultural Technician Training Project	79.3~88.3
The Remote Sensing Engineering Project for the Development of Agricultural Infrastructure	80.4~87.3
The Plant Protection Project	80.6~87.3
The Construction Guideline Service Center Project	81.4~88.3
Strengthening of Pioneering Research for Palawija Crop Production Project	86.4~91.3
Food Crops Protection Project	87.4~92.3
Centre for Development of Appropriate Agricultural Engineering Technology	87.4~93.7
Academic Development of the Graduate Program at the Faculty of Agricultural Engineering and Technology, Institute Pertanian Bogor	88.4~93.3
The Remote Sensing Engineering Project Phase II for the Development of Agricultural Infrastructure	88.6~94.6
Integrated Agricultural and Rural Development Project in Southeast Sulawesi Province	91.3~98.2
The Seed Potato Multiplication and Training Project	92.10~97.9
Research and Development for the Multispecies Hatchery Project	94.4~01.3
Irrigation Engineering Service Center Project	94.6~01.6
The Agricultural Statistics Technology Improvement and Training Project	94.10~99.9
Quality Soybean Seed Multiplication and Training Project	96.7~01.6
Development of High Quality Seed Potato Multiplication System Project	98.10~03.9
Project for Improvement of Agricultural Extension and Training System	99.9~02.3

Source: JICA

5.3 Cooperation for Increasing Rice Production in Indonesian: First Umbrella Cooperation

Of importance in the background to the cooperation for increasing rice production is the fact that on the occasion of then Prime Minister

Zenko Suzuki's visit to Indonesia in January 1981, increased food production was settled upon as one of the most important areas of economic assistance to Indonesia. In July of the same year a Record of Discussion (R/D) was concluded between the governments of Japan and Indonesia prescribing the overall framework for cooperation toward increased rice production. The method of Umbrella Cooperation was a system that managed in synthesis under unit objectives, the various forms of assistance of technical cooperation, grant aid, and loan aid in a particular sector and selected geographical areas.

Cooperation for increasing rice production was implemented over a period of five years from 1981. The objective was to increase the self-sufficiency ratio of rice in Indonesia. Concentrated assistance and increased efficiency were pursued under the umbrella method, which covered a wide scope from production through to distribution and processing. Subsectors of concentration consisted of the five subsectors of increased planting and distribution of superior seed varieties, strengthening of crop protection, regional certification and popularization of technology, development of irrigation, and postharvest processing. The geographical subject areas comprised the eight provinces of Aceh, South Sumatra, Lampon, West Java, Central Java, East Java, South Kalimantan, and South Sulawesi (Diagram, JICA Report p. 77). However, the projects were also carried out to some degree in other areas. The number of subsector-based projects and attendant costs are as set out below the foregoing is based on JICA's "Report on the Joint Evaluation on the Cooperation for Increasing Rice Production in Indonesia".

Table 5.7 Subsector Projects and Costs

		Unit: 1 million yen
SUBSECTOR	NUMBER OF PROJECTS	COST
Seed Production and Distribution	8	4,306
Crop Protection	6	3,469
Regional Certification and Popularization	1	19
Irrigation	17	21,044
Postharvest Processing	11	11,796
Other	3	468
TOTAL	46	37,156

Source: JICA, Japanese and Indonesian Evaluation Team, 1986, Joint Evaluation on the Cooperation for Increasing Rice Production in Indonesia

In 1985, JICA carried out an evaluation of assistance toward increased rice production together with the Japanese Ministry of Foreign Affairs, the Ministry of Agriculture, Forestry and Fisheries, and the Indonesian government. In this evaluation, the following appraisal was given for the entire project in connection with its impact on increased rice production:

> At the present time we cannot quantitatively judge the impact of the cooperation on increased rice production. As for results, nationwide self-sufficiency in rice was achieved during the period of the cooperation. According to the individual subsectors of cooperation, increased rice production is anticipated by means of increases to per unit yield through superior seed varieties, prevention of loss stemming from blight and insect damage through strengthening the protection of crops, expansion of production areas through irrigation development, and prevention of quantitative and qualitative loss through improved postharvest processing. The synergistic effect is similarly expected through the integrated implementation of these factors.

Further, with respect to the modality of assistance under the umbrella method, a positive evaluation was given in connection with the aspects of meeting Indonesian needs, smoothing out mutual understanding between Japan and Indonesia, and facilitating related business within the Indonesian government, and an understanding that Japan would carry out assistance in the rice sector was reached with each of the donors, international institutions, and the Indonesian government.

Evaluations of the five subsectors have been varied. With respect to seed production, even though it is thought to have contributed to increased unit yield, it has been pointed out that there were problems in that the machinery and materials provided were not used effectively enough and adequate funds could not be raised domestically. With respect to crop protection, the related projects were mostly carried out under Japanese assistance, with much achievement centering on project-type technical cooperation. Plans were formulated under development surveys. Using grant aid, observation and testing centres were set up and contributions of materials and agricultural chemicals were made. With respect to regional certification and popularization, surveys were carried out, but the projects did not proceed. In the field of irrigation, most projects remained at the preparation stage, including F/S and engineering services, and given that irrigation is a long-term operation, a conclusion on the impacts on the operation cannot be immediately drawn. With regard to postharvest processing, postharvest treatment and processing capability could not keep up with increases in rice production, and despite the fact that the amount of materials provided was increased, there was still a gap between the two.

5.4 Programme for the Promotion of Major Food Crops Production: Second Umbrella Cooperation

The Programme for the Promotion of Major Food Crops Production was also called the Second Umbrella Cooperation, and its objective was investment in staple food supplies and societal development through improvement to the regular supply and quality of rice, along with increased production of secondary crops and horticultural crops. Assistance through the umbrella method, which linked technical and financial aid, was carried out to enable this. A record of discussion prescribing the framework for the cooperation was signed in July 1986, and the period of assistance spanned five years from 1986 to 1990. For the subject crops, other than rice, soybeans were selected from secondary crops and potatoes were selected from horticultural crops. The subject subsectors were the six subsectors of increased planting and distribution of superior seed varieties, strengthening of crop protection, regional certification and exhibition of agricultural technology, irrigation and water management, improvement of postharvest processing, and mechanization of agriculture. For wetland rice there were 10 subject provinces, for soybeans 5 subject provinces, and for potatoes 5 subject provinces.

With respect to the Programme for the Promotion of Major Food Crops Production, a Japanese and Indonesian joint evaluation was conducted in 1991 and 1992. In the following, the impact of the programme is discussed based on the report of the aforementioned joint evaluation (JICA Planning Department, Evaluation and Supervision Division, Joint Evaluation for FY 1991, August 1992). Overall, the following evaluation was made:

> With respect to rice, it is extremely difficult to make a direct quantitative analysis of the correlation between the assistance in question and improvements to crop production amounts. Qualitatively, concentrated and integrated assistance was carried out, and this is estimated to have contributed to the maintenance of self-sufficiency in rice. Specifically, since attaining self-sufficiency in rice in 1984, average growth in the amount of production throughout the period of cooperation was 3.2%, and in terms of amounts, the targets in the Fifth National Economic Development Plan were attained. However, the amount of rice consumption continued to grow, and imports had to be relied on in those years in which the balance of supply and demand was upset.
>
> Annual growth in rice production was 7.7% in the first half of the 1980s. Much of this was due to increases in yield per unit area. If we compare increases in rice production between the 10 provinces falling under the umbrella cooperation and other provinces not falling under it, the

differences in impact are not very distinct given that there are many factors contributing to rice production. Moreover, it is extremely difficult to quantitatively grasp the degree to which the umbrella cooperation contributed to growth in rice production.

The evaluations in accordance with the subsectors are as follows:

(1) Planting and distribution of superior seed varieties
Seed nurseries were strengthened, resulting in efficient seed production. Seed processing centres were established in major rice producing areas, production and storage capabilities for seeds in common use were raised, and it was expected that this would contribute to seed production by farmers generally.

(2) Strengthening of crop protection
Under the Programme for the Strengthening of Crop Protection, nationwide preventative observation networks for rice damage caused by blight and insects were designed and established.

(3) Irrigation and water management
The irrigation project for the Wonogiri region was completed, and the project was being carried out in three other areas, while in yet another three areas the irrigation was under rehabilitation. Under the Remote Sensing Engineering Project for Development of Agricultural Infrastructure, technological development was carried out that was useful in selecting areas appropriate for agricultural development, based on preparation of subject and evaluation diagrams for factors including soil, geology, and water system. As a result of activities under the Irrigation and Drainage Construction Technology Center Project, the irrigation-related facilities inventory was systemized and put into the form of a highly useful manual.

(4) Agricultural mechanization
Design and testing of cultivators and husk combustion dryers was carried out under the Proper Agricultural Machinery and Technology Development Center Project, and this contributed to the development of domestically manufactured agricultural machinery.

The JICA evaluation report concluded that the subsector with the largest impact was the strengthening of crop protection, and other subsectors with considerable impact were irrigation and water management and agricultural mechanization. And, in terms of the form of assistance, the impact was largest when project-type technical cooperation was linked with financial cooperation and carried out over the long term.

With respect to the strengthening of crop protection, project-type technical cooperation in the form of the Crop Protection Strengthening

Project was carried out. Under this project, a possible outbreak of brown plant hoppers was observed in 1986 and was reported to the Indonesian government. Following Presidential Order No. 3 (issued November 3, 1986), emergency preventive measures were applied; 1,000 tons of agricultural chemicals in emergency aid was received from Japan through grant aid, and as a result, damage that probably would have extended to several hundred thousand tons of rice was prevented (same report p. 51). Moreover, the testing of agricultural chemicals in the same project revealed that some of the pesticides on the market were of no effect and proved to society the necessity of testing of agricultural chemicals (same report p. 77). With respect to the transfer of technology, the project provided training not only to leaders but also to research assistance technicians, and as a result a level was achieved in which the latter were able to participate as lecturers (same report p. 78). Regular information on damage from many patrol staff positioned in observation areas nationwide covered by observation networks was reported online to the centre, which then formulated the information into a database (same report p. 78).

With respect to Japan's technical assistance in connection with the prevention of brown plant hoppers, another report is also available. According to an article by Yuichi Sawada (Yuichi Sawada, 'Indonesia's Increased Rice Production and Pest Strategies', in Atsunobu Tomomatsu, Koichiro Katsurai, Osamu Iwamoto Editors, 1994 Kokusai Nogyo Kyorokuron [A Theory of International Agricultural Assistance], Kokon Shoin), it was from the latter half of the 1970s to the 1980s that brown plant hopper damage increased dramatically. The reasons for this were that: (1) year-round cultivation of rice was increasing, and rice as an edible grass existed in abundance; (2) rice nutrients had improved, and thus the number of eggs laid by pests and the rate of larvae survival had increased; and (3) as a result of the spread of agricultural chemicals, the natural enemy organisms of the brown plant hopper had decreased.

To deal with this damage, based on a request from the Indonesian side, JICA implemented the Crop Protection Project from June 1980 to March 1992. Its objective was the development of technology to monitor and prevent damage to rice by blight and insects and the establishment of a general management system for damage caused by blight and insects. The special features of this project-type cooperation were: (1) its direct link with an actual site, in other words the administration centre would be within the Ministry of Agriculture, but project sites would be positioned throughout the country; (2) basic research, in particular emphasis on ecological research on the occurrence of damage caused by blight and insects; and (3) implementation in combination with grant aid and training carried out in both Indonesia and third countries.

The background to the rapid increase in damage caused by brown plant hoppers was that despite the breeding of new high-yield seed varieties incorporating a blight and disease resistant factor, a new type of brown plant hopper had emerged with sufficient propagation power over this resistant variety. Moreover, the resistant variety was at times inferior in terms of yield and quality, and in the first half of the 1980s the amount of pesticides used had increased dramatically. In response, a resurgence appeared in which the degree of pest density increased to a level higher than that prior to the distribution of pesticides. The brown plant hopper damage arose through transmission in the fallow land of the plains. Inland there was no fallow land, so the plant hoppers moved to the plains. Because the density of natural enemy organisms in the fallow land in the plains had suddenly dropped, the plant hoppers that migrated from the inland suddenly increased.

Thus, the guidelines for the anti-plant hopper strategy stressed restraint of distributing agricultural chemicals inland, and on the plains monitoring was strengthened and efforts were made toward early observance and early prevention. As for the on-site prevention strategy, specifically, the following measures were taken: improvement of investigations by monitoring staff and training of monitoring staff; data analysis at outdoor test sites and guidance for this; provision of monitoring information to local government agencies; resolution on strategies for prevention by joint examination meetings; and implementation of prevention measures following the guidance by outdoor test sites and prefectures. As a result, application of insect growth inhibitors with minimal impact on natural enemy organisms and the environment was carried out with excellent effect in the prevention of plant hoppers.

6. Conclusion

If assistance funds are fungible, it is insufficient to only evaluate the impact on the aided project. However, according to Pack and Pack [1990], assistance categorized by sector in Indonesia, in most cases, was used in keeping with the purpose intended by the aid donor. Diversion into the other areas of development expenditure and diversion away from development objectives into current expenditure were not observed. Domestic revenue did not decrease due to aid inflow. With regard to assistance to Indonesia, fungibility is negligible, and it is meaningful to discuss the impact of assistance on a specified sector, such as agriculture.

If we analyze the state of increased rice production through intensification of rice production based on Indonesian government statistics, the yield rate (YR), which expresses yield per hectare, has increased almost consistently since 1974. If we check the correlation between yield per hectare on the one hand and the seven variables of seeds, pesticides, fertilizer, government expenditure on agriculture and irrigation, number of Japanese technical cooperation related personnel, grant aid disbursements, and loan aid disbursements on the other, the highest positive correlation was exhibited with loan aid disbursements. With respect to the other variables, pesticides, fertilizer, and government expenditure on agriculture and irrigation exhibited a relatively high positive correlation.

In considering the significance of ODA, in addition to the aspect of flow of ODA funds, it is also necessary that the aspects of knowledge and know-how transfer be examined. In the case of technical cooperation and the financial aid that is implemented in close relation with the former, since the impact of assistance emerges also as capacity and institution building through transfer of knowledge and know-how, it is insufficient to examine only the amounts expended. Analysis relating to whether or not transfer of the lacking technology was made is indispensable.

Even in the period prior to the Umbrella Cooperation that took place in the 1980s, Japanese technical assistance to the Indonesian agricultural sector was carried out on an organizational basis. Looking at the period until the 1970s, the West Java Food Production Increase Project was representative. The objectives of this project were increased food production and improvement of farmers' lives, and guidance and training were provided to spread agricultural technology. Subsectors of emphasis were the four areas of popularization of superior seed production, training for agricultural mechanization, promotion of model zone villages, and education of farmers' organizations and spread of rice production technology. The subject geographical areas extended to only the seven prefectures of West Java, and costs expended amounted to only 1% of the nominal expenditures of the First Umbrella Cooperation.

The umbrella method was a system that managed in unison the various forms of assistance of technical cooperation, grant aid, and loan aid under unit objectives and for specified subsectors and specified geographical areas. The First Umbrella Cooperation was carried out over a period of five years starting from July 1981. Its objective was to improve the rate of Indonesian self-sufficiency in rice. Subsectors of emphasis were the five areas of increased planting and distribution of superior seed varieties, strengthening of crop protection, regional certification and distribution of technology, irrigation development, and postharvest processing. The subject geographical areas were the eight provinces of Aceh, South Sumatra, Lampon, West Java, Central

Java, East Java, South Kalimantan, and South Sulawesi. In the evaluation carried out jointly by the Japanese and Indonesian governments, as nationwide results for Indonesia, self-sufficiency in rice was achieved during the period of assistance, and on a subject basis, increased rice production was expected through increases to unit yield as a result of superior seed varieties, prevention of damage stemming from blight and insects by strengthening crop protection, expansion of crop areas through irrigation development, and prevention of quantitative and qualitative loss as a result of improvement to postharvest processing. It was also concluded that synergies as a result of the implementation of these categories in unison could be expected.

The objectives of the Second Umbrella Cooperation lay in stable supply and quality improvement of rice, along with increased production in secondary crops and horticultural produce. The period of cooperation spanned five years from 1986 to 1990. The selected subject crops other than rice were soybeans from the secondary crops and potatoes from horticultural produce. The subject categories were the six areas of increased planting and distribution of superior seed varieties, strengthening the protection of crops, regional certification and exhibition of agricultural technology, irrigation and water management, improvement of postharvest processing, and agricultural mechanization. The geographical subject areas comprised ten provinces for wetland rice, five provinces for soybeans, and five provinces for potatoes. According to the joint evaluation carried out by the Japanese and Indonesian governments, with regard to rice, qualitatively, concentrated assistance was carried out on an integrated basis and was evaluated as contributing to the maintenance of self-sufficiency in rice. The rate of growth of amounts produced throughout the period of assistance was on average 3.2%, and in terms of quantity, the target figures were achieved in the Fifth National Economic Development Plan. However, rice consumption continued to grow, and in the years in which the balance of supply and demand was upset, imports inevitably came to be relied upon.

References

Bates, Robert H. 1981. *Markets and States in Tropical Africa*. Berkeley and Los Angeles: University of California Press.

Goro Taniguchi Translation (1984) *Daiyonji Kaihatsu Gonen Keikaku* (The Fourth Economic Development Plan) [Taniguchi Kenkyusho]

Hayami, Y. and Goudo, Y. 2002. *Nougyou Keizairon* (Agricultural Economics). Tokyo: Iwanami Shoten.

Indonesian Biro Pusat Statistik (1975-) *Statistik Indonesia*. Jakarta: BPS.

International Development Center of Japan. 1995. *Higashi Azia no Keizai Kaihatsu niokeru Nihon no ODA no Teiryouteki Hyouka* (Quantitative Evaluation of Japanese ODA in the Development of East Asian Economies. International Development Center of Japan.

Indonesia Umbrella Kyoryoku Chukan Hyoka Chosa Kikoku Hokokukai Shiryo (Materials for the Reporting Session upon Return to Japan on the Interim Assessment of Umbrella Cooperation). 1999.

The Japan Institute of International Affairs (JIIA). 2001. *The Significance of ODA in the External Relations of ASEAN*. Tokyo: The Japan Institute of International Affairs.

Japan International Cooperation Agency (JICA), Agricultural Development Cooperation Department. 1975. *Indonesia Nishijava Shokuryo Zosan Keikaku Evaluation Chosa Houkokusho* (Survey Report on the Evaluation of the West Java Food Production Increase Project).

———. Evaluation and Examinations Committee Secretariat. 1986. *Indonesia Komezosan Kyoryoku Hyoka Chosa Hokokusho* (Survey Report on the Joint Evaluation on the Cooperation for Increasing Rice Production in Indonesia).

———. Planning Department, Evaluation and Supervisory Division. 1992. *Heisei Sannendo Godo Hyoka Chosa Kekka Hokokusho (Indonesia)* (Joint Evaluation Report for FY 1991).

Hiroyoshi Kannou. 1998. *Indonesia Nouson Keizairon* (Economic Analysis of Indonesian Agricultural Villages).

Kunio Igusa Translation (1987) *Indonesia no Keizai Kaihatsu Jisseki to Kougyouka Seisaku* (Indonesian Economic Development and Industrialization Policy) [Azia Keizai Kenkyusho]

Motooka, T. 1975. *Indonesia no Kome* (Rice in Indonesia). Tokyo: Sobunsha.

Oguro, K. and Kohama, H. (1995) *Indonesia Keizai Nyumon* (Economic Development in Indonesia) (Tokyo: Nihon Hyoronsha)

Pack, Howard and Janet Rothenberg–Pack. 1990. "Is Foreign Aid Fungible? The Case of Indonesia". *Economic Journal* 100 (March).

The World Bank. 1998. *Assessing Aid – What Works, What Doesn't, and Why* [Oxford University Press] [Kohama, H. and Tomita, Y. Translation (2000) *Yukou na Enjo: Fungibility to Enjo Seisaku* (Effective Aid: Fungibility and Aid Policy) [Toyo Keizai Shimposha]]

The World Bank. 1993. *The East Asian Miracle: Economic Growth and Public Policy*. Oxford University Press. [Masaki Shiratori et al. (1994) *Higashi Asia no Kiseki* (The East Asian Miracle) [Toyo Keizai Shimposha]]

Sawada, Yuichi. *"Indonesia no"Komezosan to Gaichu Taisaku"* (Indonesia's Increased Rice Production and Pest Strategy). In *Kokusai Nogyo Kyoryokuron* (Analysis on International Agricultural Cooperation), edited by

Atsunobu Tomomatsu, Koichiro Katsurai and Osamu Iwamoto. 1994. Kokon Shoin.

Vatikiotis, Michael R.J. 1998. *Indonesian Politics under Suharto* 3rd Ed. Routledge.

Yasunaka Akio and Norio Mihira, eds. 1995. *Gendai Indonesia no Seiji to Keizai* (Contemporary Indonesian Politics and Economy). Azia Keizai Kenkyusho.

Yoshizawa, Shiro, Takayanagi, Sakio (eds.). 1995. *Nihon no ODA no Sougouteki Kenkyuu – Tai niokeru Jirei* (Comprehensive Research on Japanese ODA – Thailand Case Study). Chuo University Press

6

Official Development Assistance as a Catalyst for Foreign Direct Investment and Industrial Agglomeration

Matsuo Watanabe

1. Introduction

This chapter is intended to investigate the contribution of infrastructure development financed by Official Development Assistance (ODA) to attracting foreign direct investment (FDI) and to the formation of industrial agglomerations, with reference to the automotive industry in Thailand.

Thailand has been one of the major production bases in ASEAN, and currently there are 700 automotive-related companies. The origin of the industry in Thailand dates back to the 1960s when the country invited foreign manufacturers, mainly Japanese, under the Import Substitution Industrialization (ISI) strategy. The country subsequently changed to an export-oriented strategy at the beginning of the 1970s, which has led to remarkable success in industrialization (including that of the automotive sector) and economic development.

The success of the Thai automotive industry is evidenced by the expansion in the volume of production and exports which has been the largest of any ASEAN member. This expansion has been facilitated by a concentration of investments in the industry (known as 'agglomeration') from foreign parts suppliers, including those in the Eastern Seaboard (ESB) area.

The determinants of FDI have been analyzed fairly widely in past literature, including the issue of FDI in ASEAN economies where provision of infrastructure as well as the existence of industrial agglomeration have had a positive impact in attracting FDI.[1]

This study investigates how the agglomeration of the automotive industry has taken place in Thailand. In particular, special attention is placed on the shift in concentration on new investments over the last two decades in accordance with the development of infrastructure in the ESB and Bangkok Metropolitan area – a large part of which was financed by Japan's ODA in the same period.

This chapter is organized as follows. Section 2 reviews the Thai government's past economic policy and the path to industrialisation. Section 3 gives an overview of the development of the ESB area with particular reference to the establishment of various types of infrastructure. After outlining the situation of the Thai automotive industry in Section 4, an analysis of the formation of the automotive agglomeration follows. Section 5, which concludes this chapter,[2] discusses Thailand's attractiveness to investors.

2. Thailand's Economic Policy and the Path to Industralization

Thailand has achieved remarkable industrialization in the last two decades largely due to FDI from Japan and other countries. In particular, the country has seen an industrial agglomeration of automotive and electricity industries which account for the successful industrialization mentioned in the previous section. The following sections examine the case of automotive agglomeration in the ESB area and Japanese companies' investment behaviour which changed in accordance with infrastructural development in the ESB financed by Japanese ODA. First, Thailand's chronological industrial policy infrastructural development plan for the ESB is reviewed. Next, the agglomeration of the automotive industry in the ESB is investigated by looking at the trajectory of the industry in Thailand and the process of agglomeration in the ESB, followed by the factors which enabled the agglomeration, including Japan's ODA.

Thailand's industrialization dates back to the 1960s when the country introduced its ISI strategy. This was followed by an export-oriented strategy in the 1970s which has since been expanded by foreign capital inflows (Development Bank of Japan 2001).

The Thai government embarked on industrialization at the end of the 1950s at a time when the main source of income was agriculture, i.e., rice. In 1961, an economic development plan was introduced to establish an industrial base by encouraging foreign investment.[3] The ISI strategy, however, collapsed due to an increasing trade deficit caused by the import of capital goods. The government then altered its strategy in favour of promoting export-oriented industries by offering various incentives such as reducing customs on imports necessary for producing exportable goods and preferential financing for exporters. Through these

Table 6.1   The Thai Government's Industrialization Policies (1954–1960)

1954	- Industry Promotion Act, establishment of Board of Investment (BOI)
1957	- World Bank's recommendation (creation of economic planning agency, private sector industrialization, support of private sector and infrastructural development)
1959	- Establishment of National Economic Development Board (NEDB) and Industrial Financial Corporation of Thailand (IFCT)
1960	- Industrial Investment Promotion Act – to promote private sector industrialization

Source: Development Bank of Japan (2001)

incentives, labour intensive industries, e.g. food processing and textiles, saw a notable growth.

The National Economic Development Board (NEDB), and its successor, the National Economic and Social Development Board (NESDB), have played a significant role in Thai industrialization. The agencies report to the Prime Minister and have written nine National Economic Plans (NEP) since 1961 (Table 6.2). The first and second NEP (1961–66 and 1966–71, respectively) typically followed ISI strategy, imposing high tariffs on imports to protect domestic industries while developing infrastructure through public investment. During the NEP II, attention was directed to the mobilization of domestic resources and the promotion of labour intensive industries, textiles in particular. The domestic industries, however, lost price competitiveness due to the failure of ISI. There was also a rise in domestic prices, a decrease in foreign reserves, and a decline in exports caused by currency appreciation and the constraints of small domestic markets. As such, stagnating exports and increasing imports resulted in a deteriorating balance of payments at the end of the 1960s.

The NEP III (1971–76) saw a drastic change in which an export-oriented industrialization was introduced. In 1972 the Industrial Investment Promotion Act was replaced by the Investment Promotion Act which was intended to promote export industries, to disperse industrial areas over the country and to invite foreign capital selectively. This export-oriented industrialization policy was aimed at mobilizing domestic raw materials and labour to export industries. In addition, the government introduced various incentive schemes including tariff reduction on inputs for export goods and offered low rate loans to exporters.[4] The export-oriented policy remained throughout NEP IV and V (1976–81 and 1981–86, respectively) with the government's promotion of export industries, establishment of export processing zones

Table 6.2 Policies of National Economic Plans

	Emphasis of Economic Policies	GDP Growth Actual	GDP Growth Target
I (1961-66)	- Infrastructure development (roads, ports, dams) - Investment promotion of private sector (1962: Revision of Industry Investment Promotion Act)	8.7%	5.5%
II (1966-71)	- ISI - Protect domestic industries	7.2%	8.5%
III (1971-76)	- Promote agricultural production, export-oriented industrialization - Selective introduction of foreign capital - Disperse industrial areas (1972: Investment Promotion Act; replacement of NEDB with National Economic and Social Development Board)	6.5%	7.0%
IV (1976-81)	- Employment (investing in public enterprise – natural gas, power plants) - Narrow income gap (1977: Revision of Investment Promotion Act – to strengthen BOI)	7.4%	7.0%
V (1981-86)	- Promote heavy industries with resource development - Regional dispersion of economic activities - Double per capita income	5.4%	6.6%
VI (1986-91)	- Realise stable annual growth of 5% - Privatize energy sector - Increase employment and income distribution - Raise living standard, reduce regional gap	10.9%	5.0%
VII (1991-96)	- Maintain sustainable growth - Income redistribution and dispersion of development - Human resource development, improve living standards	8.1%	8.2%
VIII (1996-2001)	- Human and social development and economic stabilisation - Regionally balanced growth and resource development (reduce the gap between agricultural and non-agricultural sectors) - Private-public partnership (road, port, utilities, communication infrastructure)	4.9%	8.0%
IX (2001-06)	- Human resource development - Balance economies, raise living standards - Poverty elimination - Transparency of government		4-5%

Source: NESDB, Development Bank of Japan (2001)

and support for large scale exporters. The government also explored natural gas and developed the petrochemical and chemical fertilizer industries which contributed to the country's rapid industrialization. Exports of industrial products increased from 25% of total exports in 1970 to 35% in 1980 when industrial exports first exceeded those in the agricultural sector. Table 6.4 shows that Thailand's manufacturing value added (MVA) grew remarkably compared to developing countries – MVA and per capita MVA grew at 10.5% and 7.5% respectively during the 1970s while developing countries saw a 6.8% and 4.5% growth in the same period.

The decade from the mid-1980s saw increasing FDI inflows from Japan (largely reflecting the rapid appreciation of the Yen), Hong Kong, Singapore and Taiwan, and high economic growth. FDI flows were directed to technology-oriented industries, such as those in the electric/electronic and integrated circuit (IC)-related fields, which led Thailand's industrialization along with textile and metal goods. The NEP VI (1986–91) promoted investment from the private sector and the privatization of the energy sector in particular, while the subsequent NEP VII (1991–96) encouraged the diverting of investment to regions out of Bangkok such as Chenmai, with a particular focus on the food processing, textile, metal, electric/electronic, petrochemical and steel industries. As shown in Table 6.3, the country appeared to succeed in enhancing the share of the manufacturing sector from 21.5% of GDP in 1980 to about 30% in the mid-1990s, while the share of the agriculture, forestry and fishery sectors together more than halved from 23.2% to less than 10% in the same period. MVA per capita in 1990 (US$418) was twice as much as in developing countries (US$203) (Table 6.4).

From the mid-1990s onwards it appears that further technological development has become important in maintaining international competitiveness. The private sector has promoted investments in research and development (R&D), while a lack of skilled labour and a higher wage level compared to China and Vietnam has become problematic since these factors play a part in reducing the competitiveness of labour-intensive industries in particular. As such, the NEP VIII (1996–2001) emphasized the importance of increasing productivity. For instance, loan and tax reductions were granted for private companies pursuing human resource development programmes and R&D, and job training centres were established. The 1997 financial crisis, however, hit the economy hard. Real GDP growth plummeted to negative figures in 1997 and 1998 at –1.4% and –10.8% respectively. The productivity growth of whole industries also stagnated from 3.5%

Table 6.3 GDP Structure of Thailand by Sector (%)

	1980	1985	1990	1995	2000
Agriculture, Forestry, Fisheries	23.2	15.8	12.5	9.7	9.1
Manufacturing	21.5	21.9	27.2	29.6	33.4
o/w transport equipment	1.6	1.0	2.7	2.5	2.0
Commerce	17.6	18.3	17.7	16.4	16.8
Service	14.0	14.5	13.4	13.2	14.3
Others	23.7	29.5	29.2	31.1	26.4

Source: National Economic and Social Development Board, Thailand

Table 6.4 Manufacturing Value Added (MVA): 1980-1998

	Year/Period	Thailand	Developing countries	Developed countries
MVA/capita (US$ 1990 price)	1980	194	161	3,712
	1990	418	203	4,430
	1997	705	290	4,829
	1998	623	291	4,880
MVA annual growth rate (%)	1970-79	10.5	6.8	2.9
	1980-89	9.5	5.3	2.8
	1990-98	7.5	6.9	2.2
MVA annual growth rate per capita (%)	1970-79	7.5	4.5	2.1
	1980-89	7.6	3.1	2.1
	1990-98	6.4	5.2	1.5
Share of MVA in GDP (%)	1980	22.6	19.5	22.9
	1990	27.2	21.2	22.0
	1997	31.6	24.0	21.6
	1998	31.3	24.0	21.4

Source: UNIDO

in the 1986–1990 period to 0% in 1998, and hence the country rapidly became less competitive.[5]

Following the financial crisis, the Thai government formulated an Industrial Restructuring Plan in which various programmes were set up, focusing on areas such as productivity growth, technological development, and the promotion of small and medium enterprises (SMEs) – with particular emphasis on productivity growth through development of human resources, business administration and technology.

3. Eastern Seaboard Development Plan and Japan's Official Development Assistance

3.1 Overview of the Plan

The Eastern Seaboard Development Plan was originally motivated by the discovery of natural gas in the Gulf of Siam in 1973.[6] In the early 1980s, the Thai government intended to establish a new industrial cluster in the ESB area, which consists of three provinces – Chachoengsao, Chonburi and Rayong – 80 to 200 km southeast of Bangkok, to alleviate the concentration of population and industries in the Bangkok metropolitan area (JBIC 1999).[7,8]

The ESB development plan was mainly implemented in two districts, the Map Ta Phut area and the Laem Chabang area (see Figure 6.5b on p. 156). The former was expected to be a core district of heavy industries (petrochemical enterprises in particular) utilizing natural gas yielded from the Gulf of Thailand; and the latter was initially intended to host export-oriented light industries (e.g., food and textiles). In practice, however, the latter has attracted automotive, electric and machinery sectors to take advantage of its proximity to the newly constructed commercial port.

3.2 Japan's Official Development Assistance to the ESB Infrastructure

Japan's ODA has played a major role in the ESB development, providing Yen loans and technical assistance towards the construction of infrastructure from the 1980s onwards.

The Japan Bank for International Cooperation (JBIC, formerly The Overseas Economic Cooperation Fund) financed 27 loans for 16 projects (listed in Appendix A on p. 164) including the development of industrial estates, water pipelines, railways and roads. Total loan commitments amounted to ¥178.8 billion (about US$894 million) which accounted for 10% of Japan's total cumulative loan commitments to Thailand (JBIC 1999).

3.2.1 Development of the Map Ta Phut Area

In order to promote investments, particularly in heavy chemical industries, an industrial estate (380.8ha) and a port (with one multipurpose berth and two liquid cargo berths) were constructed.[9] In addition, a separation plant (of natural gas to ethane, propane and liquefied petroleum gases) and accompanying pipeline were co-financed by the JBIC and World Bank (IBRD). These facilities together with two additional plants have contributed to Thailand's energy demand and to the petrochemical industry becoming a major supplier of input materials.

3.2.2 Development of Laem Chabang Area

The projects include construction of a commercial port and an industrial estate. The port was intended to complement/substitute for Bangkok Port which could not accept large-scale container vessels.[10] In addition, due to remarkable economic growth and a rapid increase in international trade, Bangkok Port has been operating beyond its capacity. The Laem Chabang Port has two piers with eleven container terminals capable of 1.5 million TEU a year. The port has become one of the hub ports in Southeast Asia, and its handling has grown to 2.4 million TEU in 2001 which well exceeded Bangkok Port's 1.1 million TEU during the same period (LCB Container Terminal 1 Ltd 2003).[11,12]

Besides the port, an industrial estate of 420ha was developed in which an export-processing zone was instituted. The estate was fully occupied by 1999 with automotive and electric/electronics industries, and various other types of industries, and has been functioning as an important industrial base in the country.

3.2.3 Water Resource Development

This set of projects, including construction of a dam and pipelines, was intended to meet the water demand in the ESB area and to ensure the economic and social activities of near-by areas.

3.2.4 Transportation Sector

The development of railway and road networks in order to meet new demands for inland transportation was one of the important features in the ESB development plan. A railway network was constructed/renewed to meet the demand in the ESB area, particularly for the transportation of large quantities of long distance goods. First the main line between Chachoengsao and Sattahip was constructed by the Thai government followed by branch lines and long distance line between northern Thailand and the ESB (to by-pass the heavily congested Bangkok metropolitan area). These projects were all financed by Japan's ODA. The lines are used for transporting container cargos from Laem Chabang Port and fuel from Map Ta Phut.

In addition to the rail network, motorway networks were also constructed for the traffic between the Bangkok metropolitan area and the ESB, Chonburi – Pattaya (68 km) and Bangkok – Chonburi (82 km), and for bypassing Bangkok, for example, the East Bangkok Ring Road (63 km). This project was accompanied by the widening of existing roads, the cost of which was borne by the Thai Government and a World Bank loan.

4. Thailand's Automobile Industry and its Agglomeration in the Eastern Seaboard Area

4.1. Overview of the Thai Automotive Industry

The origin of the Thai automotive industry dates back to the early 1960s when Japanese manufacturers launched assembling factories in accordance with Thailand's ISI policy (Development Bank of Japan 2001).[13] The Thai Government then regarded promoting the automotive industry as a pillar of the country's industrialization strategy. To promote investment in domestic production of automotive parts, the government imposed tariffs on completely knocked down (CKD) vehicles and completely built-up units (CBU) at 40% and 80% respectively. In addition, the government also imposed a minimum local content requirement of 25% on automotive assembly (Poapongsakorn and Wangdee 2003).[14,15] These measures in fact contributed to fostering the Thai automotive industry.

Thailand has become the largest automotive manufacturer in ASEAN. As shown in Table 6.5, in 1996 the country produced vehicles equivalent to US$18 million, while Malaysia produced US$4.7 million followed by Indonesia (US$3.8 million) and the Philippines (US$1.9 million). The number of companies and employment generated by the industry accounted for more than 4% of the Thai manufacturing sector whereas the contribution of the automotive industries in other countries to their domestic manufacturing sectors was around 2% in this respect.

The industry grew steadily until 1997 when the Asian financial crisis hit the region hard after a remarkable economic growth which had been taking place since the 1980s. The number of vehicles produced and domestic sales expanded from around 85,000 in 1985 to 559, 000 and 589,000 respectively in 1996. The numbers plummeted to 158,000 and 144,000 in 1998 due to the financial crisis, followed by a recovering trend which started the next year. In 2002, production reached its

Table 6.5   Automotive Industries of ASEAN (1996)

	# of Companies		Production value		# of employment	
		% (a)	US$million	% (a)	000s	% (a)
Thailand	1,095	4.6	18,398	13.2	107	4.4
Malaysia	297	1.5	4,798	4.4	37	2.6
Indonesia	279	1.2	3,897	3.7	61	1.5
Philippines (b)	184	1.8	1,970	5.0	18	2.0

Source: UNIDO
Note: (a) Share in each country's manufacturing sector, (b) 1995 data

Table 6.6 Automotive Production and Sales Units: 1990-2002 (000's)

	1990	1995	1996	1997	1998	1999	2000	2001	2002
Production	**305**	**482**	**559**	**360**	**158**	**327**	**412**	**459**	**585**
o/w passenger car	n.a.	127	139	112	32	73	97	156	169
o/w pick-up truck	n.a.	347	358	223	122	244	299	291	377
o/w van, mini-bus, OPV	n.a.	2	4	2	2	6	6	5	20
o/w bus	n.a.	2	0.6	0.5	0.5	0.1	0	0.2	0.4
o/w heavy truck	n.a.	48	47	22	2	4	9	7	7
Domestic sales	**304**	**571**	**589**	**363**	**144**	**218**	**262**	**297**	**409**
o/w passenger car	n.a.	163	173	132	46	67	83	105	126
o/w pick-up truck	n.a.	324	328	188	81	133	155	171	241
o/w van, mini-bus, OPV	n.a.	35	40	22	10	11	14	13	13
o/w 2-4 ton truck	n.a.	16	17	9	3	4	5	5	5
o/w heavy truck	n.a.	32	32	11	4	3	5	4	6

Source: Federation of Thai Industries, Bank of Thailand
Note: Due to rounding of figures, the sum of the sub-categories does not necessarily correspond to total production and domestic sales.

Table 6.7 Thailand's Auto Vehicle Exports 2002 (Thai Baht millions)

HS8702	HS8703	HS8704	HS8705	HS8706	HS8707	HS8708
80	22,631	61,191	180	2	244	26,963

Source: Customs Department, Thailand
Note: HS8702   Motor vehicles for transport of ten or more persons
       HS8703   Motor cars and other motor vehicles principally designed for the transport of persons (other than 8702)
       HS8704   Motor vehicles for transport of goods
       HS8705   Special purpose motor vehicles (wrecking cars, crane trucks, fire engines, concrete mixer trucks, etc.)
       HS8706   Chassis with engines, for motor vehicles of 8701 to 8705
       HS8707   Bodies (inc. cabs) for motor vehicles of 8701 to 8705
       HS8708   Parts & accessories for motor vehicles of 8701 to 8705

highest level of 585,000, while sales (409,000) did not fully recover (Table 6.6).

The structure of production shows that the country's main category of vehicle is the pick-up truck which accounts for 64% of total production (377,000) in 2002. On the sales side, while more pick-up trucks are sold domestically than other types of vehicles, the share in total domestic sales was 54% (241,000 out of 409,000) in 2002. The production-sales gap implies that the country is an exporter of non-passenger vehicles (e.g., trucks). This is underwritten by the export data. Table 6.7 indicates that the country exported trucks (HS8704) to the value of TB61 billion – about three times the value of passenger vehicles exported (HS8703) in 2002.

4.2 Agglomeration of the Automotive Industry

Thailand's strong performance in the automotive industry is characterized by the agglomeration in Bangkok and the ESB area. The agglomeration is observed in two periods: up to the mid–1980s, and from the 1990s onwards (Mori 2000). The main factor regarding the former period is the reaction to the government's localization of industry, i.e., its import substitution industrialization policy. The policy encouraged foreign manufacturers (mainly Japanese) to establish assembling factories and automotive-related companies, concentrated in the Bangkok area. However, as the domestic automotive market was limited to about 100,000 units a year at the time, each assembler was forced to produce a wide range but small quantity of vehicles, and hence the number of suppliers was also limited.

In the 1990s, a new type of agglomeration took place in the ESB area. Assemblers aimed to increase competitiveness by establishing new factories and developing new models to meet an expected expansion of the domestic market (Poapongsakorn and Wangdee 2003). Toyota set up a new plant with a capacity of 50,000 units per annum in Chachoengsao followed by Honda, who set up a new plant with a capacity of 60,000 units per year in Ayuttaya province. Subsequently, in the mid-1990s, General Motors (GM) and Ford announced that they were setting up assembly plants in Thailand as a potential export hub in the Southeast Asian region.

Poapongsakorn and Wangdee (ibid.) argue that the reasons for the US manufacturers' decision were: i) Thailand's relatively well-developed automotive parts industry; ii) Thailand's commitment to trade liberalization; and iii) the Thai government's industrial promotion policy in 1994 which provided incentives to investors, including exemptions from corporate income tax and import duties.[16]

As more assembly plants were set up, a significant number of foreign automotive part suppliers appeared in Thailand. During the 1994–1997 period, the value of Board of Investment (BOI)–promoted projects was four times higher than the previous four years, amounting to TB15,070 million in 1997 (in which Japanese investors played a major role with a 65% of total incoming FDI to Thailand in 1998, equivalent to TB7,995.5 million). The capacities of the automotive industry expanded rapidly during this period. Figure 6.1 shows that the planned capacities of assemblers increased from 613,500 units in 1995 to 1,061,400 units in 1999.

Figure 6.1 Capacity Expansion Plan (Units) of Thai Automotive Industry: 1995-1999

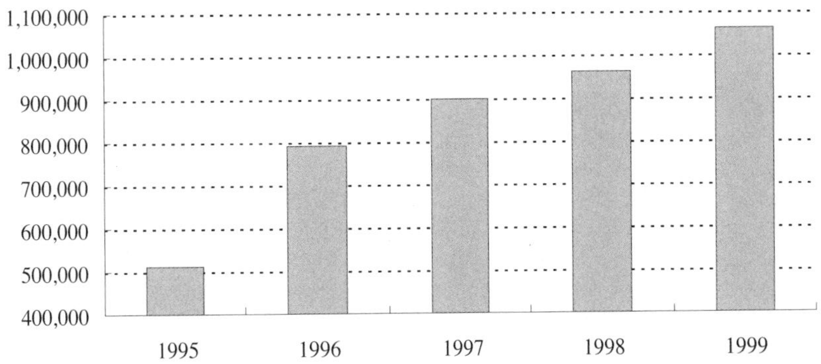

Source: Poapongsakorn and Wangdee, 2003.

4.2.1 Honda's Case

The Honda Motor Company announced in 2001 that its Thai subsidiary plant would export small size passenger cars to Japan from the following year. Many car components were procured in Thailand, where all functions except design were carried out, and Honda now plans to procure 100% of inputs domestically in Thailand (Hiratsuka 2002).[17] This plan is made feasible because of the agglomeration which allowed other Japanese parts suppliers to establish themselves in the country following Honda's establishment in the mid-1990s (when the domestic market was expanding). In addition, due to the financial crisis in 1997 and the subsequent depreciation of the Thai Baht, assemblers (including Honda) and suppliers have been localizing production and/or shifting from imported to domestic inputs in order to reduce total costs, whilst maintaining the quality (Yonetani 2002). As a result, Thai-made cars have been competitive in price and quality and can be exported to U.S. and Japanese markets.[18]

4.2.2 The Automotive Agglomeration in the Eastern Seaboard Industrial Estate (Rayong Province)

The Eastern Seaboard Industrial Estate (ESIE) is one of the industrial estates in the ESB area co-managed by a private entity (the Hemaraj Land and Development Plc) and the Industrial Estates Authority of Thailand (IEAT). It was developed in 1995 and is located in Rayong Province, 117km from Bangkok. As of June 2003, the area of 3,200 acres hosts

126 companies (of which 70 come from Japan), whose industries range from automotive, electronics, plastics/polymer, metal processing, food processing to material processing (Hemaraj Land and Development 2002).

In the automotive sector, the ESIE hosts 73 companies including Ford-Mazda AutoAlliance, GM Group (1996-), and 9 Toyota group suppliers. Other companies, include glass and plastics producers, metal processing companies, steel service centres, forging plants, chemical companies and companies carrying out other related activities (see Appendix B). The investors operating in the ESIE are entitled to receive various privileges from the IEAT and the BOI. The IEAT awards General Industrial Zone and Export Processing Zone status.[19]

There was no explicit intention to target the automotive industry when the first company, AutoAlliance, established a factory in 1995 (Nardone 2002).[20] AutoAlliance was followed by US suppliers such as TRW and Dana. Subsequently, Japanese suppliers affiliated with Toyota, Mitsubishi and Nissan also chose the ESIE as it is located within a one-hour distance of the Toyota and Mitsubishi factories. In 1996, GM selected the ESIE for its regional manufacturing. GM initially benefited from its integrated supplier base, but subsequently it relied on the existing suppliers in the ESIE affiliated to Toyota and Mitsubishi while introducing new US suppliers. As such, with additional supporting industries (including service providers and small and medium enterprises), an integrated automotive base providing supplier, logistic and source advantages for multiple manufacturers has been established in the ESIE – which is called the 'Detroit of the East'.

4.3. Infrastructural Development and Agglomeration

Iseki (2002) and Mori (2000) argue that the agglomeration of the automotive industry in the ESB has come about because of: i) the railway and road network; ii) the BOI's investment promotion measures (which encouraged those potential investors who were *already* considering operating in the country); iii) the availability of utility services such as electricity, water and communication systems; and iv) the proximity to a commercial port which allows manufacturers to establish a regional division of labour system and export complete goods.[21]

In fact, the investment behaviour of Japanese suppliers, the main actors in Thai automotive agglomeration, appears to endorse this argument. Their new investments in Thailand have clearly coincided with the development of infrastructure in the country. Figures 6.2 to 6.5 (a, b) show the change in locations and the timing of Japanese greenfield investment over time.

Figure 6.2a Location of Automotive Industry: -1979

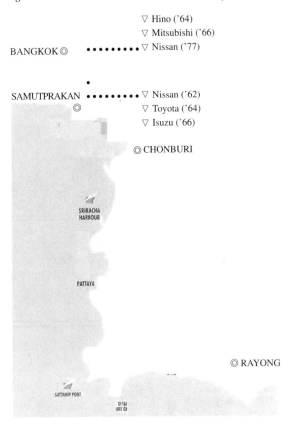

BANGKOK ◎   • • • • • • • • • ▽ Nissan ('77)
                              ▽ Mitsubishi ('66)
                              ▽ Hino ('64)

SAMUTPRAKAN • • • • • • • • • ▽ Nissan ('62)
        ◎   ▽ Toyota ('64)
                      ▽ Isuzu ('66)

◎ CHONBURI

SRIRACHA HARBOUR

PATTAYA

◎ RAYONG

SATTAHIP PORT

U-TAI URE GI

Source: Plotted from Table 6.8
Note: ▽ denotes an assembler
    • denotes a parts supplier

Up to 1979: As discussed previously, during the ISI period, Japanese assemblers and their *keiretsu* suppliers established production bases mainly in the Bangkok and Samut Prakan areas. Bangkok had the assembling factories of Hino (since 1964), Mitsubishi (1966) and Nissan (1977) and nine suppliers, while Samut Prakan hosted Nissan (1962), Toyota (1964) and Isuzu (1966) and 11 suppliers (Figure 6.2a). By this time, Thailand was hosting 22 suppliers in the whole country. At this stage, there was no infrastructure project in the ESB area (Figure 6.2b).

Figure 6.2b Infrastructure Development of Eastern Seaboard: -1979

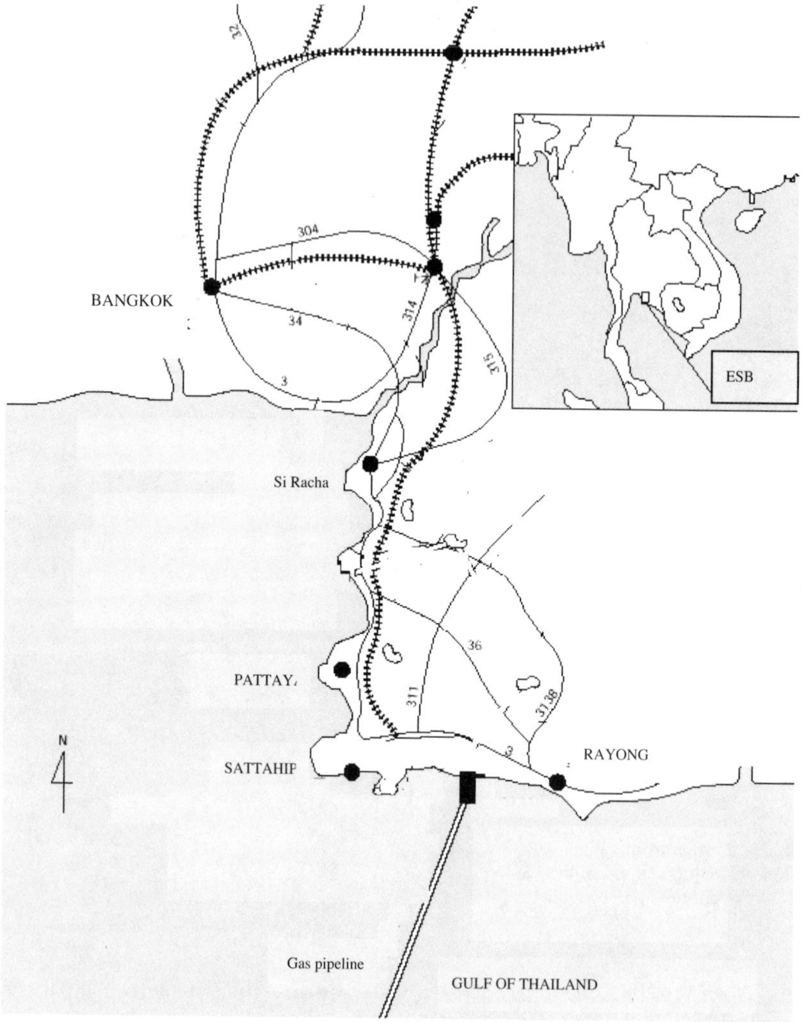

Source: JBIC (1999, 2001)

1980-89: The ESB Development Project commenced in this period with the construction of two water pipelines and the gas separation plant in Map Ta Phut (Figure 6.3b). This period also saw the country change its industrialization policy from ISI to a more export-oriented one. As production volume expanded, Japanese suppliers set

Figure 6.3a   Location of Automotive Industry: 1980-1989

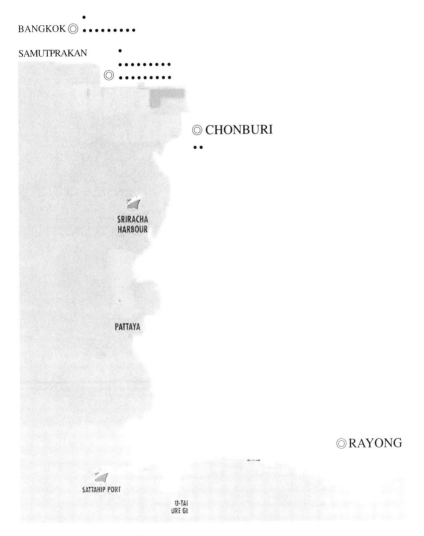

Source: Plotted from Table 6.8

up two establishments in Chonburi, while most new investments remained in Bangkok (15 companies in total) and Samut Prakan (21) areas (Figure 6.3a).

Figure 6.3b Infrastructure Development of Eastern Seaboard: 1980-1989

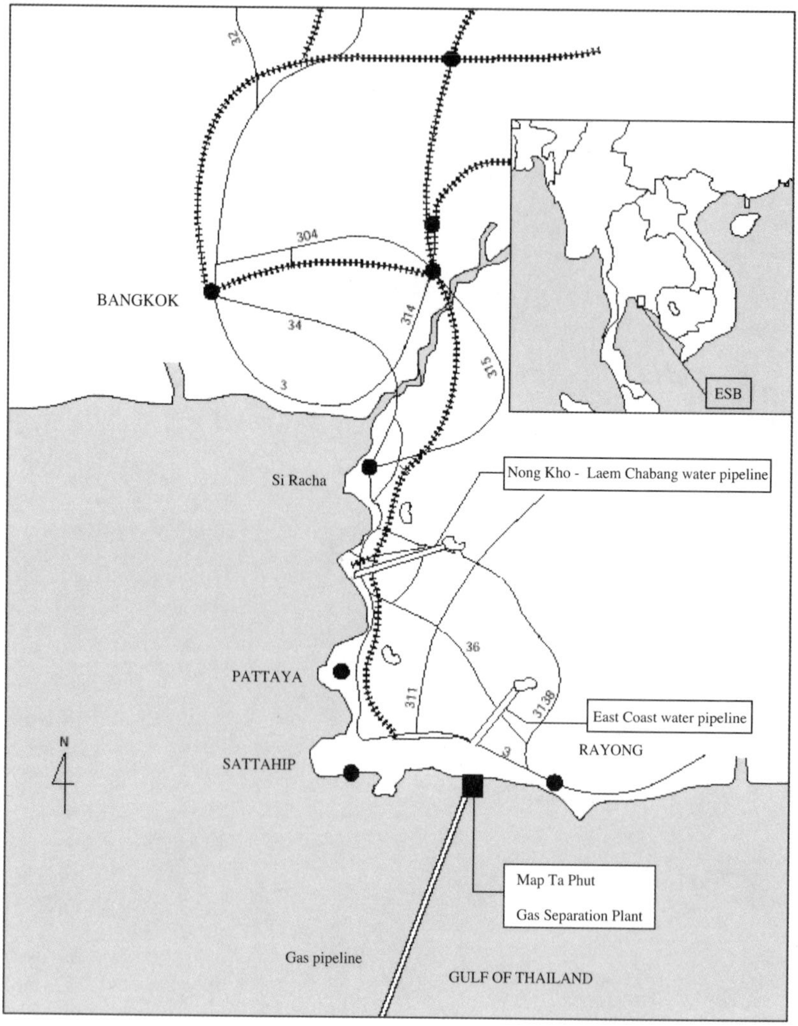

Source: JBIC (1999, 2001)

1990-95: This period saw a substantial shift in investment to Chonburi which hosted 12 new investments (14 in total), while nine new investments were made in Bangkok (bringing the total to 24) and four in Samut Prakan (bringing the total to 25) were made. In addition, Rayong Province began hosting four investments during this period

Figure 6.4a   Location of Automotive Industry: 1990-1995

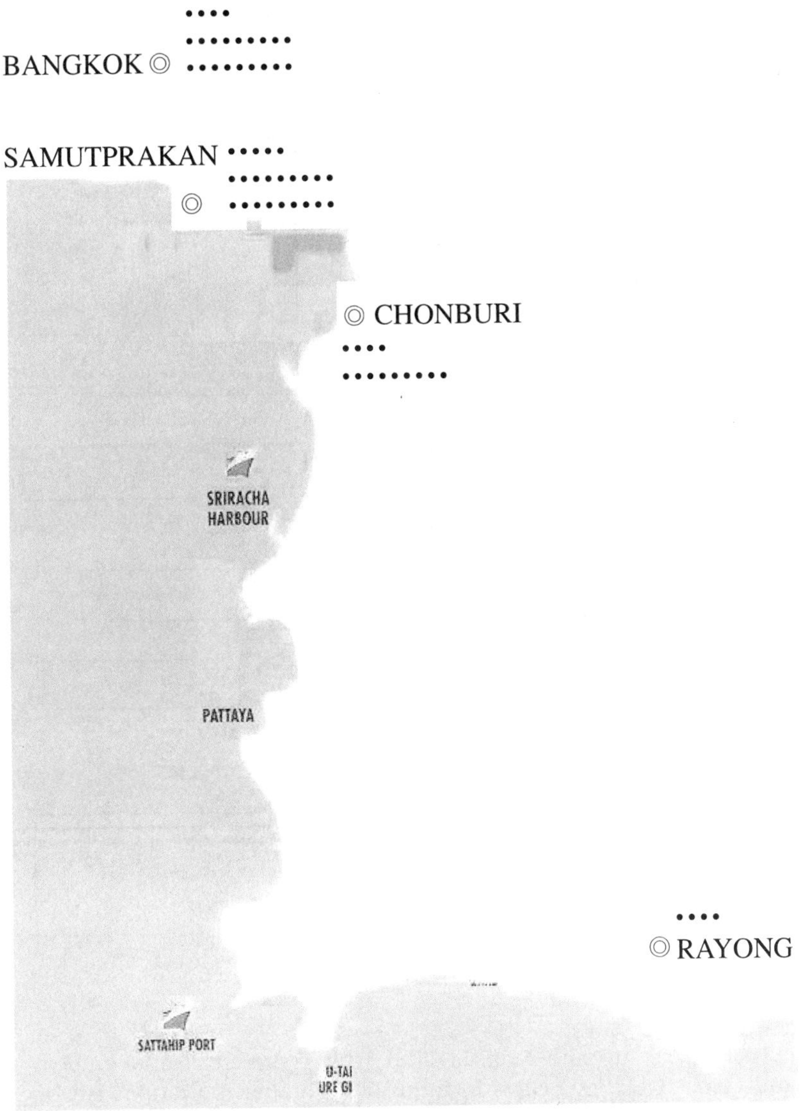

····
·········
BANGKOK ◎   ·········

SAMUTPRAKAN ·····
·········
◎   ·········

◎ CHONBURI
····
·········

SRIRACHA
HARBOUR

PATTAYA

····
◎ RAYONG

SATTAHIP PORT

U-TAI
URE GI

Source: Plotted from Table 6.8

(Figure 6.4a). The major part of the ESB Development Plan was carried out during this period as well. By 1995, industrial estates had been built

Figure 6.4b   Infrastructure Development of Eastern Seaboard: 1990-1995

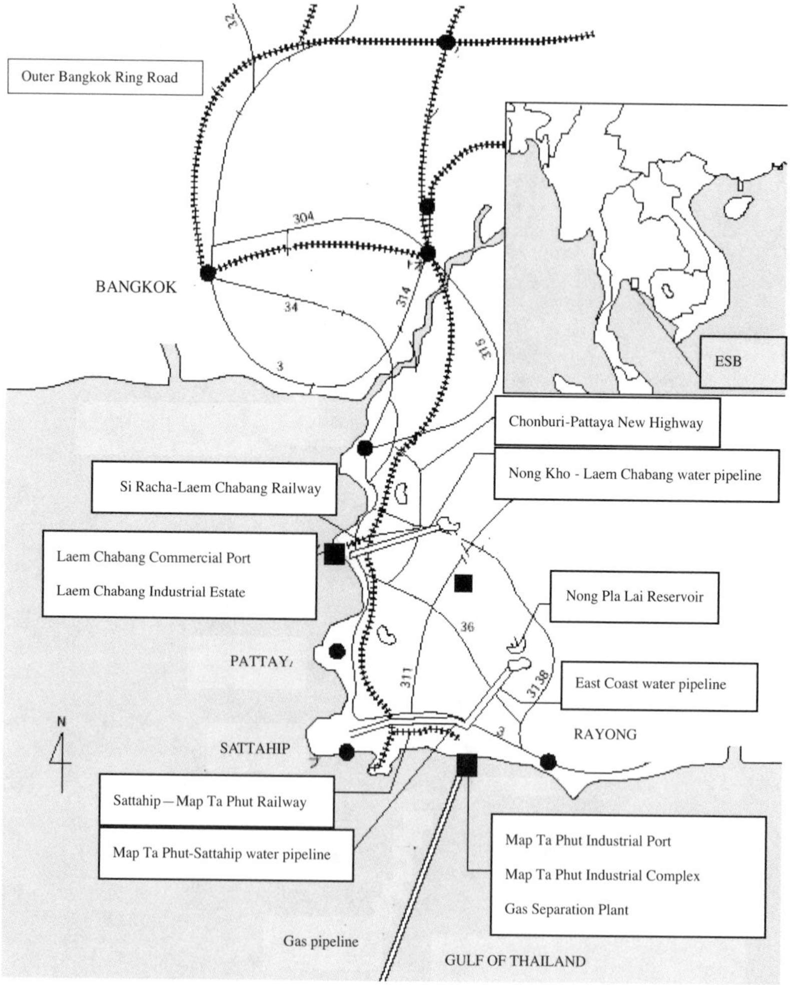

Outer Bangkok Ring Road

BANGKOK

304

34

3

ESB

Chonburi-Pattaya New Highway

Nong Kho - Laem Chabang water pipeline

Si Racha-Laem Chabang Railway

Laem Chabang Commercial Port

Laem Chabang Industrial Estate

Nong Pla Lai Reservoir

36

PATTAY,

East Coast water pipeline

N

SATTAHIP

RAYONG

Sattahip—Map Ta Phut Railway

Map Ta Phut-Sattahip water pipeline

Map Ta Phut Industrial Port

Map Ta Phut Industrial Complex

Gas Separation Plant

Gas pipeline

GULF OF THAILAND

Source: JBIC (1999, 2001)

in Laem Chabang and Map Ta Phut with commercial and industrial ports respectively, as well as in the ESIE.[22] The transportation networks have also been improved substantially: railways have been constructed between Siracha – Laem Chabang and Sattahip – Map Ta Phut, and a highway constructed between Chonburi and Pattaya. On the water resource front, water pipelines and a reservoir were constructed during this period (Figure 6.4b).

Figure 6.5a   Location of Automotive Industry: 1996-1999

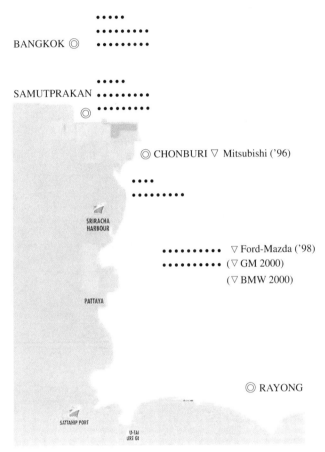

Source: Plotted from Table 6.8

1996-1999: After the completion of most features of the ODA–financed ESB Development Plan, the ESB area has emerged as the most attractive destination for new automotive industry investment. First, in response to the problem of the notorious traffic congestion in the Bangkok area, Mitsubishi decided to establish an assembling factory in Chonburi in 1996. Their example was followed by the Ford–Mazda AutoAlliance, GM and BMW who set up factories in Rayong in 1998 and 2000 (Figure 6.5a). Subsequently Japanese also suppliers set up factories in these areas. As discussed in the previous section, the businesses of Japanese suppliers are no longer confined within their *keiretsu* groups. As they see more

Figure 6.5b Infrastructure Development of Eastern Seaboard: 1996-1999

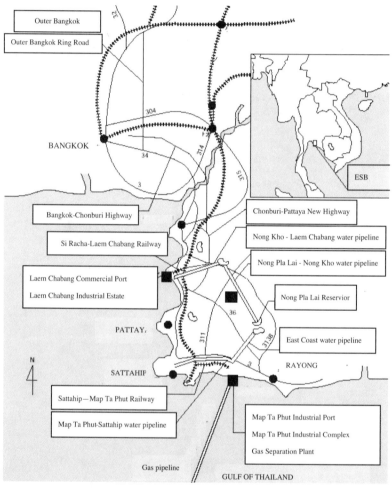

Source: JBIC (1999, 2001)

chances in the ESB area to do business beyond their group than in the traditional areas of Bangkok and Samut Prakan, the location of new investment ends up being in the ESB, although they still maintain existing business with other companies in the Bangkok and Samut Prakan areas. This strategy functions because of the construction of the Bangkok – Chonburi Highway and the Outer Bangkok Ring Road (and also because of the water pipeline between Nong Pla Lai and Nong Kho which has made the industrial estates in the ESB fully operative) (Figure 6.5b).

Table 6.8 shows that Thailand has been hosting more Japanese automotive suppliers than other major ASEAN members. 143 suppliers had invested in Thailand by 1999, while Malaysia had had 38 and Indonesia had had 72. In addition, the location of new investment in Thailand (whether assemblers or parts suppliers) has shifted over time from the Bangkok–Samut Prakan area in the 1980s to Chonburi in the first half of the 1990s, and to Rayong in the late 1990s when the country saw the largest number of new investments which have shaped the agglomeration of the automotive industry. This shift to the ESB is concomitant with the development of infrastructure in the area.

Table 6.8 Establishment of Japanese Parts Suppliers' Subsidiaries

	Thailand					(memorandum)	
	Bangkok	Samut Prakan	Chonburi	Rayong	Total	Malaysia	Indonesia
-1979	9	11	1	0	22	4	12
1980-89	6	11	1	0	28	17	11
1990-95	3	3	11	2	29	11	14
1996-99	14	5	7	18	64	6	35
Total	—	—	—	—	143	38	72

Source: Japan Auto Parts Industries Association
Note: Names of suppliers cannot be provided due to the restriction of the JAPIA

4.4. Attractiveness of the ESB

While many ASEAN countries produce auto vehicles, substantial agglomeration of the industry to make an exporting base has only been observed in Thailand.[23] Yonetani (2001) argues that assemblers have been restructuring their production network of small and inefficient units dispersed across the ASEAN region into one large scale factory, in response to the development of the ASEAN Free Trade Area (AFTA).[24] Thailand has turned out to be a leading destination for such factories. Thailand's strength is that it has an established reputation as a production and exporting base of pick-up trucks, which therefore encourages parts suppliers to invest in the country for a larger 'market' (i.e., assemblers).[25]

Botwick (2002), the president of the GM Thailand, considers Thailand's strengths to include: i) being considered as the sole exporting country in ASEAN; ii) having parts suppliers; iii) being located in the centre of Southeast Asia; iv) having a good commercial port; and v) having favourable investment conditions such as a promising domestic market, good labour and openness to competition.

A study of the JBIC (2001) shows that the main reasons for investors to locate their factories in the ESB area are: i) well-equipped transport infrastructure (e.g., roads and railways); ii) utility services such as water, electricity and communications; iii) the BOI's incentive measures; and iv) proximity to a port and to Bangkok.[26] In addition, according to the study, if the ESB Development Plan had not been implemented, the foreign investors operating in the ESB would have located in the following sites: Eastern Thailand (30.8% of the investors in the ESB), Bangkok Metropolitan area (23.1%), other areas of Thailand (2.6%), another country (7.7%), no investment (3.8%) and 'no idea' (32.1%). These results imply that the infrastructure created by the BOI's incentives did contribute to attracting FDI from those investors who had *already* decided to do business in Thailand. However, it is unclear whether the ESB attracted potential investors who had not decided their location.

5. Conclusion

It is highly likely that the development of the ESB area has substantially contributed to attracting investments in the automotive industry (as well as other industries) which has lead to agglomeration. Investors' behaviour in locating their factories has clearly coincided with the progress of the ESB Development Plan, i.e., the development of transportation, ports and industrial estates.

The concentration of investment has also been fostered by the Thai government's series of policy measures, i.e., investment incentives, local content requirement and higher customs for imported finished products. These measures and infrastructures as well as the prospective domestic market have as a whole offered good investment opportunities. In other words, provision of infrastructure does not solely account for the formation of the agglomeration.

The further development of the Thai automotive industry will depend on the progress of the ASEAN Free Trade Area. The country has been regarded as the regional centre of the automotive industry, and more and more manufacturers are concentrating their production in Thailand to seek for better utilization of the regional network of resources. For this trend to further develop, the ASEAN economies need to be more integrated. In addition, in order to increase international competitiveness so that the country can maintain its advantage in the automotive industry, as Yonetani (2002) suggests, Thailand needs to: i) develop new products (e.g., internationally strategic vehicles with small sizes in particular); ii) develop an information communication infrastructure; iii) further improve product quality; and iv) increase the credibility of delivery time. For this to happen, Japanese manufacturers in particular are urged to transfer their designing function to Thailand and to train local engineers. These measures will also contribute to doing business with non–Japanese manufacturers in the United States and Europe and hence increase the domestic (i.e., Thai) procurement rate by encouraging local companies to enter the market because of increased demand.

Notes

[1] For example, Kohama and Urata (2001) stress the importance of the host countries' condition in determining FDI location by Japanese companies. For FDI in transportation equipment in developing countries, the provision of electricity and other infrastructures, industrial agglomeration, and capacity of governance have been designated as major factors in attracting FDI (with statistical significance). Tejima (1998) argues that a significant shift in Japanese companies' motivation regarding FDI has been observed since the 1993-94 period. Traditional motivations for investing in foreign countries are: i) market seeking; ii) efficiency of production and costs; and iii) securing natural resources. In fact, Japanese investments since the 1980s onwards have been motivated by these three factors. The mid-1990s saw two emerging motivations: a) to establish an exporting base for third countries, and b) to supply parts to existing assembling factories. Interestingly, the two appeared to be important determinants of investment at the time when Japanese FDI in Asia started to resurge. In particular, the second determinant, b), is observed in automotive and electric/electronics industries in which a close network between assembling manufacturers and parts suppliers is essential to maintain competitiveness.

[2] This study centres on the formation of agglomeration and does not explicitly evaluate the impact of agglomeration on the Thai economy.

[3] Thailand's automotive industry initiated this period through ISI driven investment by Japanese assemblers.

[4] The reduction, however, did not work significantly as an incentive, due to the fact that customs revenue accounted for a major part of government revenue (Development Bank of Japan 2001).

[5] The World Competitiveness Yearbook of the IMD, Switzerland, shows that Thailand's ranking in 1998 was 41st out of 46 economies, while it was 26th in 1990 (IMD 2002).

[6] Exploration of gas fields in the Gulf of Siam had been carried since the 1960s. A submarine pipeline of 425km between a gas field found in 1973 and Map Ta Phut was later constructed.

[7] The plan was initiated as one of the main development plans of the country within the framework of the fifth and sixth Economic Plan (see Table 6.2).

[8] As of 1981, Thai industry was excessively concentrated in the Bangkok area where the manufacturing sector accounted for about 70% of total added value of the sector. The main reasons the ESB area was chosen were its proximity to Bangkok and the availability of a new topographical deep-sea port (JBIC 1999, 2001).

[9] After the completion of ODA-funded construction, the Industrial Estates Authority of Thailand (IEAT) expanded the estate to 804ha.

[10] Due to the fact that Bangkok Port is located along the Chao Phraya River, the port is shallow, and large ships with more than 10,000-12,000 of dead-weight tons cannot enter. Container vessels sailing between Bangkok and Europe and America were detained at Hong Kong and Singapore, and the cargoes were carried by feeder-service vessels in the region (JBIC 1999).

[11] TEU: Twenty-foot Equivalent Unit.

[12] The Thai government has been constructing additional terminals due for completion in 2009 to deal with a prospective increase in demand.

[13] Japanese companies control 80% of auto-assembly in Thailand, hence, Japanese manufacturers play a major role in the supply of parts (Higashi 2000).

[14] Thailand has lifted the local content requirement for automotive parts since 2000 to comply with the WTO's Trade-Related Investment Measures.

[15] The Thai government has changed the rates from time to time in order to achieve its policy objectives. In 1977, to reduce the trade deficit and boost the domestic industry, imports of CBU vehicles with an engine size of 2300 c.c. or less was banned. In addition, the government raised the tariff rates on CKD kits from 50% to 80%, and on CBU vehicles (engine capacity over 2300 c.c.) from 80% to 150%. It also raised the local content requirement on passenger cars from 25% to 50% for five years. In 1985, the tariff rate on CBU vehicles (2300 c.c. or less) was raised from 150% to 180%. During the 1990s, pressure from GATT urged the country to reduce tariff rates by 50% on CKD and CBU vehicles.

[16] Poapongsakorn and Wangdee (2003) point out as well that the expansion of the automotive industry was also fostered by the financial liberalization policy initiated in 1993. The policy allowed investors to obtain credit at low cost from foreign sources.

[17] As of 2002, the ratio of domestic procurement was 60-70%. If parts are domestically procured, the cost can be reduced by about 40%, avoiding the 33% tariff on imported parts and transport costs (Yonetani 2002).

[18] The main actors in this agglomeration are foreign companies from countries such as the US and Japan. The BOI coordinates business by matching foreign assemblers with domestic part suppliers in order to foster the latter, who also hire foreign engineers to improve operations (Hiratsuka 2002).

[19] In the General Industrial Zone, investors are given permission: to own land; to bring into the country alien skilled workers and experts; and to repatriate foreign exchange if such funds relate to imported capital, dividends or yields from such capital, or to foreign loans which are under special commitments with foreign creditors. In the Export Processing Zone, in accordance with the law on investment promotion, investors will be exempted from special fees, import duties and VAT on machinery, equipment, tools and apparatus, component parts, imported material for production as well as other products from the production processes; and will receive tax exemption or tax reimbursements on materials upon export, even though they are not exported but are brought into the Export Processing Zone. The ESIE also enjoys privileged status as the BOI's 'Zone III' in which there is: i) exemption of import duty on machinery; ii) corporate income tax exemption for eight years provided that a project with a capital investment of ten million baht or more (excluding cost of land and working capital) obtains ISO 9000 within two years from its start-up; and iii) exemption of import duty on raw or essential materials used in export production for five years (Hemaraj Land and Development 2002).

[20] The ESIE welcomes all industries except the petrochemical industry which is prohibited by regulation.

[21] Mori (2000) points out that the agglomeration in Thailand has been a simple concentration of foreign companies, and in future new types of intra-industry division of labour are expected to emerge. For local companies, however, it would become harder to take part in production processes, as the technological level is low compared to foreign counterparts. This implies that a limit to the industrial agglomeration of ASEAN is likely.

[22] During the mid-1990s, a number of industrial estates were constructed along National Road No.331 in Rayong Province by private developers in cooperation with the IEAT, including Chonburi Industrial Estate (1991), and Amata City Rayong Industrial Estate (1996).

[23] The case of Malaysia is quite the opposite. The country has been trying to foster the automotive industry by establishing a national car manufacturer, Proton. However, no agglomeration of parts suppliers has taken place, and car manufacturing in Malaysia consists only of assembling (Ito Chu 2001).

[24] AFTA is planning that the member countries reduce tariffs for intra-ASEAN trade to 0-5 percent in 2003 and to zero in 2010. The original intention behind the concentration of industry in Thailand was to export only to regional markets. In practice, largely due to the 1997 financial crisis and the economic downturn in the region, exports have been absorbed by more than 100 countries rather than just ASEAN members.

[25] In addition, Iseki (2002) argues that Thailand (including Bangkok and the ESB area) as a regional centre of the automotive industry has the advantage of intra-regional complementarity, meaning that its regional networks and business risks compare favourably to those of China.

[26] The BOI divides the country into three zones depending on the incentives. The Rayong Province and Laem Chabang Industrial Estate are classified as the Third zone in which investors are entitled to enjoy the maximum benefits offered to the zones.

References

Botwick, W.S. 2002. Interview by the Japan Automobile Manufacturers Association, *JAMAGAZINE*, October.

Development Bank of Japan. 2001. *Thai Kougyoka no Gaiyo* (The Outlook of Thai Industrialization), S-20, mimeo.

Hemaraj Land and Development. 2002. 'Welcome to "Detroit of the East" – Eastern Seaboard Industrial Estate (Rayong)', http://www.hemaraj.com.

Higashi, S. 2002. 'Tohnan Asia: Thai – Thai ni Okeru Jidosya Buhin Oyobi Kanagata Sangyo no Genjo' (Southeast Asia: Thailand – Current Situation of the Automotive Parts and Die Casting Industry in Thailand), in Yamagata, T. (ed) Nihon to Asia no Kikai Sangyo – Kyoso-ryoku wo Tsuketa Asia Syokoku-tono Kyozon ni Mukete (The Machinery Industry of Japan and Asia – Towards a Co-existence with Increasingly Competitive Asian Countries), Institute of International Economy, http://www.ide.go.jp/Japanese/Publish/Report/pdf/2001_217_06.pdf.

Hiratsuka, D. (2002) 'Globalisation Jidai no Nikkei-Kigyo no Thai Shinshutsu Jirei (Case study: Japanese Companies' Investment in Thailand in the Era of Globalisation)', in Taito-suru Asia Shokoku to Gifu-ken Seizo-gyo no Global Tenkai (Rising Asian Countries and the Global Development of the Manufacturing Industry of Gifu Prefecture), Gifu Economic and Industrial Promotion Centre, http://www.gpc.pref.gifu.jp/cyousa/houkoku/13/asia.html.

IMD. 2002. 'World Competitiveness Scoreboard', *World Competitiveness Yearbook*, www01.imd.ch/documents/wcy/content/pastranking.pdf.

Iseki, T. 2002. *Bangkok ha Detroit no Yume wo Hutatabi Miruka – Tsu-ka Kikigo no Thai Jido-shasangyojijo* (Does Bangkok See the Dream of Detroit Again? The Situation of Thailand's Automotive Industry after the Financial Crisis), Sanwa Research Institute, mimeo.

Ito Chu (2001) Saikin no Asia Josei (Asia's Recent Situation), Survey Report, 23 April, http://www.imc-itochu.co.jp/imc_web/chousa/tokubetsu/asia_1.html.

Japan Bank for International Cooperation (JBIC). (1999) Eastern Seaboard Development Plan Impact Evaluation, http://www.jbic.go.jp/english/oec/post/2000/pdf/01-01.pdf.

———. (2001) JICA/OECF Joint Evaluation: Thailand, Eastern Seaboard Development Program, http://www.jbic.go.jp/english/evaluation/report/pdf/2001-0420.pdf.

Kimata, K. (2002) 'Toyo no Detroit – Thai' (Detroit of the East), Aichi Boeki Joho, 265.

Kohama, H. and S. Urata. (2001) Higashi Asia no Jizoku-teki Hatten (The Sustainable Economic Development of East Asia), Tokyo: Keiso Shobo.

LCB Container Terminal 1 Ltd (2003) Statistic Bangkok Port and Laem Chabang Port (TEU), http://www.lcb1.com/contents/links/stat_bklcb.htm.

Mori, M. (2000) 'Thai ni Okeru Jidosha Sangyo-Shuseki no Keisei to Hatten (The Formation and Development of the Agglomeration of the Automotive Industry in Thailand)', RIM Kan-Taiheiyo Business Joho, 51, October, http://www.jri.co.jp/research/pacific/RIM/2000 RIM200004automobile.html.

Nardone, D. (2002) Detroit of the East, http://www.hemaraj.com/download/Detroit_of_the_East.pdf.

Office of Industrial Economics, Government of Thailand (2002) Automotive Industry in Thailand, http://www.oie.go.th/index_en.asp.

Poapongsakorn, N. and C. Wangdee (2003) The Thailand Automotive Industry, http://www.thaiautoparts.or.th/industrial_focus/images/auto_thailand.doc.

Tejima, S. (1998) 'Chokusetsu Toshi to Keizai Kaihatsu' (Foreign Direct Investment and Economic Development), Kaigai Toshi Kenkyusyo-ho, June, Tokyo: Export Import Bank of Japan.

Yonetani, H. (2001) 'Thai no Seizogyo no Jittai wo Yasashiku Kaisetsu-suru Series (2)' (The Situation of Thai Industry Simply Explained), JETRO Bangkok, http://www.jetrobkk.or.th/japanese/s3_9_2_4.html.

———. (2002) 'Thai-eno Toushi: Jidosya, Electronics Sangyo wo Toshite-miru Thai no Toshi Kankyo' (Investment in Thailand: the Investment Environment of Thailand through the Automotive and Electronics Industries), JETRO Bangkok, http://www3.jetro.go.jp/iv/j/fdi/step02/semminer/pdf/sem_bscs.pdf.

Appendix A

Eastern Seaboard Development Plan – List of Japanese ODA–Loaned Projects

Area	Project name	Loan agreement	Closing loan disbursement	Amount (1)
ESB	Development Plan Engineering Study	Sep. 1983	Sep. 1986	1,720
Map Ta Phut area Development	① Industrial/Urban Complex	Oct. 1985	Oct. 1991	3,207
	② Port (I)	Sep. 1984	Mar. 1995	5,611
	Port (II)	Oct. 1985	Sep. 1993	16,045
	Port (III)	Sep. 1991	Feb. 1997	3,395
	③ Gas separation plant	Jul. 1982	Jul. 1985	15,000
Laem Chabang area Development	④ Port (I)	Sep. 1984	Jun. 1993	4,172
	Port (II)	Nov. 1986	Nov. 1993	12,283
	Port (III)	Feb. 1990	May 1995	6,436
	⑤ Industrial estate (I)	Oct. 1985	Oct. 1992	2,922
	Industrial estate (II)	Sep. 1987	Sep. 1992	3,003
Water Resource Development/ Water Pipeline Project	⑥ Nong Pla Lai	Sep. 1988	Jan. 1995	4,357
	⑦ East Coast (Dok Krai – Map Ta Phut)	Jul. 1982	Apr. 1987	6,570
	⑧ Map Ta Phut – Sattahip water pipeline	Nov. 1988	Mar. 1994	1,459
	⑨ Nong Kho – Laem Chabang (I)	Sep. 1984	Apr. 1987	144
	Nong Kho – Laem Chabang (II)	Oct. 1985	Oct. 1990	1,363
	⑩ Nong Pla Lai – Nong Kho (I)	Feb. 1990	Jun. 1995	204
	Nong Pla Lai – Nong Kho (II)	Jan. 1993	May 1999	6,362
Railway	⑪ Si Racha – Laem Chabang	Sep. 1988	Jul. 1996	1,013
	⑫ Sattahip – Map Ta Phut	Sep. 1988	Jan. 1997	3,002
	⑬ Klong Sip Kao – Kaeng Khoi	Feb. 1990	Dec. 1999	8,158

Area	Project name	Loan agreement	Closing loan disbursement	Amount (1)
Road	⑭ Chonbri – Pattaya New Highway (I)	Nov. 1988	Mar. 1994	4,117
	Chonbri – Pattaya New Highway (II)	Sep. 1991	Jan. 1997	5,670
	⑮ Bangkok – Chonbri Highway (I)	Dec. 1990	Apr. 1999	15,497
	Bangkok – Chonbri Highway (II)	Sep. 1993	Jan. 2000	21,627
	⑯ Outer Bangkok Ring Road (I)	Dec. 1990	Apr. 1999	12,958
	Outer Bangkok Ring Road (II)	Sep. 1993	Jan. 2000	12,473
Total				178,768

Source: JBIC (1999)

Note: (1) ¥ million

(2) In addition to the loaned projects above, Japan provided technical assistance in the following sectors: (a) feasibility study (F/S) in water resources development including pipelines; (b) master plan (M/P) and F/S of port construction and operation; (c) M/P and F/S for industrial development of the Leam Chabang area; (d) advice on investment promotion; and (e) an environmental protection project (JBIC 2001).

Appendix B
Automotive Companies in the Eastern Seaboard Industrial Estate (Rayong)

Assemblers

Company	Product
AutoAlliance (Thailand) Co.,Ltd (Ford&Mazda)	One Ton Pick-Up Assembly Plant
General Motors (Thailand) Ltd.	Passenger Car Manufacturing & Assembly for Export & Domestic

Parts Suppliers

Company	Product
Arvin Meritor Co., Ltd.	Exhaust Assemblies
Asno Horie (Thailand) Co.,Ltd.	Auto Fuel Tanks
Bendix (Thailand) Ltd.	Automotive Disc Pads
Aoyama Thai Co., Ltd.	Fasteners
Bridgestone Matelpha (Thailand) Co., Ltd.	Steel Cords for Tyres
Cataler (Thailand) Co.,Ltd.	Catalysts, Motorcycle Catalysts, Catalytic Slurry
CCI Automotive Products Co.Ltd.	(CCI Corp. Japan) Brake Fluids for Auto
Clarion Electronics (Thailand) Co., Ltd.	Car Audio
Dana Spicer (Thailand) Ltd.	Drive Shafts & Axles
Daifuku (Thailand) Ltd.	Material Handling System Auto Industry
DE-STA-CO Manufacturing Ltd.	Valves and Tubular
EFTEC (Thailand) Co.,Ltd.	PVC Plastisols
Engelhard Chemcat (Thailand) Ltd.	Auto Catalysts
FMP Group (Thailand) Limited	Automotive Disc Pads
Furukawa Unic (Thailand) Co., Ltd.	Cranes for Trucks
Gates Unitta (Thailand) Co., Ltd.	Rubber Belts
General Seating (Thailand) Ltd.	Auto Parts Seats
GKN Driveshafts (Thailand) Co.,Ltd.	Drive shafts
Halla Climate Control (Thailand) Co., Ltd.	Radiator & Air Conditioner Systems

Parts Suppliers *(continued)*

Company	Product
Hicom Automotive Plastics (Thailand) Limited	Bumpers
ICT Automotive Co., Ltd.	Assembly of Tuk Tuk
Inergy Automotive Systems (Thailand) Ltd.	Plastic Filter Pipes, Plastic Fuel Tanks
Ingress Autoventures Co.,Ltd.	Doorsashes, Weather strips
Jideco (Thailand) Co., Ltd.	Electrical and Mechanical Components
Johnson Control&Summit Interiors Ltd.	Auto Seats
Kanemitsu Pulley Co.,Ltd.	Pulleys for Automotives
Kansai Resin (Thailand) Co.,Ltd.	Paint Resin
Keiper Summit Industry (Thailand) Co., Ltd.	Auto Seat Recliners
Kobatech (Thailand) Co., Ltd.	Fuel Injection Pump Part & Injection Parts
Kobayashi High Precision (Thailand) Co.,Ltd.	Shaft Roller
Komatsu Seiki (Thailand) Co.,Ltd.	Plate orifices and armatures
Li Tai Alloy Co., Ltd.	Alloy Wheel
Logistic Alliance (Thailand) Co., Ltd	Knock Down Making and Parts Packing
Maruyasu Industries (Thailand) Co.,Ltd.	Auto parts for Brake Fuel Tube and other parts
Maxxis International (Thailand) Co., Ltd.	Rubber Tyre
MSM (Thailand) Co., Ltd.	Electronic Part and Auto Spring
Nakatan Thai Industry Co.,Ltd.	Motorcycle Parts Forging Parts
Nisshinbo Somboon Automotive Co., Ltd.	Brake Linings, Disc Pad Brake Shoes, Drum Brakes
NT Seimitsu (Thailand) Co., Ltd.	Fuel Injection Pump Parts
NTN Manufacturing (Thailand) Co.,Ltd.	Bearings & Constant Velocity Joints
PBR Automotive (Thailand) Co.,Ltd.	Brake Calipers
PEC Manufacturing (Thailand) Ltd.	Display CRT Mold and Dies / Fuses for Automotive
Prixcar Services (Thailand) Co.,Ltd.	Automobile Touch-up
Piolax (Thailand) Ltd	Auto Parts
Plasess (Thailand) Co., Ltd.	Plastic Parts for Automotives
Plastimer Precision Co.,Ltd.	Plastic Injection Molding
Saint-Gobain Sekurit (Thailand) Co., Ltd.	Auto Glass
Sanko Gosei Technology (Thailand) Ltd.	Plastic Injection Molding
Scania (Thailand) Co., Ltd.	Trucks & Buses
Seimitsu Thai Co., Ltd.	Injector Body
Sekisui S-LEC (Thailand) Co.,Ltd.	Film for Safety-Glass
Siam Chuyo Co.,Ltd.	Springs and heat treatment
Siam Metal Technology Co.,Ltd.	Auto Forging Parts
Siam Nissan Casting Co.,Ltd.	Auto Engine Casting

Parts Suppliers   (*continued*)

Company	Product
S.N.D. Autoparts Import Export Co., Ltd.	Retouched Used Cars for export
Somboon Somic Manufacturing Co., Ltd.	Suspension Ball Joints
Star Technologies Industrial Ltd.	Power Transmission Belt
Steel Processing (Thailand) Co.,Ltd.	Wire Rods for Cold Heading
Takao Eastern Co.,Ltd.	Auto Suspension Member Parts Forging Plant
Thai Asakawa Co.,Ltd.	Fasteners for Auto & Truck
Thai Fine Sinter Co.,Ltd.	Sintering Metal
Thai Kohwa Precision Co.,Ltd.	ABS System Parts
Togo Seisakusyo (Thailand) Co.,Ltd.	Hose clips and torsion springs
Toyoda Machine Works (Thailand) Co. Ltd.	Power Steering Pumps
Toyodabo Filtration System (Thailand) Co.,Ltd.	Oil Filter
TRW LucasVarity Division Co., Ltd.	Chassis Supply
TRW Steering & Suspension Co.Ltd.	Steering & Suspension
TT Techno-Park Thailand Co.,Ltd.	Outsourcing services for Toyota Tsusho Techno Park
U-Shin (Thailand) Co.,Ltd	Car Key Sets
Visteon (Thailand) Limited	Auto Parts Instrument Plastic
Vittoria Rubber Industries (Thailand) Co.Ltd.	Rubber Tyres
World Thread Limited	Polyester Filament Thread
Yamasei Kogyo Co.Ltd.	Hydraulic Piping System
Yokohama Rubber (Thailand) Co.Ltd.	Sealants, Primers
Yorozu (Thailand) Co.Ltd.	Auto Suspension Member Parts Forging Plant
Yuan Da Electronics (Thailand) Co., Ltd.	Membrane for the car speaker
Zexel Clutch (Thailand) Co.Ltd.	Magnetic Clutches for compressors
Zexel Valeo Compressor Co.Ltd.	Compressors for Auto Air Conditioners

Source: Hemaraj Land and Development
Note: The list is as of August 2003.

7
The Role of Agricultural Exports Reconsidered: A Case of Three Southeast Asian Countries

Masayoshi Honma

1. Introduction

Expansion of agricultural exports is considered one of the most promising means of increasing incomes and augmenting foreign exchange earnings, particularly for a country stepping up its development efforts (Johnston and Mellor 1961). It is generally accepted that the supply of foreign exchange is one of the standard contributions of the agricultural sector to the promotion of economic development (Myint 1975). Therefore, agricultural exports are very important for many developing countries as a generator of overall economic growth.[1]

But in the 1950s and 1960s, it was widely believed that rapid growth in developing economies would not be achieved through increases in agricultural (primary commodity) exports because of inevitable deterioration in the terms of trade against primary commodities due to the forces limiting demand for primary products.[2] This belief underlay the foundation of import substitution strategy. Even in the 1980s the view of primary export pessimism that export prospects for agricultural products are determined predominantly by world demand was argued.[3]

Such pessimism may apply to agricultural exports as a whole since both price and income elasticities of demand for agricultural products are low in general. However, it is not necessarily true that demand is a serious constraint of export for individual commodities in each country. For a small country, the price elasticity of demand for exports of a homogeneous commodity is large and there is a huge potential to be gained if it is successful in reducing the export price by more efficient production. There are also many agricultural commodities whose demand elasticities are relatively large in terms of both price and income, such as horticultural products and processed foods. To take advantage of such opportunities for gains from agricultural exports, it is necessary that exporting countries have an ability to adjust to dynamic changes in international markets and to develop markets for commodities with large price and income elasticities of demand. Therefore, agricultural export performances of individual countries are the result of not only the external factors (demand forces) but also the internal factors (changes in supply side abilities).

The purpose of this chapter is to reconsider the roles of agricultural exports through assessing the performances of three Asian countries, Indonesia, the Philippines and Thailand over the four decades since the 1960s. First, we take a brief overview of agricultural export performances among the three. Then we try to identify the sources of the differences in performance of agricultural exports. A model is introduced to explain the growth and pattern of agricultural exports by external market conditions (world demand) and internal factors (competitiveness and export diversification), applied to aggregated agricultural exports. Next, further investigation is conducted to explore the structure of demand for exports, by commodity, in selected markets using a formal demand system model. Correspondingly, transmissibility of export prices to import markets is statistically examined. Based on these results of the statistical analyses, we conclude the sources of different performance in agricultural exports and discuss the meaning for economic growth in developing countries.

2. Performance of Agricultural Exports

2.1 Total Exports of Agricultural Products

Agricultural exports of the three Asian countries were not much different in total volume in the 1960s. As Figure 7.1 shows, export values of the three countries were stable at US$400–500 million. But afterward the agricultural export performances were clearly different among the three. The Philippines remains at a low level of agricultural exports, which is now much behind those of Indonesia and Thailand. Thailand recorded an export growth rate of agricultural products at 8.0% per year for the period from 1961–63 to 1999–2001. The Indonesian export growth rate was 6.6% per year for the same period while the average growth rate of the Philippines was just 3.3% per year.

It was Thailand's agricultural exports that grew first in the 1970s. The growth rate of Thai agricultural exports in the 1970s was more than 20% per year in US dollars and about 10% per year in volume at a 1989–91 constant price during the period (Table 7.1). Indonesia followed Thailand to increase agricultural exports in US dollars but its performance in volume at constant price was not much different from that of the Philippines in the 1970s (Figure 7.2).

Figure 7.1   Agricultural Exports of Three Asian Countries in US$

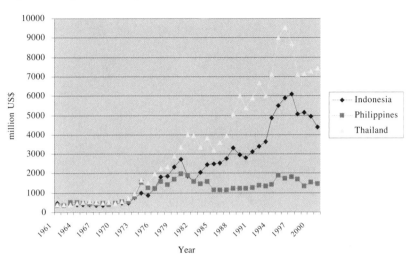

Source: FAO, FAOSTAT database.

Figure 7.2   Agricultural Exports of Three Asian Countries in at 1989-91 Price

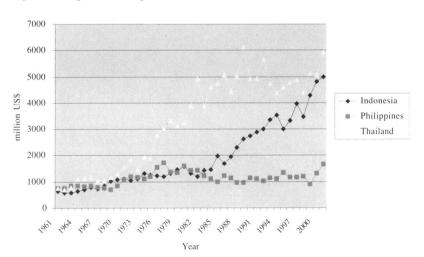

Source: FAO, FAOSTAT database.

Figure 7.3   Share of Agricultural Exports in Total Commodity Exports of Three
Asian Countries

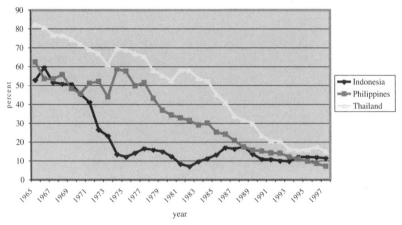

Source: FAO, FAOSTAT database and United Nations, Commodity Trade Statistics.

Table 7.1   Agricultural Export Performance of Three Asian Countries

Three year average of:	1961-63	1969-71	1979-81	1989-91	1999-2001
(a) Total value of agricultural exports (million US$):					
Indonesia	425	459	2314	2962	4817
Philippines	420	485	1849	1240	1447
Thailand	391	518	3410	5760	7285
(b) Growth rate of (a) from previous period (compound annual rate, %):					
Indonesia	-	1.0	17.5	2.5	5.0
Philippines	-	1.8	14.3	–3.9	1.6
Thailand	-	3.6	20.7	5.4	2.4
(c) Agricultural export value at 1989-91 price (million US$):					
Indonesia	596	1067	1447	2757	4700
Philippines	787	877	1462	1069	1291
Thailand	756	1341	3414	5325	5369
(d) Growth rate of (c) from previous period (compound annual rate, %):					
Indonesia	-	7.5	3.1	6.7	5.5
Philippines	-	1.4	5.2	–3.1	1.9
Thailand	-	7.4	9.8	4.5	0.1

Source: FAO, FAOSTAT database.

In the 1980s, differences in agricultural export performance among the three countries became clearer. As shown in Table 7.1, Thailand and Indonesia continued to grow their agricultural exports at a growth rate of 5.4% and 2.5% respectively in US dollars. But the Philippines' growth rate became negative and the gap between the Philippines and the other two was widening. During this period, the Philippines faced political instability that worsened overall economic performance and the country's external terms of trade. Meanwhile, the agricultural export volume of Indonesia at 1989–91 price increased at 6.7% per year which was greater than that of Thailand. This performance did not lead to the same growth rate of export value in US dollars because the unit value index of Indonesian agricultural exports fell from 149 in 1979–81 to 100 in 1989–91 (Table 7.1).

Thailand expanded its agricultural exports in US dollars in the 1990s until the currency crisis took place in 1997. Its export value reached US$9.5 billion in 1996, though it was down to US$7.3 billion on average from 1999–2001. Indonesia also increased its agricultural exports and reached US$6.1 billion in 1996. It was, though, down to US$4.8 billion on average from 1999–2001. On the other hand, Philippine agricultural exports stayed at a low level of only US$1.4 billion on average from 1999–2001, which is still less than the 1979–81 level and one fifth and one third of Thailand and Indonesia, respectively. It is noted that despite the positive growth rate in nominal terms (in US$) for Thai agricultural exports, its export volume in real terms (at 1989–91 price) declined in the 1990s and it was 2001 when it recovered the level as in 1989. This resulted from the fact that Thai exports of traditionally important commodities declined sharply while the overall export unit value index increased, which contributed to the positive export growth in nominal terms during the period. Namely, it indicates some structural changes in Thai agricultural exports in the 1990s.

Figure 7.3 shows changes in share of agricultural exports in total commodity exports of the three countries since 1965. In the 1960s the share of agriculture in exports was 50%–60% in Indonesia and the Philippines, while it was around 80% in Thailand. Agriculture's share in Indonesia declined sharply in the early 1970s because of the rapid increases in its oil export price during the period of the first oil crisis. On the other hand, agricultural share in the Philippines and Thailand increased in 1974 due to food prices soaring in the world market. The recent share of agricultural exports has declined to 10%–15% for each country.

Combining Figure 7.3 with Figure 7.1 indicates that recent rapid growth of agricultural exports in Indonesia had kept pace with that of non-agricultural exports, which resulted in the stable share of agriculture in commodity exports. In the Philippines, the agricultural share in exports declined naturally as agricultural exports had been stagnant for the last two decades. The agricultural share in exports of Thailand had also decreased sharply since the early 1980s despite the rapid growth of agricultural exports. This means that the Thai growth rate of non-agricultural exports was much higher than that of agricultural exports due to the rapid industrialization. Thailand appears to shift its comparative advantage from agriculture to industry although the performance of agricultural exports was also prominent.[4] The fact that agricultural exports as well as industrial exports were successful suggests that the structural adjustment in the process of industrialization had been smooth in Thailand, as far as changes in export composition are concerned, until the recent currency crisis.

2.2 Export Performance by Commodity

For further investigation of structural changes in agricultural exports, it is necessary to examine the export performance by commodity. Table 7.2 shows the export performance in terms of export quantity and value of the major five commodities for each of three Asian countries. The export value of the five commodities accounts for 60% to 80% of the total value of agricultural exports in each county, depending on country and year.

For Indonesia, the most important commodity in agricultural exports is natural rubber, which accounted for 67% of total value of agricultural exports in 1961–63, though the share declined to 17% in 1999–2001. The export quantity of natural rubber has been relatively stable and increased by 113% from 1961–63 to 1999–2001 (2% per year). Although natural rubber is still important in Indonesian agricultural exports, palm oil became dominant among its agricultural exports. In the 1960s and 70s, exports of coffee grew rapidly and occupied 23% of Indonesian agricultural exports in 1979–81. The growth of coffee exports was supported not only by increases in quantity but also by favourable price movements. Coffee exports, however, faced stagnation in the 1980s and 1990s. Coffee's share in value decreased to less than 7% in 1999–2001.

Meanwhile, Indonesia's export of palm oil constantly increased and its share in the value of agricultural exports reached 23% in 1999–2001. Outstanding was the export quantity expansion in the 1990s that resulted in increases in the value of palm oil exports by 240% during that decade. Tea used to be one of the major items among Indonesian exports but its importance was reduced as the share declined to 2.1% of agricultural exports in 1999–2001. Instead, cocoa beans emerged as an important crop in agricultural exports. Cocoa beans contributed 5.5% in value to agricultural exports in 1999–2001. As a whole, Indonesia seems to have been successful in diversifying export commodities not by replacing traditional products like natural rubber and tea, but by increasing exports of other products efficiently while maintaining the traditional exports as well.

The Philippines had drastic changes in the structure of its agricultural exports in the late 1970s and 1980s. In the 1960s and 1970s, the most

Table 7.2 Export Quantity and Value of Major Commodities in Three Asian Countries

Three year average of:	1961-63	1969-71	1979-81	1989-91	1999-2001
Indonesia					
Cocoa Beans					
Quantity (1000 tons)	0.05	0.40	5.0	99.7	323.2
Value (million US$)	0.05	0.24	10.5	96.1	267.3
Coffee, Green					
Quantity (1000 tons)	64.5	101.9	223.2	386.2	312.6
Value (million US$)	14.9	61.4	538.7	412.1	318.1
Oil of Palm					
Quantity (1000 tons)	109.1	182.4	356.8	1148.4	4104.1
Value (million US$)	19.7	34.6	191.6	323.3	1094.1
Rubber, Natural Dry					
Quantity (1000 tons)	672.1	787.1	872.6	1108.2	1431.9
Value (million US$)	284.1	231.9	965.1	895.5	833.2
Tea					
Quantity (1000 tons)	29.6	39.5	66.4	112.0	101.1
Value (million US$)	21.4	18.7	99.0	162.3	103.1
Philippines					
Bananas					
Quantity (1000 tons)	-	132.5	883.3	877.6	1683.0
Value (million US$)	-	7.6	111.6	155.4	276.6
Oil of Coconuts					
Quantity (1000 tons)	145.0	316.3	920.6	912.6	977.8
Value (million US$)	35.1	84.5	614.3	345.4	407.9
Pineapples, Canned					
Quantity (1000 tons)	50.7	79.3	183.0	189.0	229.7
Value (million US$)	9.9	19.3	81.4	91.7	88.0
Sugar, Total (Raw Equiv.)					
Quantity (1000 tons)	1060.4	1223.4	1380.9	244.8	112.9
Value (million US$)	149.2	187.2	467.4	105.3	46.0
Tobacco Leaves					
Quantity (1000 tons)	21.9	39.0	25.6	15.9	12.8
Value (million US$)	11.2	14.9	36.5	26.8	23.1

Table 7.2   Export Quantity and Value of Major Commodities in Three Asian Countries   (*continued*)

Three year average of:	1961-63	1969-71	1979-81	1989-91	1999-2001
Thailand					
Cassava, Total (Cassava Equiv.)					
Quantity (1000 tons)	1626.5	3206.2	13437.5	22061.8	14602.6
Value (million US$)	20.4	53.2	655.6	915.9	406.4
Maize					
Quantity (1000 tons)	594.6	1551.2	2237.0	1216.0	199.4
Value (million US$)	30.8	91.5	334.2	158.1	25.4
Rice, Total (Milled Rice Equiv.)					
Quantity (1000 tons)	1420.9	1226.0	2873.7	4887.2	6888.4
Value (million US$)	163.2	134.2	975.9	1350.4	1722.4
Rubber, Natural Dry					
Quantity (1000 tons)	188.5	286.6	482.7	1103.7	1842.0
Value (million US$)	98.1	109.0	568.7	922.8	1110.0
Sugar, Total (Raw Equiv.)					
Quantity (1000 tons)	33.1	82.5	920.7	2803.5	3652.0
Value (million US$)	2.7	8.4	273.3	673.4	628.3

Source: FAO, FAOSTAT database.

important commodity among agricultural exports was sugar, occupying 35% to 40% of agricultural exports in value. Exports of sugar in the 1960s and 1970s were supported by the quota system, in which producers could have access to the U.S. market at premium prices. Because of this quota system, the Philippines' sugar was exported exclusively to the U.S. until the quota system ended in 1973. The sugar sector in the Philippines lost competitiveness without the supporting system and sugar exports shrank rapidly. Export quantity of sugar was just 113,000 tons in 1999–2001, which was less than one twelfth of the level in 1979–81 and contributed only 3% to agricultural exports in value. Instead of sugar, coconut oil emerged as a major commodity among the Philippines' agricultural exports. The share of coconut oil in agricultural exports became 33% in 1979–81 and stayed at 28% in 1999–2001. Exports of coconut oil also depend greatly on the U.S. market. About half of the coconut oil exported goes to the U.S.

In the 1970s, banana became a major export commodity for the Philippines, targeting mainly the Japanese market. Banana exports accounted for 19% of agricultural exports in 1999–2001 and about two thirds are exported to Japan. Canned pineapples and tobacco leaves also played a role in the Philippines' agricultural exports, but remain at 6.1%

and 1.6%, respectively in the share of agricultural exports in 1999–2001. The Philippines' agricultural exports performed well in the 1960s and 70s, but faced difficulty in the era of domestic deregulation and international trade liberalization. There are no export substitutes for sugar, which lost its competitiveness in international markets. Exports of other products are slow to grow and most remain at or less than the 1979–81 level.

Thailand's agricultural exports had the most prominent performance among the three Asian countries for the last four decades. The most important commodity in Thai agricultural exports is rice, which occupied 42% of the total value of the agricultural exports in 1961–63, though the share declined to 24% in 1999–2001. The second most important commodity is natural rubber that accounted for 25% in agricultural exports in 1961–63. The share of natural rubber declined to 16% in 1989–91 and stayed at 15% in 1999–2001. In terms of quantity, exports of natural rubber expanded by 130% during the 1980s (8.7% per year) that led Thailand to become the world's largest exporter of natural rubber.

The agricultural export growth of Thailand ahead of Indonesia and the Philippines in the 1960s and 1970s was supported by the rapid export expansion of cassava and maize. Cassava exports increased from 1.6 to 3.2 million tons during the 1960s and reached 13.4 million tons in 1979–81 that contributed 19% to Thai agricultural exports. Exports of maize grew from 0.6 to 1.6 million tons during the 1960s and reached 2.2 million tons by 1979–81. The share of maize in the value of agricultural exports was as high as 18% in 1969–71 and 10% in 1979–81. However, exports of these two commodities became stagnant in the 1980s and 1990s. Exports of cassava declined from 22.1 million tons in 1989–91 to 14.6 million tons in 1999–2001 despite the favourable price (unit value), and the share of cassava in agricultural exports reduced to 5.6% in 1999–2001. Declines in cassava exports resulted mainly from the reduction of quotas in the European Union market, with which Thailand had an agreement on the total export amount of cassava products.

The reduction of maize exports was more drastic. Exports of maize were halved during the 1980s and about disappeared thereafter. Maize exports were less than 0.2 million tons in 1999–2001, which was only 0.3% of the value of Thai agricultural exports. This rapid decline of maize exports was caused by termination in 1981 of the trade contract with Japan that was the major market for Thai maize. Increases in domestic demand for maize for feeding purposes also resulted in the decline of maize exports. Thailand indeed later became a net importer of maize.

This is mainly a story of structural changes in Thai agricultural exports and explains why the growth rate of Thai agricultural exports in real terms (volume at 1989–91 price) slowed in the 1980s and became stagnant in the 1990s, as seen in Table 7.1. Unlike the Philippines, however, Thailand was successful in increasing production and exports of other products to replace the products that lost competitiveness in international markets. Strengthened in exports were natural rubber and sugar, for example. Both exports increased in quantity with favourable prices more than offsetting the negative effects of export reduction in cassava and maize, and contributed to a high growth rate of total value of agricultural exports in the 1990s.

3. Agricultural Exports by Destination

In the examination of structural changes in agricultural exports, it is useful to look at partners of each country over time. The FAO data on agricultural trade does not give trade flow data but the United Nations *Commodity Trade Statistics* provides the data of trade flows. Table 7.3 was created using the UN data on trade flows in U.S. dollars of SITC code 0 that is the aggregate of food and live animals to indicate the composition of food exports from the three Asian countries by destination.

For Indonesia, the most important partner in the 1960s (1965–67) was the E.E.C. to which Indonesia exported 41% of total food exports. The U.S. was second-most important and purchased 27% of Indonesian food exports. However, the importance of these two destinations as export destinations has declined and the share of each became 15% in 1999–2001. Instead, agricultural exports to Japan increased and Japan's share in Indonesian food exports jumped to 32% in 1999–2001 from 13% in 1965–67. It is also noted that Indonesian food exports to other ASEAN countries increased gradually as well as to other Asian countries. This means that Indonesia diversified its food exports to more partners over the decades shifting destinations from the E.E.C. and the U.S. to mainly Asian markets. The share of Asian developing countries (sum of ASEAN 6, China, and other Asian countries) in Indonesian food exports was 29% in 1999–2001.

Philippine food exports in the 1960s depended exclusively on the U.S. market. The United States purchased 82% of Philippine food exports in 1965-1967. The share exported to the United States declined sharply by the 1980s because of the termination of special treatments of Philippine exports in the United States such as the sugar quota described above. The U.S. share in Philippine food exports was 25% in 1999-2001. The Philippines strengthened its food exports to Japan over the decades and Japan's share soared to 35% in 1999–2001 from 6% in 1965–67. The Philippines diversified the destinations of food exports mainly to Asia and about 20% of Philippine food exports were for Asian developing countries in 1999–2001.

Thailand's food exports were well diversified even in the 1960s compared with Indonesia and the Philippines. As a single partner Japan was most important, purchasing 20% of Thai food exports in 1965–67.

Table 7.3 Composition of Food Exports from Three Asian Countries by Destination, %

	Indonesia			Philippines			Thailand		
Year	1965-67	1980-82	1999-2001	1965-67	1980-82	1999-2001	1965-67	1980-82	1999-2001
Destination:									
ASEAN-6*	7.9	11.5	15.6	0.2	9.3	4.8	30.9	17.4	12.8
Japan	13.2	23.9	32.4	5.7	21.6	34.8	20.3	10.3	19.3
China	0.7	0.7	3.1	0.0	2.9	2.1	0.0	2.8	7.4
Other Asia	5.4	5.1	10.0	0.7	9.2	13.3	29.4	11.0	10.7
Middle East	0.2	1.4	1.3	0.0	5.0	3.3	3.9	10.9	6.9
Africa	0.0	2.8	1.8	0.0	1.0	1.0	3.5	7.8	5.8
EC-12**	40.7	29.8	15.1	9.3	12.6	10.1	7.9	24.3	17.3
Latin America	0.0	0.2	0.6	0.0	0.8	0.4	0.0	0.8	0.7
USA	26.6	19.1	15.3	82.2	26.3	24.9	3.6	5.8	11.4
Rest of World	5.3	5.5	4.8	1.9	11.3	5.3	0.5	8.9	7.7
Total	100	100	100	100	100	100	100	100	100

Source: United Nations, Commodity Trade Statistics.
Notes: * Brunei, Indonesia, Malaysia, Philippines, Singapore, and Thailand.
**Belgium–Luxemburg, Denmark, France, Germany, Greece, Ireland, Italy, Netherlands, Portugal, Spain, and United Kingdom.

In the 1960s, Thailand exported its foods mainly to Asian countries. The share of Asian developing countries in 1965–67 was as large as 60%. Thailand, however, later diversified its food exports to other areas in the world. Japan's share remained at 19% in 1999–2001 but the share of Asian developing counties was halved to 31%, although exports to China increased. Thailand was very successful in developing new markets for its agricultural products and could diversify the destinations, which is one of the reasons why Thailand could keep its high growth rate of agricultural exports throughout the decades.

4. Effects of Market Size, Competitiveness, and Diversification

Differences in performance of agricultural exports among Indonesia, the Philippines, and Thailand are the results of differences in movement of markets that each country participates in and differences in supply responses of each country. The differences in export growth, therefore, shall be explained through an investigation of changes in demand and supply factors in the markets. The world market expansion of traditional export products is considered a major factor on the demand side. If the market expansion is external, the success of exports from a country depends on domestic supply conditions. The major factor on the supply side that influences export performance is the country's ability to maintain its competitiveness[5] in exports of traditional products and to diversify into new product lines (Athukorala 1998). Therefore, it is worthwhile comparing the sensitivity of exports among three countries to the three variables of external market expansion, competitiveness, and commodity diversification as determinants of export performance.

The conventional approach to decompose trade performance into the market expansion and competitiveness is the constant market share analysis (CMSA).[6] The CMSA calculates the effects of each factor but it cannot explain the effects of new products introduced in the markets after the base period, so that diversification effects can not be directly taken into account. The approach used in this chapter is the same as in Athukorala (1991), which adopted the methodology from Kravis (1970b) and Love (1984). It is a time series regression analysis in which the three independent factors are separately measured as indices to explain changes in agricultural export volumes in real terms. More specifically it is expressed as follows.

(1) $XVt = F(WDt, CMt, DVt)$

where XV is volume of total agricultural exports in real terms, WD is world demand for exports of traditional agricultural products for a country,

CM is competitiveness in exports of traditional agricultural products, *DV* is export diversification, and *t* represents time.

In order to see how much each factor of the determinants of exports in the model contributed to the growth of agricultural exports in each country, the growth accounting analysis is conducted. The growth accounting equation is derived from the log linear specification of equation (1) as follows:

(2) $G(XV) = b1G(WD) + b2G(CM) + b3G(DV)$

where *G* denotes percent changes in the variable in the following parentheses and *b1*, *b2*, and *b3* are estimated long run coefficients of *WD*, *CM*, and *DV*, respectively, in the ECM estimation.

Honma and Hagino (2002) conducted the growth accounting analysis using the coefficients estimated in the same manner as in Athukorala (1991) to explain the growth rates of total agricultural exports (*XV*) for the period of the initial stage (1961–65 average) to the recent one (1993–97 average for Indonesia and the Philippines, and 1986–90 average for Thailand). The results are shown in Table 7.4.

Table 7.4 Factors Accounting for Agricultural Export Growth of Three Asian Countries

		Growth rate of: XV	Contribution of changes in			Residual
			WD	CM	DV	
Indonesia	61-65,93-97	5.09	3.22	0.73	0.86	
(1961-97)	(%)	100	63.3	14.4	16.9	5.5
	61-65,78-82	4.51	3.23	0.38	0.87	
	(%)	100	71.7	8.5	19.3	0.6
	78-82,93-97	5.75	3.21	1.13	0.84	
	(%)	100	55.8	19.6	14.7	9.9
Philippines	61-65,93-97	0.68	1.28	–0.59	0.25	
(1961-97)	(%)	100	188.0	–87.5	36.4	–36.9
	61-65,78-82	2.81	2.22	–0.05	0.30	
	(%)	100	78.9	–1.9	10.8	12.2
	78-82,93-97	–1.68	0.22	–1.20	0.18	
	(%)	100	–13.3	71.7	–11.0	52.6
Thailand	61-65,86-90	6.84	4.02	2.07	0.81	
(1961-90)	(%)	100	58.8	30.2	11.8	–0.7
	61-65,73-77	7.64	4.84	1.39	1.23	
	(%)	100	63.4	18.2	16.1	2.3
	73-77,86-90	6.11	3.27	2.70	0.41	
	(%)	100	53.4	44.1	6.7	–4.2

Source: Honma and Hagino (2002).

The three determinant factors explain well the growth rates of agricultural exports of Indonesia and Thailand whose unexplained residuals are only 5.5% and –0.7%, respectively, for the whole estimation period. For the Philippines, however, the unexplained residual is –36.9% showing that the model does not fit well with her export performance. The world demand is the major contributor to agricultural exports in all three countries, accounting for 63%, 188%, and 59% of the export growth rate of Indonesia, the Philippines, and Thailand, respectively. It is noted that the competitiveness accounts for 14% and 30% of export growth of Indonesia and Thailand, respectively, but its value for the Philippines is negative meaning that the Philippines lost her market shares in traditional exports. On the other hand, the contribution of export diversification is relatively large in the Philippines, though the estimated coefficient is not statistically significant. Export diversification accounts for 17% and 12% of export growth of Indonesia and Thailand, respectively.

In observation of the contributions of the three factors divided into two periods, it is found that the contribution of world demand was greater in the first half than in the second half for all three countries. In the second half period, the contribution of competitiveness accounts more for the export performance, particularly, the negative growth in the Philippines and Thailand's stable growth up to 1990. The contribution of export diversification was more important in the first half than in the second half for both Indonesia and Thailand.

Export prospects for agricultural products are considered to be determined predominantly by the long-term pattern of world demand, leaving little room for supply side factors to achieve export success (Athukorala 1998). As indicated in Table 7.4, the demand factor, WD, accounts for more than half of the export growth rate in all three countries. But it is important to note that the high rates of agricultural export growth in Indonesia and Thailand could not have been achieved without the contribution of domestic factors of CM and DV. At the same time, the failure of the Philippines to expand her agricultural exports came from the losses in competitiveness, particularly in the 1980s and 1990s. These facts imply that there is a lot of room for the supply side to achieve export success by improving supply factors such as market promotions, infrastructure investments, and productivity increases, as well as introducing new products for export. Therefore, government policies to give incentives to improve supply side factors are one of the keys to determine the performance of agricultural exports.

5. Product Differentiation and Price Competition

In determinants of export performance, price plays an important role. Price is determined simultaneously with quantity to satisfy both demand and supply equations. Thus, it is desirable to specify the demand and supply equations to investigate the role of price and the export performance. It is difficult, however, to estimate statistically export supply equations, particularly for developing countries. On the other hand, export demand equations are easily estimated using only the trade data if the total imports in a market are considered exogenously given. In this section, the demand structure for exports of major commodities from Indonesia, the Philippines, and Thailand in selected markets is examined.

The underlying assumption is product differentiation in consumer's demand. It is assumed that consumers differentiate products of a commodity by place of production and that the commodity is weakly separable from all other kinds of commodities in the consumer's utility function. Then, the demand for imports of the commodity by source (supplying country) can be expressed as a function of import prices by supplying countries and the total expenditure on the imports of this specific commodity (Armington 1969).

In specifying the demand equations for imports by supplier, it is desirable to construct a complete system of demand equations. Honma and Hagino (2002) adopted the almost ideal demand system (AIDS) of Deaton and Muellbauer (1980) to estimate the demand equations for selective agricultural exports from Indonesia, the Philippines, and Thailand. The model was applied to estimate the import demand equations for rice, bananas, raw sugar, coffee, natural rubber, palm oil, and coconut oil in major countries to which each Indonesia, the Philippines, and Thailand are exporting.

Using the estimated parameters of the AIDS model of import demand systems for seven commodities and mean values of the import shares, uncompensated own price elasticity of import demand and elasticity of import demand to expenditure on the total imports of the given commodity can be calculated. Elasticities calculated are summarized in Table 7.5.

The calculated own price elasticity is relatively large in most cases. For Indonesian exports, of the 16 markets, the own price elasticity is greater than one in absolute value. For Philippines exports, the own price elasticity is greater than one in five of the 10 markets while there are only two of the 12 markets that have an own price elasticity greater than one for Thai exports. Among the commodities, palm oil and coconut oil in particular have large values of own price elasticity in most markets.

Table 7.5   Elasticities Calculated from AIDS Estimates of Import Demand Equations for Major Products from Three Asian Countries in Selected Markets

Commodity:		Coffee		Natural rubber		Palm oil	
Exporter	Importer	Price	Expend.	Price	Expend.	Price	Expend.
Indonesia	Canada			−0.36	0.43		
	China					−2.85	−0.13
	Germany	−1.89	2.99				
	India					−1.07	1.16
	Japan	−0.82	2.29			−1.75	0.37
	Korea	−0.53	−0.49	−5.23	2.52		
	Netherlands	−0.66	0.10	−0.55	0.24		
	Singapore						
	U.K.	−1.34	0.85	−2.06	1.75	−1.55	1.44
	U.S.A.	−0.46	0.37	−1.08	0.81	−0.41	0.77

Commodity:		Bananas		Coconut oil	
Exporter	Importer	Price	Expend.	Price	Expend.
Philippines	France			−1.74	2.39
	Germany			−1.54	1.07
	Hong Kong	−0.85	1.02		
	Italy			−5.99	2.69
	Japan	−0.92	0.91	−1.08	0.98
	Korea	−0.94	0.91		
	Netherlands			−2.32	1.30
	Saudi Arabia	−0.65	0.46		
	U.S.A.			−0.79	1.21

Commodity:		Rice		Raw sugar		Natural rubber	
Exporter	Importer	Price	Expend.	Price	Expend.	Price	Expend.
Thailand	France					−0.46	0.62
	Hong Kong	−0.64	1.36				
	Indonesia	−0.85	0.91				
	Japan					−0.61	0.37
	Korea			−0.92	0.85	−0.58	0.03
	Malaysia	−0.40	0.97	−0.59	2.35		
	Saudi Arabia	−2.23	1.27				
	Singapore	−0.64	0.97			−0.79	1.34
	U.K.						
	U.S.A.					−2.04	1.79

Notes: 1) Figures in the "Price" column are uncompensated own price elasticity of import demand.
2) Figures in the "Expend" column are elasticity of import demand to expenditure on the total imports of the given commodity.
Source: Honma and Hagino (2002).

Expenditure elasticity of import demand denotes the percent change in demand for imports from the given country to the percent change in total expenditure on imports from all countries. If the expenditure elasticity is greater than one, the share of the given country is increasing as the market is expanding. The expenditure elasticity is greater than one in six of 16 markets for Indonesian exports, six of 10 markets for the Philippine exports, and five of 12 markets for Thai exports. It is interesting that for exports of coconut oil from the Philippines and rice from Thailand, the expenditure elasticity does not vary much by markets but for other exports it varies from a small value to a large one depending on the market. The expenditure elasticity can be interpreted as an indicator of non-price competitiveness in each market. Thus, coconut oil from the Philippines and rice from Thailand seem to have maintained their shares well in most markets in the world due to the strong non-price competitiveness. But other exports failed to establish the competitiveness uniformly and could not take advantage of the success in one market to another.

The information on the characteristics of the markets is important and useful for exporters to consider export strategies. In the markets in which the price elasticity of demand is greater than unity, it is expected to increase export earnings if the export price falls by increasing production efficiency, for example. In the markets in which the expenditure elasticity is greater than unity it is expected to increase the market share as the market expands and to raise the price as far as the export supply curve has a positive slope.

For exporting countries, however, the strategies to take advantage of such characteristics of the markets do not work well if there are factors disturbing the transmission of the changes from exporters to importers, such as variable transportation costs, inefficient distribution systems, and traders' marketing power. So, it is important to examine the degree of transmission of changes, particularly, in prices from exporters to importers. To examine the degree of transmission between the export prices of major commodities from three Asian countries and the corresponding import prices in selected importing countries, a regression analysis was conducted according to the following specification:

(3) $$\ln PM_{ijt} = \alpha_{ij} + \beta_{ij} \ln PX_{ijt} + \varepsilon_{ijt}$$

where *PM* and *PX* are the c.i.f. import price and the f.o.b. export price, respectively, of a commodity traded from county *i* to country *j*, *t* is time, and *e* is an error term. Unit values of imports of importing countries by source and unit values of exports of exporting countries by destination were used for the c.i.f. import prices and the f.o.b. export prices, respectively. Data was obtained from *Commodity Trade Statistics* of the

United Nations stored in the International Economic Data Bank of Australian National University.

The regression was conducted for the 38 trade flows to which the AIDS model was applied in the previous section. Prior to estimating the equations, non-stationarity was tested for each data series. Judging from the test results, all the data series were used in the first differential form for regression. The price transmission elasticities estimated by regression are summarized in Table 7.6.

If the transmission is perfect, the coefficient is expected to be unity. Therefore, a hypothesis for the coefficient to be unity was statistically tested for all the estimated equations. The elasticities that are significantly different from unity are those with asterisks in Table 7.6. For Indonesian exports, the hypothesis is rejected in 11 of 16 trade flows. In particular, the price transmission elasticities of coffee exports to all six destinations are significantly less than unity. For the Philippines, the elasticities are significantly less than unity in seven of ten trade flows and the unity hypothesis is not rejected only for the elasticities of bananas to Hong Kong and Saudi Arabia and coconut oil to Japan. For Thailand, one half of 12 trade flows rejects the hypothesis. The elasticities, of all five rice trade flows and one of natural rubber to Japan are significantly less than unity while the two of raw sugar and four of natural rubber cannot reject the hypothesis.

In the trade flows in which the price transmission elasticity is significantly less than unity, the export price changes are partly absorbed in the process of international distribution. One possible explanation for the imperfect price transmission is the behaviour of distributors who may take risks of price changes to guarantee a certain quantity of supply offsetting by reduction (inflation) of market margins when export prices rise (fall).

A second possible explanation is the behaviour of traders. If they have enough market power to set prices in import markets, they set each price monopolistically making the marginal revenue derived from the import demand curve equal to the marginal cost that is basically the export price. The marginal revenue curve is less elastic than the demand curve so that the changes in monopolistic import price along the demand curve are less than the changes in the marginal cost (export price). Therefore, PM became less elastic in response to changes in PX. This could happen for the commodities whose price elasticities of demand are greater than unity among those with low transmissibility such as Indonesian coffee to Germany and the United Kingdom, Philippine coconut oil to Europe, and Thai rice to Saudi Arabia.

Third, if commodities are traded in an integrated system such as a transnational corporation, it is not necessary to transmit the export price onto the import price perfectly because they can transfer the pricing

Table 7.6   Price Transmission Elasticities and Ratios of Import Price to Export Price for Major Export Products from Three Asian Countries in Selected Markets

Commodity:		Coffee		Natural rubber		Palm oil	
Exporter	Importer	Elasticity	*PM/PX*	Elasticity	*PM/PX*	Elasticity	*PM/PX*
Indonesia	Canada			0.94	1.11		
	China					1.01	1.05*
	Germany	0.74**	1.23				
	India					0.68	1.09
	Japan	0.86**	1.14			0.91**	1.13*
	Korea	0.72**	1.17	0.80**	1.06*		
	Netherlands	0.67**	1.25	0.67**	1.14		
	Singapore						
	U.K.	0.75**	1.26	0.90	1.16*	0.82**	1.22
	U.S.A.	0.84**	1.15	0.98	1.15*	0.46**	1.08

Commodity:		Bananas		Coconut oil			
Exporter	Importer	Elasticity	*PM/PX*	Elasticity	*PM/PX*	Elasticity	*PM/PX*
Philippines	France			0.60**	1.23		
	Germany			0.79**	1.10		
	Hong Kong	0.76	2.31*				
	Italy			0.62**	1.17		
	Japan	0.47**	2.43	1.00	1.11*		
	Korea	−0.10**	2.91				
	Netherlands			0.86**	1.09		
	Saudi Arabia	0.44	2.53				
	U.S.A.			0.85**	1.07		

Commodity:		Rice		Raw sugar		Natural rubber	
Exporter	Importer	Elasticity	*PM/PX*	Elasticity	*PM/PX*	Elasticity	*PM/PX*
Thailand	France					0.87	1.13*
	Hong Kong	0.93**	1.08*				
	Indonesia	0.45**	1.21				
	Japan					0.92**	1.05*
	Korea			1.03	1.20	0.91	1.06*
	Malaysia	0.87**	1.09*	1.07	1.16		
	Saudi Arabia	0.70**	1.15*				
	Singapore	0.90**	1.10*			0.98	1.03*
	U.K.						
	U.S.A.					0.94	1.09*9

Notes: 1) Figures in the columns for elasticity are price transmission elasticities obtained from regressions of import price (PM) on export price (PX) in differential form after logarithmic transformation.
2) Figures in the columns for PM/PX are mean values of the ratio of import price to export price for each trade flow over the estimation period.
3) Figures with ** in the columns for elasticity are significantly different from *unity (1)* at 5% level. All other figures are *not* significantly different from *unity* at 10% level.
4) Figures with * in the columns for PM/PX are those whose coefficient of variation (CV) over the sample period is less than 10%.
Source: Honma and Hagino (2002).

mechanism from one sector to another within the integrated organization. This happens particularly in the case where production and international trading are integrated, such as in transnational corporations that manage banana plantations in the Philippines.

Fourth, it may be simply a data problem. There is a time lag between the date of export and the date of import for a shipment. Data is annual so that for some shipments exports were recorded in one year and imports in the following. This may have appeared as low transmissibility in estimations. Further investigation is necessary to identify the source of low transmissibility by commodity and by country.

Table 7.6 also shows mean values of the ratio of import price (*PM*) to export price (*PX*) for each trade flow over the estimation period. The ratio minus one multiplied by 100 is the percentage of distribution cost and market margins to the export price. The distribution costs and market margins are in a range of 3% to 26% of export prices, except for bananas of the Philippines whose values are more than 100%.[7] There are four factors considered to affect the differences in the ratio of *PM/PX*. First is the mark-up or market margin for international distributors. Second is the transportation cost that is assumed to be proportional to the distance from origin to destination. Third is the cost associated with the different treatment in shipping that is a commodity-specific factor. Fourth is the factor depending on the structure of an industrial organization on trade management that may vary by country and market.

The ratios in natural rubber from both Indonesia and Thailand are very likely to be proportional to the distance but the ratios of the United States in coffee, palm oil and coconut oil are clearly low compared with the ratios of other destinations in the same commodity exports. Also, the ratios cannot be explained by the difference in the cases of bananas for Korea and rice for Indonesia. More information is needed to clarify the differences among the ratios of *PM/PX*. It is important for exporting countries to know the structure of international distribution costs and structures because if there is any room to improve the efficiency, the improvement directly affects the market prices and makes for greater gains from exports even under the same domestic supply conditions.

6. Conclusion

In the 1960s, agricultural export performance was similar among Indonesia, the Philippines and Thailand, both in nominal and real value terms. But in the decades since then, the three countries have shown different performances in agricultural exports. What brought the differences in the export performances among the three countries? One important factor resulting in the differences is the ability of diversification and adjustment of agricultural exports when the market conditions changed. Indonesia shifted the weight of agricultural exports from natural rubber, which was dominant in the 1960s, to coffee in the 1970s, to palm oil in the 1980s, and to cocoa in the 1990s, while keeping the exports of natural rubber steady. Indonesia also diversified the destinations of exports from the United States and European countries to Japan and other Asian countries in the last decades.

The changes in the structure of Thai agricultural exports are more drastic, although rice has been dominant in agricultural exports. Dramatic were the emergence of cassava and maize as major items in agricultural exports in the 1970s and then their rapid disappearance from the markets in the 1990s. Exports of cassava and maize were targeted at the European Community and Japan by quota and contract, respectively. The reduction of quota and the termination of contract resulted in the sharp decline of exports of these commodities. Thailand, however, prepared alternative commodities to strengthen its agricultural exports, substituting for cassava and maize. Agricultural export growth was sustained by expansion of natural rubber and sugar exports and the introduction of new commodities like processed and horticultural products in its list of exports. Thailand used to export agricultural products mainly to Asian countries but developed new markets over the world.

The Philippines, however, could not adjust its agricultural exports to changes in the market conditions. Philippine agricultural exports totally depended on the U.S. markets, particularly for sugar and coconut oil. After the Philippines lost the sugar market in the United States by the termination of special treatments, it could not find alternative markets, nor could it introduce new products to export. Coconut oil and bananas have remained as major export items since the 1980s but have not contributed to growth of agricultural exports of the country.

The differences in export performance among the three countries are characterized clearly in the contribution of each factor to explain the export growth rate. Among the factors contributing to the export growth rate for principal agricultural products, commodity diversification plays a significant role in Indonesia compared with the other two countries. In Thailand, competitiveness (increasing market share) has contributed significantly to its export growth for the last four decades. On the other hand, the growth rate of Philippine exports is explained mostly by the expansion of the markets. Namely, the high growth rates of agricultural exports in Indonesia and Thailand were the result of internal efforts in diversification and/or strengthening competitiveness in addition to the market expansions. But agricultural exports of the Philippines that depended mainly on external factors could not grow much because of the stagnation of market growth and lack of the ability to diversify to new product lines.

Agricultural exports are often considered less promising because of the inelastic demand for agricultural products to both price and income. However, at the level of trade flows by commodity and by market, there are a lot of opportunities to gain from exports. Demand elasticities are not necessarily small for individual trade flows as estimated in this study. For the commodities whose price elasticity of demand is more than unity, export earnings are expected to increase during price falls due to increases in production efficiency, for example, in exporting countries.

But changes in exporting countries are not directly transmitted to the markets because of the existence of distributors and transportation costs. Transmission elasticity between export and import prices was significantly less than unity in 24 out of 38 trade flows estimated in this study. For exporting countries to capture the total gains from exports, it is necessary that the efficiency and transparency in international distribution systems be improved. At the same time, domestic distribution systems also should be efficient for producers in rural areas to gain from exports of their products. Indeed, farm gate prices of most agricultural products are very low compared to retail prices in importing countries.[8]

The factors to determine comparative advantage have become more complicated than before as agricultural exports change composition, shifting to more value-added products like processed foods and horticultural products, which was observed particularly in Thailand and to some extent in Indonesia. In addition to the production efficiency at the farm level, exports of processed foods and horticultural products requires more efficient technologies, marketing systems, and infrastructure, such as transportation facilities, than traditional agricultural exports. In others words, comparative advantage is shifting from labour-intensive products to capital- and technology-intensive products even within the agricultural sector in the process of economic development.

In pricing agricultural commodities nowadays, such post-harvest activities as processing, distributing, marketing, and transporting products all benefit from economies of scale, largely from the use of public infrastructures such as airports, docking facilities and fumigation plants. Improving public infrastructure, therefore, is key to enabling developing countries to pursue their potential comparative advantage in agriculture and to strengthen their competitiveness in the world market. Success in agricultural trade depends on price mechanisms that work well without too much government intervention. But governments have an important role to play in providing public goods, which are difficult for the private sector to supply because of the 'free-rider' problem. Governments of importing countries like Japan can also contribute to improving the infrastructure in developing countries through foreign aid programmes, which would result in import price declines and, in turn, benefit consumers in importing countries as well.

Notes

This article is heavily drawn from Honma, M. and T. Hagino (forthcoming), 'A Comparative Study on Agricultural Exports of Three Southeast Asian Countries,' paper prepared for the World Bank study: "Dynamism of Rural Sector Growth: Policy Lessons from East Asian Countries".

[1] On the relationship between export expansion and economic growth in general, see, for example, Maizels (1968), Michaely (1977), Feder (1982), Hsiao (1987), and Dutt and Ghosh (1996).

[2] This pessimistic view was embodied in the works of Prebisch (1950), Singer (1950), Nurkse (1952), and Myrdal (1957). For a useful survey of their works and relevant literature, see Myint (1979), Lewis (1989), and Krueger (1997).

[3] For example, Lewis (1980) argued that the slowing down of the engine of growth in developing countries, which is trade, is attributed to a secure decline in the rate of economic growth in developed countries. See also Riedel (1984). For an empirical study of the long-run terms of trade of developing countries for the 1900-86 period, see Grilli and Yang (1988).

[4] This shows that the relationship between agricultural and industrial exports is best looked upon not as a dichotomy, but as a continuum in the development process. See Findlay (1984 and 1985), Lewis (1989) and Athukorala (1998).

[5] "Competitiveness" is improved for an exporter if the market share of the exporter increases in a given market. See Kravis (1970a and 1970b) for the terminology.

[6] For the details of CMSA, see Yotopoulos and Nugent (1976).

[7] This large ratio of distribution costs of bananas is not necessarily due to the commodity-specific characteristics but due to the structure of the banana export industry in the Philippines. See Honma (1991) for the comparison of banana export prices between the Philippines and Taiwan.

[8] Honma (1991) emphasises the high share of the benefits from trade that often go not to the producer or the consumer but to the intermediary.

References

Akiyama, T. and K. Kajisa. 2000. "Agricultural Pricing Policies in Three Asian Countries: Time Series Analysis over Four Decades". (mimeo).

Armington, Paul S. 1969. "A Theory of Demand for Products Distinguished by Place of Production". *IMF Staff Papers* 16: pp.159-176.

Athukorala, Prema-chandra. 1991. "An Analysis of Demand and Supply Factors in Agricultural Exports from Developing Asian Countries". *Weltwirtschaftliches Archiv* 127 (4): pp. 746-91.

Athukorala, Prema-chandra. 1998. *Trade Policy Issues in Asian Development*, London: Routledge.

Bourguignon, F. and C. Morrison. 1989. *External Trade and Income Distribution*, Paris: Development Centre, Organisation for Economic Cooperation and Development.

Deaton, A. S. and J. Muellbauer. 1980. "An Almost Ideal Demand System". *American Economic Review* 70: pp.312-326.

Dutt, S. D. and D. Ghosh. 1996. "The Export Growth-Economic Growth Nexus: A Causality Analysis". *Journal of Development Areas* 30, pp.167-182.

Engle, R. F. and C. W. J. Granger. 1987. "Co-integration and Error Correction: Representation, Estimation, and Testing," *Econometrica* 55, pp.251-276.

Feder, G. 1983. "On Exports and Economic Growth". *Journal of Development Economics* 12, pp.59-74.

Findlay, R. 1984. "Trade and Development: Theory and Asian Experience". *Asian Development Review* 2, pp.23-42.

Findlay, R. 1985. "Primary Exports, Manufacturing and Development". In *The Primary Sector in Economic Development*, edited by M. Lundahl. London: Croom Helm.

Grilli, E. R. and M. C. Yang. 1988. "Primary Commodity Prices, Manufactured Goods Prices, and the Terms of Trade of Developing Countries: What the Long Run Shows". *The World Bank Economic Review* 2, pp.1-47.

Honma, M. 1991. *Growth in Japan's Horticultural Trade with Developing Countries: An Econometric Analysis of the Market*, Research Report 89, Washington, D. C.: International Food Policy Research Institute.

Honma, M. and T. Hagino (forthcoming), "A Comparative Study on Agricultural Exports of Three Southeast Asian Countries", paper prepared for the World Bank study: "Dynamism of Rural Sector Growth: Policy Lessons from East Asian Countries."

Hsiao, Mei-Chu W. 1987. "Test of Causality and Exogeneity Between Export Growth and Economic Growth". *Journal of Development Economics* 12, pp.143-159.

Johnston, B. F. and J. W. Mellor. 1961. "The Role of Agriculture in Economic Development". *American Economic Review* 51, pp.566-593.

Kravis, I. B. 1970a. "Trade as a Handmaiden of Growth: Similarities Between the Nineteenth and Twentieth Centuries". *Economic Journal* 80, pp.850-872.

Kravis, I. B. 1970b. "External Demand and Internal Supply Factors in LDC Export Performance". *Banca Nazionale del Lovoro Quarterly Review* 24, pp.157-179.

Krueger, A. O. 1997. "Trade Policy and Economic Development: How We Learn". *American Economic Review* 87, pp.1-22.

Lewis, W. A. 1980. "The Slowing Down of the Engine of Growth". *American Economic Review* 70, pp.555-564.

Lewis, S. R. 1989. "The Experience of Primary Exporting Countries". In *Handbook of Development Economics*, vol. II, edited by Hollis B. Chenery and T. N. Srinivasan. North Holland: Elsevier, pp.1542-1600.

Love, J. 1984. "External Market Conditions, Competitiveness, Diversification, and LDC Exports". *Journal of Development Economics* 16 (3), pp.279-291.

Maizels, A. 1968. *Exports and Economic Growth in Developing Countries*, London: Cambridge University Press.

Michaely, M. 1977. "Exports and Growth: An Empirical Investigation". *Journal of Development Economics* 4, pp.49-53.

Myint, H. 1975. "Agriculture and Economic Development in the Open Economy". In *Agriculture in Development Theory*, edited by L. G. Reynolds. New Haven and London: Yale University Press.

Myint, H. 1979. "Exports and Economic Development of Less Developed Countries". In *Economic Growth and Resources*, edited by I. Adelman. New York: St. Martin's Press, pp.102-120.

Myrdal, G. 1957. *Economic Nationalism and Internationalism*, Melbourne: Australian Institute of International Affairs.

Nurkse, R. 1952. "Some International Aspects of the Problem of Economic Development". *American Economic Review* 42, pp.571-583.

Prebisch, R. 1950. *The Economic Development of Latin America and its Principal Problems*. New York: United Nations.

Riedel, J. 1984. "Trade as the Engine of Growth in Developing Countries, Revisited". *Economic Journal* 94, pp.56-73.

Singer, H. 1950. "The Distribution of Gains Between Investing and Borrowing Countries". *American Economic Review* 40, pp.473-485.

Yotopoulos, P. A. and J. B. Nugent 1979. *Economics of Development: Empirical Investigation*. New York: Harper and Row.

8
Seeking New Development Strategies: The Role of Government and ODA in Southeast Asia[1]

Fukunari Kimura

1. Introduction

Although major players have alternated, the East Asian region has continued to serve as the world's growth centre for four decades. Justifying its claim for the 'East Asian Miracle', the World Bank emphasized in its 1993 report (World Bank 1993) the existence of well-managed macroeconomic fundamentals and wisely designed microeconomic policies. Over the last decade, another important element was added to the characteristics of the East Asian economies; i.e., the formation of international production/distribution networks.

The Southeast Asian (SEA) countries[2] after the latter half of the 1980s, as well as China in the 1990s with some important differences, present a new development model of less developed countries (LDCs) in the globalization era. An important turning point was in the mid-1980s. Before that, these countries were cautious about accepting too much FDI, as many LDCs still are, and foreign companies were allowed to come only into selected industries with various restrictions. In the latter half of the 1980s and the early 1990s, the SEA countries switched their policies and started hosting nearly every kind of FDI with facilitating measures, which ended up with the unprecedented formation of international production/distribution networks taking advantage of fragmentation and agglomeration.

The development pattern of the SEA countries is fundamentally different in many respects from the pattern of preceding economies such as Japan and Korea in which industrialization started from import substitution by local indigenous firms. The role of FDI is different from that in Latin America and other parts of the world in terms of the number of countries involved in international production/distribution networks. Market forces are of course important, but the policy framework is not simple laissez-faire; rather, the new role of government is pursued.

Now the SEA countries are facing new challenges. China has emerged as a great attractor of FDI, and competition over location advantages has become intense. The difficulties include stubborn technological gaps between local indigenous firms and foreign affiliates, lack of human capital, highly distortive investment incentives to keep footloose foreign affiliates in the territory, and others. How to remove inefficiencies in import-substituting industries and how to further activate international production/distribution networks are the issues. In these contexts, the Japanese official development assistance (ODA) programme for the East Asian countries should also be evaluated.

This chapter argues the new role of government in the context of new development strategies applied by the SEA countries and partially by China and discusses some implications for economic cooperation programmes implemented by the Government of Japan. The next section presents the development strategies the SEA countries applied from the mid-1980s. Section 3 investigates the pros and cons of traditional import-substituting FDI policy. Section 4 explains the economic logic behind the formation of international production/distribution networks and claims the importance of government policies. Section 5 interprets current issues on industrial development in the SEA countries. The last section discusses the implication for economic cooperation programmes.

2. Development Strategies of the SEA Countries: Overview

There are a few peculiar features in the development strategies of the SEA countries throughout their history of development. First, in the literature of development economics, we often classify development strategies into two distinctive categories, import substitution and export orientation, and regard these two strategies as contradictory with each other. However, the SEA countries have continuously tried to have two types of industries at the same time. This is the so-called "dual track approach". To accelerate import substitution, the government must provide a certain level of incentives for the industries concerned. Trade protection is one of the typical policies for such purposes. Trade protection naturally tends to affect exporting industries negatively. In order to mitigate the inconsistency between the two objectives, the SEA countries have tried to manipulate this delicate policy combination for a long period.

Second, hosting FDI has been an essential element in their development strategies, and their industrialization has virtually proceeded with foreign companies as a core. Foreign companies have been introduced to both import-substituting industries and export-oriented industries.

The significance of foreign companies in the whole picture of development strategies is qualitatively different from that in Japan and Korea in the 1950s and 1960s.

Keeping these peculiar characteristics in mind, let us review the transition of development strategies in the SEA countries, particularly Malaysia, Thailand, the Philippines, and Indonesia. The basic structure and over-time changes of their trade and FDI-related policies would be summarized in Table 8.1.

From the 1970s to the mid-1980s, the SEA countries applied selective introduction policies for FDI, mainly in selected import-substituting industries. Although FDI for export promotion was also invited, competing domestic industries were typically protected by the policy that limits the activities of export-oriented FDI, for example, to geographically segregated export-processing zones.

After the mid-1980s, on the other hand, these countries switched their FDI hosting policy from selective acceptance to basically "accept everybody" policy. While keeping trade protection for import-substituting industries, they started trying to host as many foreign companies as possible and formulated a critical mass of industrial clusters. The extensive application of duty drawback system as well as various kinds of FDI facilitation at least partially offsets the policy bias against exports. This important policy change allowed these countries to effectively utilize the wave of globalization of corporate activities and to capture the benefits of fragmentation and agglomeration. They successfully formulated unprecedented international production/distribution networks.

Table 8.2 presents rough estimates of the significance of Japanese and U.S. firms in the East Asian economies in terms of value added, employment, exports, and imports in 1996, i.e., just before the Asian crisis. Taking into account that a major portion of FDI is going to manufacturing activities, the core of manufacturing sector in the SEA countries consists of foreign companies.[3] Table 8.3 shows that values and shares of exports/imports of machineries in the East Asia economies in 1996. Machineries are defined as HS 84-92; i.e., they include general machinery, electric machinery, transport equipment, and precision machinery. The shares of machineries in each country's total exports and imports are astoundingly large. Furthermore, the shares of parts and components in machinery trade are also very high. These indicate that the international production/distribution networks, particularly well developed in machinery industries, are truly significant in the East Asian economies.

The SEA countries are now facing new challenges. A triggering factor was the Asian currency crisis where various structural problems revealed themselves. A more fundamental issue is the intensified competition with China over location advantages for multinational enterprises (MNEs).

Table 8.1 The Dual Track Approach in Development Strategies: the Case of the SEA Countries

	Phase 1 1970s - mid-1980s	Phase 2 Mid-1980s - 1998	Phase 3 1998 - present
Import-substituting industries	Selective acceptance of FDI for import substitution	Acceptance of FDI for import substitution	Reorganization of protected sectors required; more competition must be introduced
Export-oriented industries	Selective acceptance of FDI in export-processing zones	Emphasis on forming agglomeration; formation of international production/ distribution networks	Further activation of international production/ distribution networks required
Development strategies re. Hosting FDI	Acceptance in selective sectors with capital share restriction and performance requirements	"Accept everybody" policy; duty drawback system; various FDI facilitating measures	Structural adjustment; utilizing FTAs as a booster
External factors	"New international economic order"	Globalizing corporate activities; reduction of service link cost	Asian currency crisis; China shock; FTA boom

Table 8.2 The Significance of Affiliates of Japanese and U.S. Firms in the East Asian Economies, 1996

	Value added		Employment		Exports		Imports	
	Affiliates of Japanese firms	Affiliates of U.S. firms	Affiliates of Japanese firms	Affiliates of U.S. firms	Affiliates of Japanese firms	Affiliates of U.S. firms	Affiliates of Japanese firms	Affiliates of U.S. firms
Korea	0.46	0.49	0.33	0.17	6.95	n.a.	6.34	n.a.
Hong Kong	5.24	1.91	2.66	3.18	17.02	17.17	16.38	n.a.
Singapore	11.90	7.69	4.73	5.68	33.17	55.13	33.38	n.a.
Malaysia	4.61	4.68	2.67	1.62	13.11	18.47	15.19	n.a.
Thailand	4.54	1.89	0.89	0.26	33.28	n.a.	29.76	n.a.
Philippines	1.56	2.60	0.34	0.24	13.98	31.02	9.70	n.a.
Indonesia	1.12	2.61	0.26	0.06	11.33	18.93	15.26	n.a.
China	0.42	0.26	0.05	0.02	3.82	5.32	4.51	n.a.

Affiliates of Japanese firms: Affiliates abroad with more than 10% Japanese ownership (except those whose parent firms are in finance & insurance or real estates). Data for 1996 F/Y.

Affiliates of U.S. firms: Affiliates abroad with more than 50% American ownership (neither parents nor affiliates are banks). Data for 1996.

Note that the ratio of returned questionnaires is as low as 59.1% for the data of affiliates of Japanese firms.

The definition of "value added": "sales minus purchases" for affiliates of Japanese firms, and "gross product" for affiliates of U.S. firms.

Value added and exports/imports for affiliates of Japanese firms are estimated by using the data for total NIEs and total ASEAN4.

Source: MITI (1999), U.S. Department of Commerce (1998), and IMF (2000).

Table 8.3 Machinery Trade in the East Asian Economies, 1996

	Exports	Imports
Japan		
Value (US$1000)		
Total	410,944,244	349,185,062
Machinery (HS84-92)	307,646,521	98,088,775
Parts and components in machiney goods	145,594,106	42,244,407
Share		
of machinery goods in total	74.9%	28.1%
of parts and components in total	35.4%	12.1%
of parts and components in machiney goods	47.3%	43.1%
Korea		
Value (US$1000)		
Total	129,696,331	150,320,064
Machinery (HS84-92)	70,265,289	61,430,373
Parts and components in machiney goods	31,300,305	31,107,314
Share		
of machinery goods in total	54.2%	40.9%
of parts and components in total	24.1%	20.7%
of parts and components in machiney goods	44.5%	50.6%
Hong Kong		
Value (US$1000)		
Total	27,426,223	201,282,410
Machinery (HS84-92)	10,178,998	83,881.726
Parts and components in machiney goods	7,360,808	40,664,744
Share		
of machinery goods in total	37.1%	41.7%
of parts and components in total	26.8%	20.2%
of parts and components in machiney goods	72.3%	48.5%
Singapore		
Value (US$1000)		
Total	122,882,738	131,337,708
Machinery (HS84-92)	86,464,800	82,698,546
Parts and components in machiney goods	45,255,689	51,240,888
Share		
of machinery goods in total	70.4%	63.0%
of parts and components in total	36.8%	39.0%
of parts and components in machiney goods	52.3%	62.0%
Malaysia		
Value (US$1000)		
Total	78,308,476	77,901,213
Machinery (HS84-92)	44,883,017	48,816,398
Parts and components in machiney goods	26,416,051	33,052,487
Share		
of machinery goods in total	57.3%	62.7%
of parts and components in total	33.7%	42.4%
of parts and components in machiney goods	58.9%	67.7%

Table 8.3   Machinery Trade in the East Asian Economies, 1996   (*continued*)

	Exports	Imports
Thailand		
Value (US$1000)		
Total	55,672,988	72,311,216
Machinery (HS84-92)	22,414,630	36,457,745
Parts and components in machiney goods	12,095,832	21,896,420
Share		
of machinery goods in total	40.3%	50.4%
of parts and components in total	21.7%	30.3%
of parts and components in machiney goods	54.0%	60.1%
Phillipines		
Value (US$1000)		
Total	20,537,617	34,697,094
Machinery (HS84-92)	12,058,695	18,657,072
Parts and components in machiney goods	9,543,414	12,381,556
Share		
of machinery goods in total	58.7%	53.8%
of parts and components in total	46.5%	35.7%
of parts and components in machiney goods	79.1%	66.4%
Indonesia		
Value (US$1000)		
Total	49,811,786	42,923,875
Machinery (HS84-92)	5,305,267	18,128,354
Parts and components in machiney goods	2,216,286	9,311,469
Share		
of machinery goods in total	10.7%	42.2%
of parts and components in total	4.4%	21.7%
of parts and components in machiney goods	41.8%	51.4%
China		
Value (US$1000)		
Total	151,046,318	138,831,036
Machinery (HS84-92)	40,190,931	58,949,579
Parts and components in machiney goods	15,050,765	26,684,923
Share		
of machinery goods in total	26.6%	42.5%
of parts and components in total	10.0%	19.2%
of parts and components in machiney goods	37.4%	45.3%

Data source: Based on PC-TAS. Figures appeared in Ando and Kimura (2003).

To further activate international production/distribution networks, they must restructure inefficient import-substituting industries as well as reduce service link cost and formulate critical mass of agglomeration.

The author believes that the SEA countries are pioneers in effectively utilizing the forces of globalization in the context of development strategies. These countries have similar initial conditions to many other LDCs in terms of narrow domestic market, immature human capital, weak local indigenous firms, and others. Despite these handicaps, they have made sustained economic growth with impressive industrialization. The development strategies applied by SEA countries is worth investigating in detail. It is particularly important to examine the role of government in their development process and clarify the pros and cons of new development strategies. In the following two sections, detailed discussion is provided on policy packages for import-substituting industries and export-oriented industries.

3. FDI for Import Substitution

Let us now examine the logical structure of a policy package for hosting import-substituting FDI and discuss its blessings and curses in the SEA countries.

The textbook of development economics has taught the infant industry protection argument for long. The infant industry protection policy is a policy that allows an immature industry to expand production by temporarily providing some protection such as import tariffs and tries to make the industry internationally competitive by picking up dynamic economies of scale. There are three checkpoints to judge whether such an infant industry protection policy can be economically justifiable or not. The first criterion is the so-called Mill's criterion; i.e., the concerned industry should have good prospects to stand alone without protection in the future. The second is the so-called Bastable's criterion; i.e., the sum present value of future benefits generated by the protection must be larger than the cost of protection. The third is to check whether some sort of externalities exist to justify government intervention in the market.

Such a traditional infant industry protection argument clearly targeted the promotion of local indigenous firms. Selective trade protection policies applied in the Northeast Asian countries in the past were primarily along this tradition. However, the SEA countries have taken quite different development strategies. One of the key factors is the globalization of corporate activities. Particularly when the technological gap with foreign companies is large, hosting FDI can be a powerful tool to boost industrialization.

A key departure from the traditional infant industry argument is the interpretation of low productivity in domestic production. The traditional argument implicitly assumes that the main cause for low productivity is low technological and managerial capability of local indigenous firms. And, once production starts with proper protection, local indigenous firms are supposed to gain productivity through dynamic economies of scale and end up with a lower domestic supply curve. In the case of import-substituting FDI, on the other hand, there should be essentially no handicap in technology or managerial ability at the firm level because MNEs' firm-specific assets must be competitive. Then the issue is why LDCs still suffer from low productivity even with foreign companies and how productivity should be improved.

An advantage of introducing FDI for import substitution is to save the required protection cost compared with the case of directly fostering local indigenous firms. However, because of the existence of negative factors, even MNEs cannot necessarily operate in LDCs in an internationally competitive manner. Hence, the government must still allow foreign companies to capture the domestic market by setting trade barriers or some other incentives in order to compensate for location disadvantages.

A primary factor for low productivity is inferior macro/sectoral economic conditions and social capability of the host country that is mostly external to individual corporate firms. These include the lack of human capability, poor economic infrastructure, inferior policy environment, and others.

Another factor is the size of domestic market. A small market makes it difficult for a firm to clear the minimal scale of efficiency. Therefore, the smaller the domestic market, the higher and the more prolonged trade barriers are required to encourage MNEs to invest. In addition, a small market makes the competition of multiple MNEs more difficult, possibly resulting in strengthened politico-economic pressure demanding continuous provision of preferential status. Furthermore, the higher the trade barriers, the slower the expansion of the domestic market. Thus, the smallness of domestic market is a curse in multiple ways. Actually, countries with a large domestic market, such as China, have a lot of advantages in this regard. If the domestic market is large, MNEs may be willing to invest, even without any policy incentive, in order to capture the forerunner's advantage. The problem is that few LDCs do not have large enough markets.

The third factor is related to local industrial structure. One major disadvantage in operating in LDCs comes from a lack of local suppliers of parts and components. For parts and components for which there is no prospect of domestic production in the short run, the government must set the trade barriers as low as possible to reduce the cost of inviting downstream assemblers from abroad. However, complete knockdown operations barely generate technological spillovers and close the development path that leads to greater industrialization. That is why the government tries to make MNEs supply parts and components locally. The domestic production of parts and components is not easy at all. In many cases, the government must provide additional trade protection for local firms or foreign affiliates to produce parts and components, which pushes up production costs in the downstream and results in higher protection.

Once foreign affiliates are introduced, how to then push productivity to an internationally competitive level? MNEs must of course have some room for productivity growth in their plants. However, we should not forget other factors that shift the supply curve; that is, the improvement of macro/sectoral economic condition and social capability, the growth of the domestic market, the formation of parts and components supply networks, and others. Taking these factors into account, the Bastable's test must be applied to check whether it is worth providing policy incentives to invite FDI for import substitution.

Strategies utilizing import-substituting FDI were popular in the past, but the difficulty of designing and implementing a proper policy package has recently been recognized. The author does not claim that a proper policy design is impossible. In the cases of mobile phones in China, automobiles in Thailand, and steel products in Vietnam, for example, import-substituting FDI seems to work, at least clearing Mill's criterion. In addition, long-term efforts to faster import-substituting industries perhaps provides a certain basis of further industrial development. However, we must admit that the proper designing of a policy package is not always an easy task.

One of the current issues in the SEA countries is how to reorganize import-substituting industries. The cost of protection is enormous, but the results are not always favourable. Possible inconsistency with hosting export-oriented FDI is also not a negligible issue. Policymakers in the SEA countries have started recognizing that the re-organization of import-substituting industries must be eventually conducted by removing trade barriers and other costly incentives.

4. International Production/Distribution Network under Globalization

The SEA countries were hit by economic slump in the mid-1980s, and various problems in their industrial structure were revealed. The period was a turning point, and the SEA countries switched to an aggressive FDI hosting policy though the timing was slightly different across countries.

Such policy changes began to be adopted in Malaysia and Thailand in the mid-1980s and in the Philippines, Indonesia, and China in the early 1990s. They loosened foreign entry restrictions on selected industries and foreign capital shares and started offering an inviting economic environment for foreign companies by constructing basic economic infrastructure and giving tax incentives. Various types of FDI facilitation were provided, which were particularly effective for accelerating FDI by foreign small and medium enterprises (SMEs). They tried to build up a critical mass of industrial clusters demonstrating efficient upstream-downstream inter-firm relationships and hook them up to international production/distribution networks.

International production/distribution networks formulated in the 1990s in East Asia are virtually unprecedented in their sophistication of vertical production/distribution division of labour across a number of countries. To understand the mechanics of the networks, we must add new flavours to the traditional international trade theory. The theory of comparative advantage based on the relative advantages in autarky (no trade situation) is still valid in various circumstances; technological gaps and factor price differences explain location patterns of industries to some extent. However, in the globalization era, we must at least incorporate three new lines of thought into our analytical framework.

The first line of thought is the fragmentation theory. It is a powerful tool when we analyze FDI to LDCs and the formation of international production/distribution networks.[4] The traditional international trade theory primarily explains an industry-wise location pattern. However, in East Asia, for example, we often observe a product-process-wise location pattern. A typical example is the semiconductor-related electronics industry. This industry as a whole is obviously capital-intensive or human-capital-intensive, but its production activities are finely segmented and located in various places. The fragmentation theory neatly presents an economic logic behind such a location pattern.

There could be various patterns of fragmentation. For example, we could initially have a big factory located in Japan taking care of all the production activities from upstream to downstream. If we look carefully at individual production blocks, however, we may find that some production blocks require close watch by technicians while others are purely labour-intensive. If we can locate production blocks separately in Japan, Malaysia, and China, for example, we may save on the total production cost.

Fragmentation becomes economical when the cost of service links (SLs) connecting production blocks (PBs) is low enough. The SL cost includes transport costs, telecommunication costs, and various coordination costs between PBs. The SL cost depends heavily on the nature of technology in each industry. For example, a full-scale iron mill plant cannot be economically fragmented because of its energy efficiency. However, globalization reduces the overall SL cost and enables firms in many industries to fragment further. Because the SLs tend to carry strong external economies of scale, globalization may accelerate concentration and fragmentation at the same time, ending up with countries that enjoy the fruit of globalization and countries that do not.

The second line of thought is the agglomeration theory. This is an extension of international trade theory with external economies of scale while introducing the concept of 'space' from city planning and other academic fields.[5] Although the microfoundation of spatial agglomeration has not fully been investigated, the importance of agglomeration as a source of location advantage is increasingly recognized. The traditional comparative advantage theory defines comparative advantage based on relative production costs between two locations in autarky. However, economies of scale or agglomeration effects do not necessarily depend on the initial condition under autarky; in an extreme case, a country may start having agglomeration purely by chance. In this sense, the source of gains of trade in the 'new' international trade theory is logically different from those in the traditional theory of comparative advantage.

Among the factors that generate location advantage for MNEs to invest, agglomeration is one of the crucial elements, particularly in LDCs. There are several types of agglomeration or industrial clusters. In cases of East Asian agglomeration we observed so far, vertical links along the value chain are important though there typically exist multiple assemblers. Assemblers take advantage of both fragmentation and agglomeration. For standardized parts and components particularly, the inventory cost is not very high, as they look for the cheapest suppliers by utilizing network information. For customized parts and components for which intimate information exchange with suppliers is important, they enjoy the benefit of agglomeration.

The third line of thought is the internalization theory of corporate firms. For example, a firm typically does not do everything from upstream to downstream. It sets its upstream-side boundary by purchasing materials or parts from other firms and determines its downstream-side boundary by selling their products to other firms or consumers. Such a boundary setting decision is called an "internalization decision". In addition, a firm cuts its internalized activities into thin slices and places these slices in appropriate places. This is called the "location decision". A firm makes internalization and location decisions at the same time, considering its own firm-specific assets such as technology and managerial know-how. Internalization may have different dimensions. For example, an internalization would be made across different functional activities such as financial management, personnel management, R&D activities, parts procurement, sales activities, and others.

206 Asian Development Experience, Vol. 1

In East Asia, various kinds of internalization patterns with innovative inter-firm relationships emerge in the effort of concentrating on core competencies. Such sophistication is particularly salient in the machinery industries and the textiles and garment industries. International trade theory has not yet fully digested elements of ownership advantages and internalization advantages that Dunning's OLI theory presents (Dunning 1993).

The SEA countries have effectively utilized global economic forces that are presented with these three lines of new thought and have successfully gained rapid economic growth. What was the policy package used to attract export-oriented foreign firms and connect their own countries with international production/distribution networks?

Because the SEA countries had immature local indigenous firms, they chose the path of accepting as much FDI as possible in order to quickly form a critical mass of agglomeration. How could they attract FDI? The answer was simple; they tried to enhance location advantages for foreign companies to produce internationally competitive products for exports in order to make the location best (or second best, in case of hedging purposes) in the world.

The SEA countries made significant effort to provide good economic infrastructure. Transportation, telecommunications, energy and water supply, and industrial estate services were drastically improved. A part of the public investment was financed by Japanese ODA. The countries also tied up with general trading companies and other private agencies for the construction and operation of industrial parks. In addition, various types of trade/FDI facilitation worked substantially.

Government policies were also crucial to providing a competitive supply of parts and components. Fostering domestic parts and components suppliers is very important whenever it is accomplished with economic efficiency. When local indigenous firms are too immature, they must invite foreign parts suppliers and make them form agglomeration. For intermediate inputs that cannot be produced domestically, at least in the short run, the government must facilitate imports of those inputs by removing trade barriers or by at least providing a duty drawback system on imported parts and components to produce goods for exports. In the case of parts and components of electronic machinery, the SEA countries had substantial tariff cuts particularly in the mid-1990s under the initiative of APEC. In addition, when trade protection was kept, the duty drawback system was extensively used.

In the past, LDCs' governments typically tried to control their industrial organization by applying a complicated policy combination of entry regulations for FDI and various performance requirements together with investment incentives. However, this complicated policy mix often caused self-contradiction and made the economy inefficient. From a number of bitter experiences, we have learned that at least for export-oriented FDI, it is important to design before- and after-entry regulations/incentives to be as simple as possible and to think much about the stability and transparency of policies. We had better stop selecting firms or industries and in principle welcome all foreign companies that are willing to invest and set up a certain size of industrial cluster as soon as possible.

5. Toward Sustained Growth: Current Agenda

The SEA countries are now facing new challenges. They have so far extensively hosted foreign companies and have successfully formed agglomeration at a certain level. However, local indigenous firms are still largely immature so that they cannot fully penetrate the international production/distribution networks. Meanwhile, big and competitive China has emerged. China is also aggressively utilizing incoming FDI to accelerate growth, and the significance of foreign companies including firms with Chinese heritage is substantial. Because both the SEA countries and China depend heavily on foreign companies, competition with China for location advantages has become a serious issue for the SEA countries.

China's advantages ultimately reside in its abundant human resources. Human resources include not only unskilled labour but also skilled labour and, more importantly, entrepreneurs. Entrepreneurship is the basis of local indigenous firms, some of which are very competitive. Firms with different nationalities, including local indigenous firms, form active agglomeration with many possible choices of inter-firm relationships. The potentially large domestic market is also a big charm. Poor economic infrastructure and a bad policy environment were weak points in the past, but these are quickly improving. The SEA countries were forerunners in hosting FDI, but China is clearly catching up with them in the competition for attracting foreign companies.

The SEA countries' weak points are scarce human resources, immature local indigenous firms, and narrow markets. In particular, the development of human resources must have priority though it is rather a long-term objective. The short-run agenda should be to further activate international production/distribution network as well as to form larger industrial clusters. There are many things that the governments can do in this regard.

6. Implication for Economic Cooperation Programmes

We have so far discussed development strategies that the SEA countries have applied, as well as the role of government in development. In the development process of these countries, there have been both successes and failures in policies. Utilizing market forces is obviously important, but simple laissez-faire policy is not enough for successful industrialization. There surely exists the role of government. And the role of government in the SEA countries was different from that of Japan or Korea in the 1950s and 1960s. With globalizing corporate activities today, we should write up a new policy package.

When the role of government exists, there is also room for government-based economic cooperation programmes including both ODA and OOF. Economic cooperation policy would have multiple purposes; however, here we treat it as purely a part of economic policy and discuss the desired form of cooperation by the Japanese Government.

As for promoting import-substituting industries, Japan has conducted economic cooperation in various forms such as financing the construction of physical infrastructure, training technicians, and promoting local supporting industries. A typical problem in these programmes is that neither donors nor recipients are very much cost-conscious. For these industries, a lot of distortive policies are already imposed, and thus policymakers are less sensitive to the efficiency of cooperation programmes. Another related problem is that the governments of LDCs almost always try to control the path of development too far and the role of economic cooperation is also over-stated. This makes the demarcation of government jobs and private activities vague, ultimately killing private dynamism. The development of physical infrastructure as well as human resources is not entirely a waste, of course. But the feasibility of import substitution itself must be strictly checked. The current task of economic cooperation is to support a quick fading-out of protection policies.

As for further promotion of export-oriented or networking-type industries, the role of government is clearer; policies must head for reducing SL costs, support the formation of agglomeration, and allow various forms of internalization of firms. Economic cooperation should pursue the common goal. In this context, physical infrastructure development is still of great importance though the focus must be properly placed. Considering the efficient demarcation of government jobs and private activities, the government and economic cooperation have a lot of room for further activating the formation of agglomeration and tightening the connection with international production/distribution networks. The governments of LDCs must conduct further liberalization/

de-regulation, trade/FDI facilitation, and institution building where economic cooperation could help. And, last, human resource development is the key for the long-term location advantage of industries. If economic cooperation can contribute, it must also be conducted.

Lastly, in the globalization era, coordination or coherence across policy channels is increasingly important. Economic cooperation policy does not stand alone; rather, by properly coordinating with other policies, such as international commercial policy, effectiveness would greatly be enhanced. Particularly in the case of Japanese cooperation for East Asia, explicit coordination is needed, in the author's opinion, in order to achieve further economic integration.

Notes

[1] This chapter is partially drawn from Kimura (2003) though the main contents are newly added.

[2] In this chapter, the Southeast Asian countries include the original ASEAN (Association of South-East Asian Nations) member countries, namely, Singapore, Malaysia, Thailand, the Philippines, and Indonesia.

[3] In the case of China, the figures in Table 8.2 may seem to be too small. Actually, FDI from Japan and the U.S. occupies less than 10%, respectively, in the total inward FDI in China. About two-thirds of inward FDI are from Taiwan, Hong Kong, and other Chinese connections.

[4] As for the fragmentation theory, see Jones and Kierzkowski (1990), Deardorff (2001), and Cheng and Kierzkowski (2001).

[5] As for the agglomeration theory, see Krugman (1991, 1995) and Fujita, Krugman, and Venables (1999).

References

Ando, Mitsuyo and Kimura, Fukunari. 2003. "Unprecedented Formation of International Production/Distribution Networks in East Asia". Presented at the Fourteenth NBER Annual East Asian Seminar on Economics, "International Trade," held in Taipei, Taiwan on September 5–7, 2003.

Cheng, Leonard K. and Kierzkowski, Henryk. 2001. *Global Production and Trade in East Asia*. Boston: Kluwer Academic Publishers.

Deardorff, A. V. 2001. "Fragmentation in Simple Trade Models". *North American Journal of Economics and Finance*, 12: 121–137.

Dunning, John H. 1993. *Multinational Enterprises and the Global Economy*. Wokingham: Addison-Wesley.

Fujita, Masahisa, Paul, Krugman and Anthony J. Venables. 1999. *The Spatial Economy: Cities, Regions, and International Trade*. Cambridge: The MIT Press.

International Monetary Fund (IMF). 2000. *International Financial Statistics*, June.

Jones, R. W. and Henry Kierzkowski. 1990. "The Role of Services in Production and International Trade: A Theoretical Framework". in Ronald W. Jones and Anne O. Krueger, eds., *The Political Economy of International Trade: Essays in Honor of Robert E. Baldwin*, Oxford, Basil Blackwell.

Kimura, Fukunari. 2003. "New Development Strategies under Globalization: Foreign Direct Investment and International Commercial Policy in Southeast Asia". Forthcoming in Akira Kohsaka, ed., *New Development Strategies: Beyond the Washington Consensus*, Hampshire: Palgrave Macmillan.

Krugman, Paul. 1991. "Increasing Returns and Economic Geography". *Journal of Political Economy* 99: 183-199.

Krugman, Paul. 1995. *Development, Geography, and Economic Theory*. Cambridge: The MIT Press.

Ministry of International Trade and Industry (MITI), Government of Japan (GOJ). 1999. *Dai 27 Kai Wagakuni Kigyou no Kaigai Jigyou Katsudou (The 27th Survey on the Foreign Activities of Japanese Firms)*. Tokyo: Ministry of Finance Printing Office.

U.S. Department of Commerce (Economics and Statistics Administration/ Bureau of Economic Analysis). 1998. *U.S. Direct Investment Abroad: Operations of U.S. Parent Companies and Their Foreign Affiliates, Preliminary 1996 Estimates*.

World Bank. 1993. *The East Asian Miracle: Economic Growth and Public Policy*. Oxford: Oxford University Press.

9
A New Japanese Approach to Nation Building: People-Centred Human Security

Kaoru Ishikawa

1. Introduction

The last decade of the twentieth century was characterized by the demise of communist illusion and a massive embracing of democratic values. It was most typically illustrated in the Charter of Paris, issued in 1990 by the Conference on Security and Cooperation in Europe (CSCE) nations summit. American and European leaders, including President of the Soviet Union Mikhail Gorbachev, President of the United States George Bush and President of France Francois Miterrand, gathered there to celebrate democracy. They declared in the Charter of Paris that democracy was the only system of government for CSCE nations and that an abiding adherence to shared values and their common heritage are the ties which bind North American and European states together.

A year and a half later, the Soviet Union collapsed and people learnt after more than seven decades that communism did not produce freedom nor a happy life. Thus, the collapse also meant the end of a world divided into two opposite values: communism or democracy. Yet to many people's regret, contrary to the expectation for peace, after the cold war ended, armed conflicts increased and economic growth did not bring its dividend to all nations. Though the reasons must be multifaceted, we must note that the end of an era of two opposing values gave birth to a world where multitudes of values mushroomed. It is a difficult situation for people who can no longer justify their positions only by accusing those who belong to the other side as wrong. Indeed, in each society, every person now needs to think for himself to justify his way of life and the way their community/society is governed. This is the difficult side of the coin in a world community where 'ready made' values do not tell you what to do.

During the last decade of the twentieth century, when people began to cope with diversifying values, another important phenomenon changed the world: very rapid deepening of globalization promoted by new technologies, such as the introduction and rapid advancement of new information and communication technology (ICT). New ICT gave birth to many new business models and made a strong impact on cultural diversity on the one hand, but at the same time, it allowed criminals to engage in new dimensions of crime. Economic crises took on new forms, such as the sudden downturn shown in the Asian financial crisis in 1997. Not only did the crisis affect the global economy, moving well beyond country borders, but also highlighted the different measures that the Thai and Malaysian authorities introduced to fight back the crisis, reminding us that in an economic dimension, the notion of the nation state had become obsolete. But is it obsolete only in an economic dimension?

The time has come to reflect on what we all learnt in school: Peace of Westphalia in 1648 changed the Western world, then the whole world, from a medieval system to a new system where nation states became the sole playing units in international relations. But the reality was, in many regions of the world, that such a notion was not true. The most typical and tragic example is sub-Saharan Africa,[1] where highly developed civilized kingdoms were invaded and destroyed by Europeans since the sixteenth century. To make the situation worse, Europeans unilaterally drew sub-Saharan African borders at the Berlin Conference in 1884–85, neither consulting with the Africans nor taking into consideration the political, social and ethnic situation in Africa. Thus, the notion of nation building based on nation state became unrealistic in sub-Saharan Africa. In many sub-Saharan African states, people have been obliged to ask themselves whether they should identify with their cousins across the border or be loyal to their president whose mother tongue is different.

All these elements lead us to think about the importance of the role of rule making in light of a newly emerging situation in the world, as well as that of a people-centred approach to build communities, and the role of communities in nation building. This is why some highly industrialized countries such as Japan started to seek a new way of employing development assistance.

In this chapter, the first part will deal with an overview of global issues in the post-cold war era. The second part will review the Japanese approach to sustainable development expressed at the World Summit on Sustainable Development (WSSD), held in Johannesburg in August and September 2002. The third part will have a look at the concept of Human Security that Japan is promoting through ODA and other policies.

2. Global Issues in a Post-Cold War Era

Figure 9.1 shows a notion of global issues in a post-cold war globalized world. Given the change of the world in the post-cold war era, where

Figure 9.1 A View of Global Issues in the Post-Cold War World

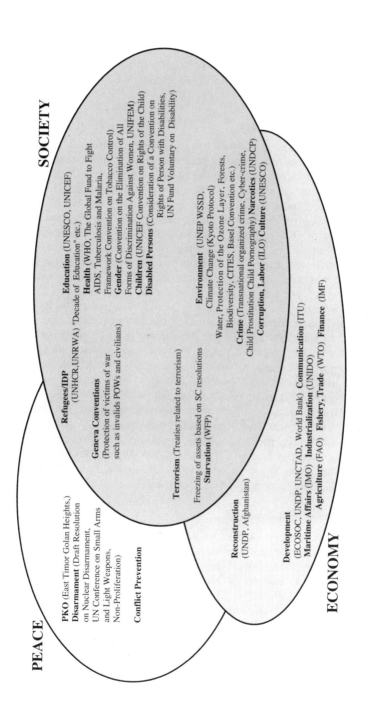

PEACE

PKO (East Timor Golan Heights,)
Disarmament (Draft Resolution
on Nuclear Disarmament,
UN Conference on Small Arms
and Light Weapons,
Non-Proliferation)

Conflict Prevention

SOCIETY

Refugees/IDP
(UNHCR,UNRWA) "Decade of Education" etc.)

Geneva Conventions
(Protection of victims of war
such as invalids POWs and civilians)

Terrorism (Treaties related to terrorism)

Freezing of assets based on SC resolutions
Starvation (WFP)

Education (UNESCO, UNICEF)

Health (WHO, The Global Fund to Fight
AIDS, Tuberculosis and Malaria,
Framework Convention on Tobacco Control)
Gender (Convention on the Elimination of All
Forms of Discrimination Against Women, UNIFEM)
Children (UNICEF Convention on Rights of the Child)
Disabled Persons (Consideration of a Convention on
Rights of Person with Disabilities,
UN Fund Voluntary on Disability)

Environment (UNEP WSSD,
Climate Change (Kyoto Protocol)
Water, Protection of the Ozone Layer, Forests,
Biodiversity, CITES, Basel Convention etc.)
Crime (Transnational organized crime, Cyber-crime,
Child Prostitution Child Pornography) **Narcotics** (UNDCP)
Corruption, Labor (ILO) **Culture** (UNESCO)

Reconstruction
(UNDP, Afghanistan)

Development
(ECOSOC, UNDP, UNCTAD, World Bank) **Communication** (ITU)
Maritime Affairs (IMO) **Industrialization** (UNIDO)
Agriculture (FAO) **Fishery, Trade** (WTO) **Finance** (IMF)

ECONOMY

globalization is deepening year by year, it is useful to analyze the actual world by looking at it from political, economic and social dimensions as well as their overlapping areas. Figure 9.1 shows a way to overview actual global issues.

2.1 Political Issues

One important agenda of the twenty-first century, which remains even after the cold war, is peace building. Peace building can only be realized when individual people get their peace, both materially and in their minds.

Increase of regional conflicts makes peace building and consolidation of peace building more and more important. As of May 2003, 14 Peacekeeping Operation (PKO) missions are dispatched in the world.[2] About 40,000 persons from around 90 countries are participating in those missions. The total number of PKO since 1948 is 56, out of which 43 were sent after 1988. In spite of great expectations for peace after the cold war, this fact may be telling us of the paradoxical negative situation to which the end of the cold war gave birth.

When reflecting on armed conflict, it is not to be forgotten that in sub-Saharan Africa where most of the armed conflicts occur, no country other than South Africa has the capability to produce firearms. This fact leads to the logical conclusion that those belligerents are spending foreign currencies to import firearms on one side, and there are countries that export arms to these poorest countries on the other. Indeed, almost all of the countries in conflict coincide with the poorest countries in the world. In those conflicts, arms used are small fire arms such as pistols, revolvers, rifles, heavy machine-guns, mortars, portable anti-tank/anti-aircraft guns, rockets, missiles, grenades and land-mines etc. In 1995, military expenditure/GDP ratios in the African countries were as follows:[3] Sudan 6.6%, Sierra Leone 6.1%, Libya 6.0%, Egypt 5.7%, Mozambique 5.4%, Botswana 5.3%, and Rwanda 5.2%.

2.2 Economic Issues

The foundation of a prosperous world lies in robust growth, which is shown by the world economic statistics.

The world GNI in 2000 was US$31,315 billion,[4] out of which US$9,601 billion was earned by the United States, US$4,519 billion by Japan, US$2,064 billion by Germany, and US$1,460 billion by the United Kingdom. In Asia, some main figures include China (US$1,063 billion), India (US$455 billion), Republic of Korea (US$421 billion), Hong Kong China (US$176 billion), Indonesia (US$120 billion), Singapore (US$99 billion), and Thailand (US$122 billion).

In sub-Saharan Africa, the Republic of South Africa represents almost 40% of the region's GNI. The GNI of the giant of sub-Saharan Africa is

US$129 billion. Second largest in the region, Nigeria's GNI is US$33 billion, and Kenya's GNI is less than US$11 billion dollars.

Per capita income has even larger discrepancies. For example, among above mentioned countries, Singapore's per capita GNI is US$24,740 dollars which is as high as West European countries, whereas China's per capita GNI is US$840, ranking 141st in the world. South Africa is US$3,040, Nigeria US$260 and Kenya US$350.

Taking this into account, it would be surprising to learn that, according to the World Bank statistics, per capita GNP in the 1960s was higher in many sub-Saharan African countries than in South East Asia such as Thailand and Indonesia (see Figure 9.2). This tells us of the importance of robust growth as so mentioned in the G8 Communiqué Okinawa 2000.[5]

'The East Asian Miracle' of the World Bank[6] has given detailed analysis on the rapid economic growth of Southeast Asian countries. One of the most important factors is that the primary school enrolment ratio was high even during their 'poor' days (see Table 9.1). According to the World Bank research report, 'Levels of human capital were higher in the High-performing Asian economies in the 1960s than in other low- and middle-income economies. Educational investment resulted in universal

Figure 9.2 GDP Per Capita of Thailand, Indonesia and Selected African Countries 1960–1999

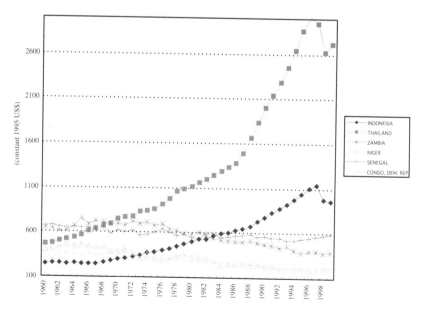

Table 9.1   Gross Enrolment Ratio: Primary School (%)

	1960	1965	1970	1975	1980	1985	1990	1995
Indonesia	71.0	72.0	80.0	86.0	107.2	117.0	115.2	113.4
Malaysia	96.0	90.0	88.7	94.5	92.6	100.7	93.7	103.4
Philippines	95.0	113.0	108.3	108.6	111.9	107.4	111.3	114.1
Singapore	111.0	105.0	105.5	109.7	107.7	108.1	103.7	95.2
Thailand	83.0	78.0	81.4	83.6	98.9	96.1	99.1	86.5
Zambia	42.0	53.0	89.7	96.0	89.9	104.5	98.7	88.5
Niger	5.0	11.0	13.3	18.5	25.3	25.5	28.8	29.0
Senegal	27.0	40.0	38.8	40.0	46.3	56.4	58.9	64.3
D.R.Congo	60.0	70.0	95.0	92.7	92.4	86.5	70.3	72.2

Source: World Development Indicator Database

Gross Enrolment Ratio : Primary School

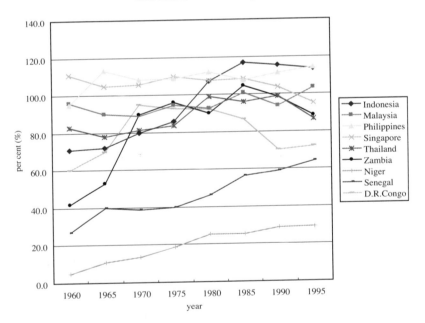

primary education and in widely available secondary education.'[7] More equitable income distribution in these countries also played important role for this.[8]

Table 9.1 and the related graph show some typical cases of primary school enrolment ratio.

Another feature of the deeply and rapidly globalized world is that almost every country is de facto obliged to think about the external market. Given the fact that the level of industrialization differs from country to country, international rules must be established reflecting the reality. Bearing this in mind, Japan is proposing to raise, in the New Round of World Trade Organization Negotiations, the following points:[9]

(a) The response to economic globalization,
(b) Prevention of dividing the world economy into blocks through the strengthening of the WTO,
(c) The aim to make the New Round a comprehensive one so that various WTO members will see the benefit,
(d) The active engagement of the developing countries, in the New Round and proper response to the demands of the developing countries inter alia in the field of agriculture.

2.3 Social Issues

Figure 9.1 includes typical issues in the social sector in the globalized world. Rule making activities, mainly in the United Nations, became active especially regarding the weak part of the society. Conclusion of Convention of Rights of the Child (entered into force in 1990) is a major achievement after the successful conclusion and functioning of Convention of the Elimination of All Forms of Discrimination against Women (entered into force in1981). In accordance with the Convention, the world has started dealing seriously with trafficking of women and children. Mounting international interest further led to a successful conclusion of United Nations Convention on Transnational Organized Crime (concluded in December 2000).[10]

The situation of women in the world still needs a great deal of improvement in spite of the above-mentioned Convention. For example, the female adult (age 15 and above) literacy rate in developing countries in 2000 was 66.0% (least developing countries 42.8%, Arab states 50.1%, East Asia and Pacific 79.4%, Latin America and the Caribbean 87.4%, South Asia 43.8%, sub-Saharan Africa 53.6%). The female youth (age 15-24) literacy rate shows improvement (80.5%) but further actions for literacy are needed especially in South Asia and sub-Saharan Africa (least developing countries 58.1%, Arab states 72.5%, East Asia and the Pacific 96.4%, Latin America and the Caribbean 94.4%, South Asia 61.2%, sub-Saharan Africa 73.0%).[11] Gender inequality persists in economic activities, work burden and political participation.

With regard to health, the establishment of the Global AIDS and Health Fund to fight AIDS, tuberculosis and malaria should be mentioned. Based on the discussions following the Okinawa Infectious Disease

Initiatives launched at the G8 Okinawa Summit in 2000, the Fund was officially established at the Genoa G8 Summit in July 2001. According to the WHO and The Global Fund, as of December 2002, the number of people living with HIV/AIDS was 42 million persons (38.6 million adults, out of which were 19.2 million women, and 3.2 million children under 15 years). People newly infected with HIV in 2002 were 5 million persons (4.2 million adults, out of which were 2 million women, and 0.8 million children under 15 years). AIDS deaths in 2002 were 3.1million in total (2.5 million adults, out of which 1.2 million were women, and 0.61 million children under 15 years). In 2001, 1.1 million persons died of malaria and 1.64 million died of tuberculosis.[12] The three infectious diseases not only kill people, but also threaten national economy and security, given the fact that in the case of HIV/AIDS, the working population is hit. Those with a regular salary and intellectuals are the ones who are killed more often. In other words, the emerging middle class is often touched, thus the indispensable bid for socio-economic development will perish. HIV/AIDS hits the future. For example, according to the Joint United Nations Programme on HIV/AIDS (UNAIDS), in South Africa 'the number of AIDS-related deaths among young adults is projected to peak in 2010-2015. It is estimated that there will be more than 17 times as many deaths among young persons aged 15-34 as there would have been without AIDS.'[13]

Based on these facts, UN Secretary General Kofi Annan gave four priorities to the Fund on the occasion of the establishment of the Global AIDS and Health Fund:

> First, to ensure that people everywhere – particularly the young know what to do to avoid infection. Second, to stop perhaps the most tragic form of HIV transmission – from mother to child. Third, to provide treatment for all those infected. Fourth, to redouble the search for a vaccine, as well as a cure. Fifth, to care for all whose lives have been devastated by AIDS, particularly the orphans – and there are 13 million of them today – and their numbers are growing.[14]

The Fund was established by the Japanese initial commitment of US$200 million together with American and European commitment. As of June 2003, US$1.4 billion are committed in total. Japan placed importance on the prevention of HIV/AIDS, given the fact that an effective prevention campaign alone can truly fight back the pandemic. Africa certainly is an important target but Asia is also deeply affected. At the same time, Japan is reminding the world not to forget tuberculosis and malaria, which actually continue to kill. Emergence of the Severe Acute Respiratory Syndrome, or SARS, in China and its spread to other countries also reminded us of the importance of the international networking of surveillance, alertness and cooperation.[15]

2.4 Overlapping Issues

In the globalized world, there are issues which have overlapping natures among political, social and economic sectors.

The problem of refugees and internally displaced persons are usually caused by political reasons, but it has a social dimension as well. Actually, there are about 20 million refugees around the world (45% in Asia, 25% in Europe and 21% in Africa).[16] Refugees are the weakest elements of the world, the poorest, often surviving in camps without basic human needs such as safe water, sanitation, educational facilities and health facilities. Among them, elderly persons, women, and children need special care, but it is not easy to provide for them. In many cases, host countries themselves are the poorest and least developed countries, and thus have inevitable difficulties in bearing the burden. Under these circumstances, a new approach has been launched in Zambia since 2002. This Zambia initiative is to conceive of refugees not as burden but as agents of development through their integration to local communities' socio-economic activities. Donor countries and UNHCR, UNICEF and other relevant agencies are cooperating to implement the new approach.[17]

To solve the refugee problem, UNHCR is promoting 4Rs (repatriation, reintegration, rehabilitation and reconstruction). This is to make the process from repatriation to reconstruction smooth, in cooperation with development assistance agencies. In this connection, the UNDP implemented in Sierra Leone a project which consists of reintegration of ex-combatants through a capacity building and self-employment project (US$3.09 million), financed by the Trust Fund for Human Security (Japan's financial contribution to UN). Following her basic development assistance policy line, Japan is placing importance on each and every person's empowerment.

Environment is also a typical case of an overlapping issue. Since the Rio de Janeiro Summit in 1992, global rule making has been taking concrete shape: on climate change, protection of ozone layer, forest preservation and sustainable use, biodiversity, hazardous waste, hazardous chemicals, etc. It is of utmost importance that the same rule applies to all so that planet earth can continue to bear human activities.[18]

Transnational organized crime is a typical problem on the negative side of globalization. While judicial authorities inevitably work inside each country's sovereign border, transnational organized criminals ignore national borders and use the most advanced technology such as information and communication technology. Their main activities are smuggling of people, especially women and children, as well as smuggling of firearms, illegal drugs, clandestine migrants, etc. To overcome national border barriers in their fight against these criminals, states should harmonize their crime law, and police and judicial authorities should cooperate closely. Cooperation among financial authorities is also crucial to fight against money laundering. The United Nations Convention against Transnational Organized Crime was agreed under these circumstances. Contracting parties are obliged to criminalize participation in an organized criminal group, agreeing with one or more other persons to commit a serious crime, the laundering of proceeds of crime, corruption, and obstruction of justice. This Convention also stipulates international cooperation in confiscation of property, extradition of criminals, and mutual legal assistance.

3. How to Realize a Society with People's Participation

3.1 People's Hope as the Engine of Growth

At the World Summit on Sustainable Development (WSSD) held in Johannesburg in August and September 2002, the government of Japan proposed a new approach to realize sustainable development and proposed to share experiences and information, strategy, and responsibility with developing countries.

The Japanese approach was based on the honest recognition that not a single country has ever realized 'sustainable development', i.e., attaining at the same time both economic development and environmental preservation. To share its own experiences, the Japanese Government and NGOs held seminars and symposiums in the Japanese Pavilion in UBUNTU Village and continuously showed videos on the suffering of people from pollution during the economic 'miracle' and the cost of recovering from it to regain blue sea and blue sky. To realize sustainable development, it was pointed out that every country and every person should be aware of the need to realize a recycling society.

At the same time, the importance of governance was pointed to as a prerequisite to realize sustainable development. The Japanese Government distributed the 'Conceptual Flow of Global Sharing (Partnership)' to realize sustainable development.[19]

As is shown in Figure 9.3 peace, security and good governance are the prerequisites for sustainable development. Without peace, it is unrealistic to think that people will invest, cultivate or go to school. Security includes social security that allows 'normal' life for ordinary people. Governance assures ordinary people's peaceful life assuring them that they will not to go to jail or their goods will not be confiscated unless they breach the law. In other words, these three prerequisites give ordinary people 'predictability' and 'political and economic participation' and will nurture a 'culture of conflict prevention'.

Peace is often said to be the most important basis upon which was realized the British industrial revolution. Two hundred years of peace

Figure 9.3 Conceptual Flow of Global Sharing (Partnership)

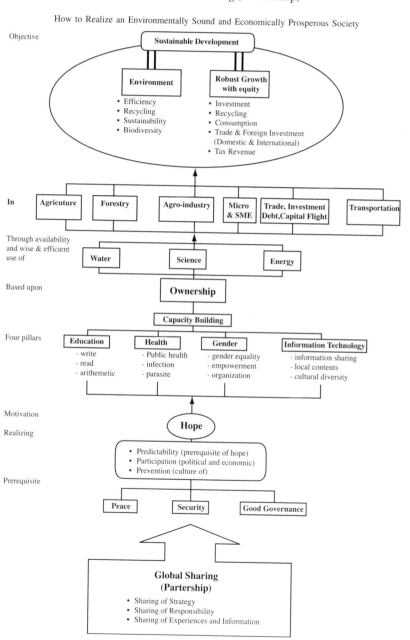

in England gave birth to solid agriculture, capital accumulation and innovative entrepreneurs. The Japanese Edo period (1603–1868, with the Tokugawa Shogun government with its political capital in Edo, which was renamed Tokyo after the Meiji revolution) was a peaceful era with a solid agricultural and commercial network around the nation, and a mining industry as well.[20] For example, the copper and silver mining industry was the origin of a Japanese modern industrial giant, the Sumitomo group: during the last decade of the sixteenth century founders of Sumitomo innovated new refinery technology to separate silver and copper. In the early seventeenth century, annual production of copper in Japan was about 7,800 tons, with 5,400 tons exported to China, Holland, etc. In 1668, 70% of Japanese total export was copper (note: Japan continued to trade with China, Korea and Holland during its closed door policy.). The copper mining industry was so prosperous that the Shogun government established in Osaka the copper refineries association in 1701. Incidentally, Sumitomo founded its bank in seventeenth century and lent money to feudal lords. Another Japanese economic giant, Konoike, has its origin (Shinroku KONOIKE founded in 1578) in the innovation of brewing transparent 'sake' (rice wine). Their successful brewing business led them to launch in the commercial sector, first opening a large shop in Osaka in 1619 and then in Edo. Shinroku's son opened a bank in 1656 and established a nationwide commercial network using navigation. A similar experience led the Mitsui group to establish a textile industry and textile retail shop (today's Mitsukoshi department store), then launched in the banking sector as well to establish today's giant. One additional point concerning these giants is that they did their best to survive the Meiji revolution, while many of the then-economic giants were crushed by the new government.

It is not by coincidence that the poorest countries today have been suffering from regional or domestic conflicts. Therefore, Japan is making a significant contribution for peace building and consolidation of peace. At present, Japan has participated in eight PKO,[21] such as those in Mozambique, the Golan Hights, Cambodia and Timor-Leste (East Timor). Further to the traditional peacekeeping operations, Foreign Minister Kawaguchi has launched a new concept, accompanied by actions, called 'the consolidation of peace' initiative,[22] bearing in mind that from humanitarian activities during the conflict to post conflict reconstruction, there should be seamless support, including during the chaotic period which usually follows just after the end of conflict when social disorder occurs due to the collapse of the civilian police. Asian countries, i.e., Afghanistan, Timor-Leste and Sri Lanka, are some examples where Japan is taking the lead for the consolidation of peace, placing importance on the role of each individual and community. This human and community-centred approach has a basic notion common with the concept proposed by the Commission on Human Security in its report, 'Human Security Now',[23] submitted to UN Secretary General Kofi Annan on May 1, 2003.

The feature of this new pillar of Japanese foreign policy, 'consolidation of peace', is that Japan has started to provide support to benefit the local communities even before a formal peace agreement is concluded. This approach not only brings assistance to the local people at a crucial time of need, but also gives crucial momentum to the peace process by helping the local populace to enjoy the dividends of peace. This approach is more proactive than conventional ones, which have been focused on rehabilitation and reconstruction after peace accords have been signed. Currently, there is a significant movement toward peace in Sri Lanka, Mindanao and other parts of the world, and Japan is trying hard to implement programmes of support and contribute to peace in such regions.

The issue of small arms is another area where Japan is taking the lead through its numerous activities, i.e., submission of draft resolutions to the UN General Assembly over the past years, chairmanship of the UN Panel (1996–97) and the Group of Governmental Experts (1998–99), and hosting the Tokyo Follow-up Meeting of the UN Conference on the Illicit Trade in Small and Light Weapons in All Its Aspects in January 2002, 'Regional Seminar for Pacific Island Countries' again in Tokyo in January 2003, and 'Regional Seminar' in Bali, Indonesia in February 2003. Japan has also provided substantial financial assistance for post-conflict weapons collection and economic recovery.

Japan is the only highly industrialized country that does not export arms. This spirit is also reflected in the Japanese ODA principle as follows:

(a) Environmental conservation and development should be pursued in tandem.

(b) Any use of ODA for military purposes or for aggravation of international conflicts should be avoided.

(c) Full attention should be paid to trends in recipient countries' military expenditures, their development and production of weapons of mass destruction and missiles, their export and import of arms, etc., so as to maintain and strengthen international peace and stability, and from the viewpoint that developing countries should place appropriate priorities in the allocation of their resources in their own economic and social development.

(d) Full attention should be paid to efforts for promoting democratization and introduction of a market-oriented economy, and the situation regarding the securing of basic human rights and freedom in the recipient country.

Security is another prerequisite for sustainable development. In the above-mentioned Japanese Edo period cases, security inside the country assured the establishment of a commercial and banking network through investment and consumption, giving birth, for example, to the world's first futures transaction of a commodity in the Osaka Dojima Rice Market. Needless to say that a futures transaction is feasible only where market confidence is consolidated.

Governance reflects democratic values, ensuring rule of law and an institutionalized system. OECD mentioned governance as 'the use of political authority and exercise of control in a society in relation to the management of its resources for social and economic development'. It also said, 'It is often useful to distinguish between three aspects of governance; the form of political regime, the process by which authority is exercised in the management of a country's economic and social resources, and the capacity of government to formulate and implement policies and discharge government functions'[24].

In WSSD, the Japanese delegation pointed out that peace, security and good governance will give predictability to ordinary people's lives.[25] With predictability, people can make a plan and programme of their economic activities: farmers can seed when thinking of harvest in several months, entrepreneurs can invest with their market strategy in mind. If they are not confident, they will understandably put their money in a safer place, as most unfortunately is the case in developing countries where capital flight occurs and hampers their country's development. It is not surprising to see that capital flight and economic underdevelopment often happen in the same countries.

Political participation means free election under a multiparty system with guaranteed secrecy of vote. In this connection, it is encouraging to see that 29 sub-Saharan African countries are now choosing their governments through multiparty elections.[26]

Economic participation means market economy where ordinary people can freely express their entrepreneurship without a central planning authority or political intervention. Dynamic micro and small enterprise does promote economic growth as typically shown by the success in Bangladesh of micro-financing by Grameen Bank to female farmers, which gave them not only a cash income, but also, and more importantly, self confidence and self identity. A female farmer answered in an interview that when she signed her own name for the first time in her life to get a micro-credit she realized that she was she.[27]

A culture of conflict prevention, promoted by Mr. Kofi Annan, United Nations Secretary General, will be nurtured through acceptance of those who are different and enhance dynamism based on diversity. In other words, a culture of conflict prevention will be realized through tolerance of those who do not belong to the same group and enhancement of cultural diversity. In July 2000, at the G8 Kyushu-Okinawa Summit hosted by Japanese Prime Minister Yoshiro Mori, G8 leaders declared in the 'G8 Communiqué Okinawa 2000' that 'Cultural diversity is a source of social and economic dynamism which has the potential to enrich human life.'...'promoting cultural diversity enhances mutual respect, inclusion and non-discrimination, and combats racism and xenophobia.' The Communiqué also declared that 'we must encourage peoples to learn to live together by nurturing interest, understanding and acceptance of different cultures.'[28]

With this 'treble p' (predictability, participation and prevention), ordinary people may be able to think that tomorrow can be better than today, i.e., to have HOPE. Hope indeed is the best motivation for ordinary people who are actually the protagonists of growth and nation building.

3.2 Four Principal Pillars

3.2.1 Education

With hope, people will invest for the future and the most typical case is education. Statistics show that already in early 1960's, South East Asian countries were at a record high primary school enrolment ratio as mentioned above. It is to be noted that it was even so in the early 1960's when their per capita GNP was lower than sub-Saharan African countries (see Tables 9.2 and 9.3 above)

Data in the UNDP Human Development Report show that the school enrolment ratio of Asia is higher than that of sub-Saharan Africa generally, and that the ratios have fluctuated sharply in sub-Saharan Africa.

Asian countries have put emphasis on a continuous flow of investments in education, although these countries have the good fortune to have stable international situations. Below are net primary enrolment ratios (%) of some countries in 1998 all belonging to the 'low human development' category:

Sudan 46, Togo 88, Madagascar 63, Djibouti 32, Tanzania 48, Zambia 73, Senegal 59, Chad 55, Ethiopia 35, Burkina Faso 34, Niger 26.... Laos 76, Bangladesh 100.

Belief in ordinary people's potential has been at the centre of Japanese development assistance. Thus, education and human resources development has been its main pillar. Prime Minister Koizumi reiterated his belief in human resources development on May 14, 2003 in Tokyo in his welcoming speech to President Wade of Senegal and said that he regarded human-centered development as a priority area. He also expressed his intention to intensify policy dialogues with heavily indebted African countries so that they will invest in education and other socio-economic development priorities with financial resources made available by Japanese cancellation of their debt.

In fact, Koizumi had emphasized in his WSSD speech in September 2002 as follows:

We must determine the key factors in ensuring sustainable development once peace is *achieved*. I believe that the answer is "People". Japan, a country poor in natural resources, has grown to be what it is today on the strength of its human resources. It has attached paramount importance to education as the basis of development. My government, together with Japanese non-governmental organizations, has proposed that the United Nations declare a "Decade of Education for Sustainable Development". We shall provide no less than 250 billion yen in education assistance over a five-year period'.

He also stated at the press conference that each country is facing a different situation on education and human resources development. Japan would like to find what are the largest needs for each country and in order to do so, would like to listen to them. We must recognize that each developing country's wishes and requests differ and we must extend our hand of solidarity accordingly. This is Japan's basic position for development assistance.

Japanese ODA in 'social infrastructures and service' including education and human resources development amounted to US$2,066 million in 2001. 'Social infrastructures and service' is one of most important areas of Japan's ODA, following the 'economic infrastructures and service' area. That is because we recognize the important role of education and human resources.[29]

In Asia, one of the most successful cases of partnership in ODA between Japan and a recipient country may be Thailand. In fact, Japan and Thailand signed a partnership agreement for technical cooperation for third countries in 1994. For example, 'Project for the Asian Center for International Parasite Control' which aims to strengthen the basis of parasite control in Southeast Asia has established a human resources and information network system in cooperation with Mahidon University and the Ministry of Health. In this project, Thailand is not a recipient country but rather a donor country towards other countries. The project is a follow-up of the Hashimoto Initiative against infectious and parasite diseases launched at the G8 Birmingham Summit in 1998, and is supposed to produce managers who engage in parasite control in Thailand and in Asian and African countries.

A future oriented and rather unique way of human development in Asia has been organized since 1990 by NHK (Japan Broadcasting Corporation) and education institutions:[30] a series of Robot Tournaments are held at the senior industry high school level (Japanese domestic event) and at the university level (international). Students participate in the tournament, for example, in a ball game using only robots which are made by themselves under a strict budget limit. The purpose is to enhance creativity and originality of Asia-Pacific youth through competition. Each year, students are given a specific theme of a ball game (e.g., basket ball) to be played by robots. The tournament started from a domestic competition and little by little enlarged its scope to include mainly Asian students.

A more classic form of Japan-Asia cooperation for Asian human resources development includes Asian students studying in Japanese universities. In 2002, 88,664 foreign students including 6,167 government-financed students from Asia were studying in Japan.[31]

In fact, according to an old Japanese saying, 'people are castle's wall, people are the main tower of the castle after all'. Given the fact that most of the Southeast Asian countries do not have natural resources, the only reasonable explanation for their success must be attributed to the high quality of their human resource development.

3.2.2 Health

A second sector people will be concerned about is health, his or her own health and that of his or her family and members of their community and country.

In 1994, the Government of Japan announced 'Global Issues Initiatives (GII) on population and AIDS' and committed US$3 billion over seven years. After seven years, it turned out to be US$5 billion dollars, making Japan a leading nation in combating infectious and parasitic diseases. As a follow-up to the successful GII, Japan further announced its commitment of US$3 billion over five years on holistic initiatives to fight back infectious diseases at the G8 Okinawa Summit ('Okinawa Infectious Diseases Initiatives (IDI)'). 'IDI' states three important principles: (i) combating infectious diseases is a main pillar for development; (ii) global solidarity and regional measures in accordance with regional characteristics are both necessary; and (iii) combination of public health measures and infectious diseases measures are to be pursued[32].

In line with these basic policy lines, the outbreak of the Severe Acute Respiratory Syndrome, or SARS, in early 2003 led the Japanese Government to move swiftly to contain the new infectious disease. Japan immediately extended ¥2 billion (US$17 million) worth of emergency assistance to eight affected countries, mainly to China. In other countries, for example in Vietnam, Japanese emergency teams arrived as early as March 16 for two weeks, providing expertise and necessary materials. Expert teams also went to Taiwan in late May. In the case of SARS, the recent trend in Japanese ODA is shown, i.e., combination of bilateral and multilateral assistance. The Japanese Government proposed together with ASEAN countries a resolution on SARS to this year's World Health Assembly to recognize SARS as the first severe infectious disease to emerge in the twenty-first century, and to enhance international cooperation and coordination in the fight against SARS, which was adopted with consensus.[33] At the G8 Evian Summit held in June 2003, Japanese Prime Minister Koizumi expressed his intention to support the WHO.

The Japanese initiative in combating infectious disease in the world is also a reflection of its own experience after its complete defeat in 1945. Infrastructure was almost totally destroyed by severe bombing all over the nation, and the defeated country tried to rebuild the nation firstly by reconstructing schools and secondly by introducing a simplified, safe water distribution network, especially in rural areas. The hygiene situation was thus reestablished and strengthened, and female farmers realized a sort of kitchen revolution, giving them more free time that led to female empowerment. Post-defeat public health reestablishment went further and a nationwide network of health posts, mother and child health care, together with education of public health nurses and a solid school health system gave strongly positive results in infectious and parasitic diseases eradication.

Japan is expanding these experiences in Asia. For example, the distribution of the 'Mother and Child Pocket-book'[34] in which all the relevant records of a child since his or her mother became pregnant, such as periodically recorded weight, height, and vaccinations are written in, is now carried out in Indonesia. This is bringing positive results in the improvement of mother and child health.

3.2.3 Gender

As of 2003, there are 6.3 billion human beings, of which 3.13 billion are female.[35] With their full participation, based on full appreciation of their potentiality and role, the world community will enjoy greater economic growth, a lower infant mortality rate, and more dynamic cultural diversity.

Gender equality is another important pillar in Japanese ODA. In 1995, Japan announced the 'Women in Development Initiative' and is pursuing ODA for women's education, health including reproductive health, and participation in socio-economic activities. Japan provides gender-related ODA through such means as support for small-in-scale and community-based programmes conducted by NGOs, etc. (Grant Assistance for Grassroots, etc.) and the dispatching of experts or accepting trainees (Technical Cooperation).[36]

Gender balance in education is another important target. Providing basic facilities, such as water wells, is an important ODA objective. In sub-Saharan Africa, 'the average distance walked from household to the traditional source is about three kilometers'.[37] And girls are doing this water-carrying job. With water wells in their villages, girls would gain several hours that could be used for education.

3.2.4 Information Technology

Information technology is a fourth pillar in realizing ownership. Before information and communication's rapid innovation occurred, it was difficult for weaker people to get information freely and even more so to send out information. Today, with rapidly advancing technology, information is becoming accessible to even the remotest parts of the world or even to those living under a single party system country. Certainly the question of affordability remains, yet it is now possible for villagers in the remotest rural areas to send out to the world their cultural performances through the Internet.

The importance of realizing 'digital opportunities for all' was stressed in the report by the IT Dot Force,[38] set up by the G8 Okinawa Summit and presented to the G8 Genoa Summit in 2001. The report proposed the following measures: (a) Help establish and support developing countries' and emerging economies' e-strategies; (b) Improve connectivity, increase access and lower cost; (c) Enhance human capacity development, knowledge creation and sharing; (d) Foster enterprise and entrepreneurship for sustainable economic development; (e) Establish and support universal participation in addressing new international policy and issues raised by the Internet and ICT; (f) Establish and support dedicated initiatives for the ICT inclusion of the least developed countries; (g) Promote ICT for health care and in support against HIV/AIDS and other infectious and communicable diseases; (h) National and international effort to support local content and applications creation; (i) Prioritize ICT in G8 and other development assistance and programmes and enhance coordination of multilateral initiatives.

On the other hand, information sharing should be rapid enough to match the requirements of a globalized world. Recent experience with SARS, which was spread across the world through jet aircraft because information was not revealed at the outset in the country where the outbreak started, is a clear warning from this view point. Information and communication technology can realize transparency and information sharing, allowing people to receive and send information.

Together with *education, health, and gender mainstreaming, information technology* will empower ordinary people. As the Figure 9.3 flow chart (on page 219) shows, their capacity building will enhance ownership of a nation.

3.3 Some Key Sectors

Ownership of a country, supported by partnership with other countries, is the important engine to realize sustainable development. Based on ownership and partnership, countries can use water, science and energy to enhance their socio-economic activities.

Water was the mother of four ancient civilizations. Human history saw prosperity with ancient irrigation, but also saw the decline of agriculture and eventually civilization due to salt pushed up close to the soil surface by irrigation over the centuries.[39] Water is now becoming a scarce resource and such campaigns as 'more crop per drop' by UN Secretary General Kofi Annan illustrate the importance of the issue. In fact, UN Secretary General declared 'WEHAB' as the five key sectors in WSSD. W is for water, E for energy, H for health, A for agriculture, and B for biodiversity.

In WSSD, Japan placed great importance on the water sector. In fact, in quantitative terms, Japan has provided ODA for water amounting to more than ¥650 billion (approximately US$5.7 billion) from fiscal year 1999 to fiscal year 2001. Included in that amount was US$1 billion for drinking water and sanitation.[40]

Japan's emphasis on water in her ODA is partly based on her own experience after defeat in WW II in 1945, and of creating a subsequent successful simplified water distribution system in rural areas, as mentioned above in 3.2.2. In addition to positive results in combating infectious and parasitic diseases, female farmers could introduce a sort of kitchen revolution and could use freed time for more productive activities than water well pumping.

The Ministerial Declaration on water issued on 23 March 2003, states as follows: 'In managing water, we should ensure good governance with a stronger focus on household and neighborhood community-based approaches by addressing equity in sharing benefits, with due regard to pro-poor and gender perspectives in water policy'. This community-based approach is in line with the post-defeat Japanese experience. The Ministerial conference was held at the end of the third World Water Forum (WWF III) held at Lake Biwa and the Yodo River Basin[41] in March 2003. About 24,000 participants – including representatives from NGOs, UN agencies, the private sector and local governments, as well as ordinary citizens, members of parliament and other officials – attended the eight-day event.

The flow of world opinion making on water issues continued at the G8 Evian Summit held in June 2003. Based on WSSD and the WWF III, the G8 action plan on water issued at Evian says: 'As water is essential to life, lack of water can undermine human security'. The action plan stresses the importance of promoting good governance, utilizing all financial resources, building infrastructure by empowering local authorities and communities, strengthening monitoring, assessment and research, and reinforcing engagement of international organizations. Man needs safe water for life, but one out of five persons have no access to water, and 6,000 children die every day of water-related diseases.[42]

4. Human Security

4.1 State and People

Kwame Nkrumah, the father of African independence, has been asking himself during his fight for independence which area he was fighting for. Was he fighting for the independence of the British Gold Coast or for the independence of the former Kingdom of Ashanti?[24] Indeed, European invaders came from the sea and drew their demarcation line totally ignoring existing states, civilizations and peoples who were living there. The Berlin conference of the nineteenth century was just a reconfirmation of what King Affonso I (Mbemba Nzinga, 1506-45) of the Kingdom of Kongo wrote in 1526 and throughout the 1530s in his letters addressed to Pope Paulus III and the Portuguese King John III: He told the Portuguese to tell his people to stop grabbing Kongolese, including noblemen and even royalty and selling them, a practice so common which was so great that his country was being completely depopulated. The King also wrote it was doing great harm to the security and peace of the Kingdom.[44] In sub-Saharan Africa, states and civilizations, together with ownership, died little by little during the centuries-long slave trade, exploitation of wealth and finally, colonization by Europeans.

This led to the above-mentioned question by Nkrumah. After reflection, he decided to lead the independence movement for the British Gold Coast since it was the only pragmatic reality. The newly independent state needed a name and the leader chose the name Ghana. Ghana was the ancient Empire that flourished from around the fourth century to 1280 in West Sudan, but had no direct link with modern Ghana. The name was understandably a wise choice because it was a reminder of African glory and civilization. The sad reality was that, in any event, the new state needed an 'artificial' name since it was not possible to have a 'nation state'. It may be noted that history was not kind to Africa.

In order to overcome this harsh reality that hit almost all of the newly independent states, new African leaders ran were idealistic, believing that Africa is united as one. Thus, the Organization of African Unity was born.

But, again history was not kind to Africa. In spite of their idealism, newly independent states needed to consolidate their own national identity, for peoples who were speaking 250 languages (in the case of the Congo) in one nation, asking their people to be loyal to their new president speaking another language and not to their cousins across the border who were speaking their own language.

To further worsen the situation in Africa, the continent did not see the 'Cold War', because there was a 'hot' war, with shelling and killing in the context of 'cold' war. After the end of the cold war in the 1990s, as outsiders' interest faded away from the continent, regional conflicts erupted as described in Section 2.1 above.

African history illustrates a typical contradiction emerging from the notion of nation state, about the relationship between a nation and her people, resulting in a lack of security for ordinary people.

On the other hand, the terrorist attacks on September 11, 2001 revealed that even the mightiest state cannot assure its people of total security in the globalized world of the twenty-first century. Furthermore, weapons used for the attack were civilian aircraft with innocent, ordinary people on board. The target was innocent ordinary people working in civilian buildings. And the attacker was not a state, but a group without territory or national authority. Normally a state is composed of authority/power, territory and people. But 9.11 revealed that an entity without any of these three basic elements of a state can pursue attacks without armed forces.

This leads us to think that in a globalized world, national borders do not serve the traditional role of a wall, protecting people living inside from outside danger. International society has been composed of nation states, with borders in between. But as mentioned earlier in this chapter, the Asian financial crisis revealed that global free movement of capital can boost the economy when massively invested, but can also turn it down very rapidly when drawn out in a short period. It also revealed that in the financial sectors national borders do not exist. A characteristic of the globalized world is that nation-to-nation relations are not in parallel, existing side by side with their respective peoples staying inside their borders. They are in fact overlapping and peoples are not only directly linked to their counterparts through their jobs in the same sector but also exposed directly to the outside world as shown in the 9.11 attack. An apparent phenomenon is the migration of people realized through transportation and information technology innovations. A globalized world thus renders people fragile and we may need to rethink how to ensure people's safety.

There are, however, states that destroy people's security. Lack of governance or bad governance as seen in part 2 above of this chapter does not give predictability, or allow political and economic participation, nor harness a culture of conflict prevention. These states exploit their own people, do not trust their own people and even oppress and kill their own people. In such cases, people flee their homes to become refugees or internationally displaced persons. This still happens in the twenty-first century, though it is not necessarily directly caused by globalization. It occurs rather in the context of classic relations between state and people, yet here again a key element is migrating people.

Then a question to be asked in the twenty-first century is 'who should protect ordinary people, and from what sort of danger'. Another difficult question is 'whom to protect'. Here arises the question of citizenship as well.

4.2 People-Centred Approach[45]

Such are some of the questions studied by Human Security Commission,[46] 'established in response to the UN Secretary General's call at the Millennium Summit in September 2000 to achieve the twin goals of "freedom from fear" and "freedom from want"'.[47] The commission was co-chaired by Sadako Ogata and Amartya Sen, and they presented the commission's report to UN Secretary General on May 1, 2003 in New York.

Not all of the people living in the twenty-first century can live with human dignity, nor can they claim their identity in society. Often they die before their first birthday[48] or reaching the age of five, or do not have basic human needs met, or they do not have access to information because of illiteracy. On the other hand, a state can not completely guarantee its people's security. Here arises the need to find ways in which people can pursue their lives and protect themselves. Ways to realize this include empowering people through education and vocational training, assuring good health by strengthening public health and other means, realizing gender mainstreaming, and realizing a more equitable economic environment, including better international trade rules, etc. A new direction for international development assistance should be researched from these view points.

Empowerment of each person in order to further strengthen resilience against the above-mentioned risks and dangers and engendering a human network of empowered persons will be effective and necessary. Such networking will build a solid community and furthermore, networking of communities will make for a resilient society. Such a resilient society will become a basis for nation building. In other words, in cases where good governance exists, the government tries hard to provide security for its people but it is not perfect, because of poverty of the country itself or because of the negative side of the coin of the globalized world, so the question to be addressed is how to make people more resilient and make them secure in their own lives. This new notion of security is called 'human security'. Human security can be realized by a combination of top down national security and bottom up people's security.

In cases where good governance does not exist or conflict occurs, there are two dimensions. Inside such a country, people would be less vulnerable if there is human networking and community networking. If they are to flee their homes, internationally displaced persons and refugees could be less vulnerable if humanitarian assistance can support them in a timely manner and without interruption through different stages of conflict or bad governance. How to assure human dignity to refugees is a difficult question, but it must be recognized that those tens of millions of people also have an authentic right to live and not merely to survive. Humanitarian assistance should thus also be people-centred, recognizing each individual's face and name. At the same time, most of the countries that receive refugees are often very poor, as is the case of the Great Lake Region in Africa, West Africa, Horn of Africa, etc. Refugees are often a 'burden' for their host community and host country, and international humanitarian assistance does not necessarily cover all needs.

Zambia has started an interesting and positive approach to the refugee issue. Zambia has eight borders and refugees arrive at Zambia, a country of ten million persons, from neighbouring countries, namely Angola, the Democratic Republic of the Congo and Burundi. Many of the refugees have stayed for the past 20 years. In 2002, the Zambian government made a drastic change of approach and began trying to define refugees not as a burden, but on the contrary, to incorporate them as an element of socio-economic activities. This is called the 'Zambia initiative'[49] and the key notion of the initiative is to construct a new community composed of local people and refugees, focusing on the western region of the country. At the International Symposium on Refugees in Africa, held on 19-20 June 2003 in Tokyo,[50] the initiative was discussed and drew attention of participants as a new approach to the refugee issue. One facet of its feasibility is the fact that many of the refugees' groups in the western region of Zambia speak the same language as their host community, according to Peter Mumba, Permanent Secretary of Ministry of Home Affairs of Zambia.[51] The initiative is supported by donor countries, including Japan, as well as the UNHCR and UNOPS.

If the approach brings positive results, a new form of community building will be launched. At the same time, it would also bring an answer to countries which have been struggling to overcome a gap between ethnic identity and national identity because of external colonial factors as is often the case in sub-Saharan African countries. Building a common community among those who belong to different nationalities and integrating refugees into the nation building process would bring a win-win solution. If that is the case, hopefully the refugee issue will enhance regional cooperation and integration. The Southern African Development Community (SADC) would be a good example.

This reminds us of the importance of tolerance. The Commission on Human Security recommends that we learn 'to develop a method of teaching that respect diversity'.[52] Easier said than done, but there are some efforts in that direction. G8 education ministers met in Tokyo in April 2000 to discuss 'Education in a Changing Society', and decided to promote education, including lifelong learning, to learn about different cultures. The Chair's Summary of the meeting is, as follows:

> It (lifelong learning) builds the base for economic and social development, develops the capacity of individuals to contribute to and benefit from that development, sustains and enriches both individual and overall culture of a nation and builds mutual respect and understanding that transcends cultural differences.[53]

Innovation of information and communication technology enables this kind of education only if there is a political will to do so. The G8 Okinawa Communiqué stated that cultural diversity is the source of human dynamism. The fact is that 3,000 out of 6,000 languages are disappearing. Ignorance of other people's culture and history still prevails. UNESCO is promoting cultural diversity and adopted the topic at its 2001 General Conference 'UNESCO Universal Declaration on Cultural Diversity'.

The Commission on Human Security recommends the following actions to be taken by the international community. The commission arrived at a policy conclusion to promote Human Security as follows;

1. Protecting people in violent conflict
2. Protecting people from the proliferation of arms
3. Supporting the security of people on the move
4. Establishing human security transition funds for post-conflict situations
5. Encouraging fair trade and markets to benefit the extreme poor
6. Working to provide minimum living standards everywhere
7. According higher priority to ensuring universal access to basic health care
8. Developing an efficient and equitable global system for patent rights
9. Empowering all people with universal basic education
10. Clarifying the need for a global human identity while respecting the freedom of individuals to have diverse identities and affiliations.

4.3 Japanese Support

Japan took the lead in launching the notion of human security in line with its new dimension of development assistance.

In the 1990s, when Europe decreased its development assistance citing 'aide fatigue' and transferred its financial resources to the former socialist bloc in Europe, Japan decided to stand by the forgotten region. Japan proposed a New Development Strategy that respects developing countries' ownership and based on ownership establishes partnership. The New Development Strategy was adopted at the Development Assistance Committee (DAC) of the OECD in 1996. It is significant that development assistance was recognized as an equal footing endeavour and not a sort of nineteenth century-like charity that had a connotation of vertical relations. In this context, the Tokyo International Conference on African Development (TICAD) process was launched in 1993.[54] TICAD in fact proposed the twin notions of ownership and partnership. It was based on the confidence in ordinary people's potentiality and their entrepreneurship.

TICAD II in 1998 further stressed the importance of self-help based on human resource development and the same basic philosophy prevailed in Japanese basic policy at the World Summit for Sustainable Development (WSSD) in Johannesburg in 2002 as described in Section 2 of this chapter.

Consistent support for ordinary people's empowerment based on the confidence in their potentiality made the Japanese Government a strong supporter of the notion of human security. Then Minister of Foreign Affairs and later Prime Minister of Japan, Keizo Obuchi, was deeply affected by the sudden economic downturn in South East Asia following the financial crisis. The sudden economic downturn in Indonesia, for example, forced many girls to leave school, followed later by boys.

In the 'Intellectual Dialogue on Building Asia's Tomorrow', held in December 1998, Keizo Obuchi, now in the capacity of Prime Minister of Japan, expressed his views on human security. Later in the month, in his policy speech in Hanoi entitled 'Toward the Creation of a Bright Future of Asia', he clearly identified human security in Japan's foreign policy and announced that a Trust Fund for Human Security would be established in the United Nations with contributions from Japan. This commitment was fulfilled in 1999, when Japan made an initial contribution of about US$4.63 million. By May 2003, the total contribution had amounted to some US$203 million.

In addition, Prime Minister Yoshiro Mori stated in his speech at the UN Millennium Summit in September 2000 that Japan positioned human security as one of the key perspectives of its foreign policy and that it would establish an international commission on human security to further deepen the concept of human-centred initiatives.

Following this announcement, a Commission on Human Security was established in January 2001, with 12 internationally prominent members. The Commission's mandate was to develop the concept of human security and make recommendations that would serve as guidelines for concrete action to be taken by the international community. After holding five meetings and convening dialogue events with stakeholders in various venues throughout the world, the Commission has just published a final report. The summary of the report was presented to Prime Minister Jun'ichiro Koizumi in February 2003, and the report itself was presented to United Nations Secretary-General Kofi Annan in May 2003.

To implement recommendations by the Commission on Human Security, the Japanese Government is supporting developing countries' human security-related projects through the Human Security Grass Root Grant Aid, and United Nations Specialized Agencies through the Human Security Fund established at the United Nations Secretariat by Japanese financial contributions. For example, assistance through the Human Security Grass Root Grant Aid was extended to an international NGO, CARE UK, to support their activities in hospitals in Baghdad 'to prevent unnecessary death and suffering among the people of Iraq by supplying hospitals with emergency medical supplies'.[55]

Other typical types of support in the area of human security include a project in Southeast Asian countries (Cambodia, Indonesia, Laos, Thailand and Vietnam) to support community efforts to empower socially weak persons. The UN Economic and Social Commission for Asia and the Pacific (ESCAP) implemented the project, encouraging ordinary people to talk on issues and problems and ways to overcome them. Community solidarity was enhanced and concrete results were achieved, such as the building of small bridges. Assistance for the prevention of trafficking in Cambodia, Vietnam and Laos is another case. 'The objective of the project is to build community capacity to prevent trafficking in children and women in a participatory manner' in provinces and localities 'where trafficking is recognized as one of the most serious problems. Activities include awareness raising on danger and prevention of trafficking and assistance to families whose children are at risk of trafficking through rural skills training for food security and income generation'. In Laos, activities include 'teacher training to improve quality of basic education'.[56]

Human security is a new notion that needs to be implemented in concrete terms. Respect for human dignity of each and every individual, and the realization of life with dignity – this should be the endeavour for the twenty-first century.

Notes

[1] K. Ishikawa 'Nation building and development assistance in Africa', Macmillan Print Ltd. 1999.

[2] They are: United Nations Truce Supervision Organization (since 1948 in Israel, Egypt, Syria, Lebanon), United Nations Military Observer Group in India and Pakistan (since 1949 in Kashmir), United Nations Peacekeeping

Force in Cyprus (since 1964), United Nations Disengagement Observer Force (since 1974 in Golan heights), United Nations Interim Force in Lebanon (since 1978 in southern Lebanon), United Nations Iraq-Kuwait Observation Mission (since 1991 in demilitarized zone between Iraq and Kuwait), United Nations Mission for the Referendum in Western Sahara (since 1991), United Nations Observer Mission in Georgia (since 1993), United Nations Interim Administration Mission in Kosovo (since 1999), United Nations Mission in Sierra Leone (since 1999), United Nations Organization Mission in the Democratic Republic of the Congo (since 1999), United Nations Mission in Ethiopia and Eritrea (since 2000), and United Nations Mission of Support in East Timor (since 2002) and United Nations Mission in Cote d' Ivoire (since 2003).

[3]   World Bank Atlas, 1998

[4]   2002 World Development Indicators. Also for the following GNI figures.

[5]   'Robust, broad-based and equitable economic growth is needed to fight poverty and rests on expanding people's capabilities and choices.' (Paragraph 15)

[6]   'The East Asian Miracle: Economic Growth and Public Policy Price' by World Bank ISBN, Oxford University Press 1993.

[7]   Ibid, Summary, page 20.

[8]   'The East Asian Miracle', page 196.

[9]   Japanese Ministry of Foreign Affairs homepage (http://www.mofa.go.jp)

[10] cf. 1.(4) of this chapter.

[11] UNDP, Human Development Report 2002.

[12] WHO, the World Health Report 2002.

[13] UNAIDS, 'Report on the global HIV/AIDS epidemic, 2002', page46

[14] The Secretary –General statement at press event, Genoa, 20 July 2001

[15] cf. WHO homepage on SARS and 2003 World Health Assembly's declaration on SARS.

[16] source: UNHCR

[17] 'International Symposium on Refugees in Africa', held jointly by Japan and UNHCR in Tokyo, 19-20 June 2003.

[18] See more elaboration on environment in part 2 of this chapter.

[19] http://www.mofa.go.jp/policy/environment/wssd/2002/concept.html.

[20] Series of radio programmes, 'PERSPECTIVES ECONOMIQUES', by Radio Zaire, directed by K.Katamba and K.Ishikawa, 1987-88. cf. Sumitomo, Mitsui and Konoike company's respective history.

[21] UNAVM II, UNTAC, ONUMOZ, ONUSAL, UNDOF, UNAMET, UNTAET, UNMISET

[22] 'Changing Security Environment and Japanese Diplomacy', Y. Kawaguchi, RONZA, March 2003 (in Japanese)

[23] Co-chaired by Mrs. S. Ogata, former UNHCR and Prof. A. Sen, Cambridge University and Nobel Prize Laureate. cf. Part 3 of this chapter.

[24] 'Orientations on Participatory Development and Good Governance', DAC/ OECD, 1995

[25] Press conference given by Japanese delegation on August 25, 2002 at Library council chamber in WSSD.

[26] UNDP, Human Development Report 2002, Table 1.1.

[27] A female farmer interviewed by NHK TV programme 'Mirai heno Kyoushitsu (classroom for future)' series. Mohammad Yunus, President of the Bank stressed the importance of commitment to self help. http://www.nhk.or.jp/ tv50/archives/db/2001/2720001018n.html

[28] G8 Communique Okinawa 2000, paragraph 39 to 42

[29] 'Japan's ODA White Paper', 2002

[30] http://www.official-robocon.com/jp/

[31] Source: Ministry of Education, Culture, Sports, Science and Technology, Japan.

[32] ODA white book, 2002

[33] Adopted on May 27, 2003 at 56th World Health Assembly

[34] ODA white paper, 2002.

[35] World Population Prospects, The 2002 revision, United Nations Population Division.

[36] ODA white paper, 2002.

[37] 'Atlas of the African Child', UNECA and UNICEF.

[38] http://www.library.utoronto.ca/g7/summit/2001genoa/dotforce 1.html.

[39] Nikkei Science ,May 2001

[40] http://www.mofa.go.jp/policy/environment/wwf/initiative.html

[41] Kyoto, Shiga and Osaka prefectures in Japan.

[42] United Nations WEHAB Working Group, 'A Framework for Action on Water and Sanitation', August 2002.

[43] K. Nkrumah, 'I speak of Freedom', Westport, 1976, Greenwood Press.

[44] B. Davidson, 'African Civilization Revisited', Trenton, Africa World Press, 1991.

[45] cf. Sadako Ogata's interview, Asahi Shimbun, February 20, 2003

[46] Members are Co-chairs; Sadako Ogata (Scholar in Residence, The Ford Foundation, Former United Nations High Commissioner for Refugees), Amartya Sen (Master, Trinity College, Cambridge University) Commissioners; (in alphabetical order); Lakhdar Brahimi (Special Representative of the UN Secretary-General for Afghanistan and UN Under Secretary-General), Lincoln C. Chen (Director, Center for Global Equity Initiative, Harvard University, and former Vice President of the Rockefeller Foundation), Bronislaw Geremek (Historian, Former Foreign Minister of Poland), Frene Frenny Noshir Ginwala (Speaker of the National Assembly, Parliament of the Republic of South Africa), Sonia Picado S. (President of the Board of Directors of the Inter-American Institute of Human Rights), Surin Pitsuwan (Member of Parliament and Former Minister of Foreign Affairs of Thailand), Donna E. Shalala (President of University of Miami and Former Secretary of Health and Human Services of the United States), Peter Sutherland (Chairman and Managing Director, Goldman Sachs International, Chairman of BP and former Director-General of the General Agreement of Tariffs and Trade and the World Trade Organization), Albert Tevoedjre (Special Envoy of the UN Secretary-General for Ivory Coast, Former Deputy Director General of the International Labour Organization and Former Minister of Planning in Benin), Carl Tham, Swedish Ambassador to Germany and former Secretary General of the Olof Palme International Center).

[47] Commission on Human Security, 'HUMAN SECURITY NOW', New York, 2003.

[48] The infant mortality rate (the number of deaths of children under one year of age per thousand live births) exceeds 100 in the following countries (World Bank Atlas 2002): Afghanistan, Angola, Burkina Faso, Burundi, Chad, Cote d'Ivoire, Djibouti, Equatorial Guinea, Guinea-Bissau, Liberia, Malawi, Mali, Mauritania, Mozambique, Niger, Rwanda, Sierra Leone, Somalia, Zambia

[49] UNHCR 'Zambia Initiative', http://www.unhcr.ch

[50] Co-chaired by Ruud Lubbers, UN High Commissioner for Refugees (2001–), Sadako Ogata, former UN Commissioner for Refugees (1991–2000), and Sam Ibok, Director of Peace and Security Diretorate, African Union

[51] Permanent Secretary Peter Mumba participated to the symposium as a panelist.

[52] HUMAN SECURITY NOW, page 141.

[53] 'G8 Education Ministers' Meeting, Tokyo, 1–2 April 2000, Chair's Summary, para.4

[54] K.Ishikawa, 'Nation Building and Development Assistance to Africa' p.38, Macmillan Press Ltd, 1999

[55] CARE International UK, http://www.careinternational.org.uk/cgi-bin/display_project.cgi?project_id=122.

[56] Japanese Ministry of Foreign Affairs press releases dated May 8, 2003 and June 17, 2003.

References

Annan, K. 2001. The Secretary-General statement at press event, 20 July 2001, Genoa.

CARE International UK. 2003. *Emergency Medical Supplies for Hospitals*, http://www.careinternational.org.uk/cgi-bin display_project.cgi?project_id=122

Commission on Human Security. 2003. *Human Security Now: Human Security Now: Protecting and Empowering People*, http://www.humansecurity-chs.org/finalreport/index.html.

Davidson, B. 1991. *African Civilization Revisited*. Trenton: Africa World Press.

G8 Education Ministers' Meeting (2000) *Chair's Summary*, Report of G8 Education Ministers' Meeting and Forum, Tokyo, 1–2 April, http://www.mext.go.jp/english/topics/g8/000101x.htm

Ishikawa, K. 1999. *Nation Building and Development Assistance in Africa*. London: Macmillan.

Joint United Nations Programme on HIV/AIDS (UNAIDS). 2002. *Report on the Global HIV/AIDS Epidemic, 2002*. New York: UNAIDS.

Katamba, K and K. Ishikawa. 1987. Radio programme, *Perspectives Economiques*, on Radio Zaire.

Kawaguchi, Y. 2003. 'Henka-suru Anzen-hosho-kankyo-to Nihon-gaiko (Changing Security Environment and Japanese Diplomacy)', Ronza, March. Tokyo: Asahi Shimbun, pp.180–9.

Ogata S. 2003. Interview by Asahi Shimbun, *Asahi Shimbun*, February 20.

Organisation for Economic Co-operation and Development (OECD). 1995. *Orientations on Participatory Development and Good Governance*. Paris: OECD.

Ministry of Foreign Affairs, Japan. 2003a. Japan's Official Development Assistance: White Paper 2002. Tokyo: Ministry of Foreign Affairs.

————. 2003b. *Assistance for Prevention of Trafficking in Cambodia and Viet Nam*, May 8 and June 17, http://www.mofa.go.jp/announce/announce/2003/5/0508.html

Mori, Y. 2000. G8 Communique Okinawa 2000, http://www.mofa.go.jp/policy/economy/summit/2000/documents/index.html.

Nikkei Science. 2001. 'Shinobiyoru Mizu-Shigen Kiki (Creeping water resource crisis)', *Nikkei Science*, May.

Nkrumah, K. 1976. *I speak of Freedom*, Westport, CT: Greenwood Press.

United Nations Development Programme (UNDP). 2002. *Human Development Report 2002: Deepening democracy in a fragmented world*, New York: Oxford University Press.

United Nations Economic Commission for Africa (UNECA) and United Nations Children's Fund (UNICEF). 1995. *Atlas of the African Child*, Paris: UNICEF.

United Nations WEHAB Working Group. 2002. *A Framework for Action on Water and Sanitation*, http://www.johannesburgsummit.org/html/documents/summit_docs/ wehab_papers/wehab_water_sanitation.pdf

World Bank. 1993. *The East Asian Miracle: Economic Growth and Public Policy*. Washington, D.C.: World Bank.

World Bank. 1998. *World Bank Atlas 1998*. Washington, D.C.: World Bank.

————. 2002a. *World Development Indicators 2002* (CD-ROM). Washington, D.C.: World Bank.

————. 2002b. *World Bank Atlas 2002*. Washington, D.C.: World Bank.

World Health Organization (WHO). 2002. *The World Health Report 2002: Reducing risks, promoting healthy life*. Geneva: World Health Organization.